"In Prabhu's book there is something more than just a story about an ancient martyr. Restoring to us the times in which the discrepancy between science and mysticism was unknown, he encourages us to direct our efforts to both these objectives simultaneously and to derive therefrom the paradigm for scientists who today are confused about the mystery of God. And although I resent some of Prabhu's remarks about Christianity, I find the purpose of his novel admirable."
— *Professor Maria Dzielska,* Author of *Hypatia of Alexandria,*
www.amazon.com

"A masterful piece of fiction, enlivening the debate on the search for truth. I read it in five hours straight and thoroughly enjoyed it."
— *Amrit Yegnanarayan*

"I finished the book in 4 days, very quickly!! I was absorbed by it and you succeeded in maintaining the reader's interest from the beginning until the end. The book made me think a lot about the values in this life and the purpose of it. I tend to believe there is a universal religion no matter what is the religion you practice or you are taught when you are a child and I found this trend in the book. You have all my admiration."
— *Angie Trius*

"A book that I will treasure for its insights into the most fundamental question of first cause. I prefer biographical novels to straight biographies, and especially enjoyed this allegorical unification of philosophy, science, and religion. It's a book I can come back to again with interest and enthusiasm."
— *Professor Art Gittleman*

"I really enjoyed the book and found the idea very original. It is such a joyful book and should be read by many people. With all the wars over religion and science it is refreshing to see that they do have a common meeting ground. I know I would enjoy reading this more times."
— *Robert Krol*

"A delightful book that forces one to think about things that one is too afraid to think by oneself. The conversations between children and adults are very illuminating. I have recommended this book to a number of people and all of them find something dear to their hearts from reading it."

— *Professor M. S. Krishnamoorthy*

"Having known the real Major K for so many years, I found this book to be a fitting tribute to him. The ending brought tears to my eyes."

— *Shyamsundar*

"I found the book's theme to be very powerful and the story enjoyable and gripping."

— *Sunita Lodwig*

"If you want one book on your reading list, this is the one. I could not put it down until I finished reading it!"

— *Professor Sree Nilakanta*

"I finished the book in a pretty short time. The middle parts gave me a chill and excitement as if I was reading some mystery. Major Kay and Anita were very likable characters and I simply loved them both. The book made me think a lot about the unbearable heaviness of nonexistence. It is a very nice book and I enjoyed reading it a lot."

— *Okan Zabunoglu*

"The book was very captivating and it forced me to ponder the purpose of my existence. I would enjoy reading this over again."

—*Rajshri Agarwal*

"The fascinating aspect of the book is that it can be read with different levels of interpretation. The story is but a brilliant façade, which reveals more than it hides the most challenging queries into our deepest beliefs. Our religious, spiritual, and even scientific notions are challenged. It is left to the reader to develop his/her own queries and answers. An absolutely brilliant book!!"

— *B. Prabhakar*

"I have read your book more than once and enjoyed it very much. I've highlighted many passages where your power of expression has been fantastic."

— *Professor V. Krishnamurthy*, Author of *Science and Spirituality*, www.geocities.com/profvk/

ANITA's LEGACY
An inquiry into First Cause

By

Gurpur M. Prabhu

Viresh ● Publications

This book is a fictional dramatization of a metaphysical and spiritual journey. Names, characters, places, and incidents are all imaginary or, if real, are used fictitiously. Any resemblance to actual events or locales or persons, living or dead, is entirely coincidental.

Grateful acknowledgment is made for permission to reprint the following:
- Excerpt from *Zen and the Art of Motorcycle Maintenance* by Robert M. Pirsig. Copyright 1974 by Robert M. Pirsig. Reprinted by permission of William Morrow and Company.
- Lyrics from *Welcome Back Kotter* by John Sebastian. Reprinted by permission of John Sebastian Music.

Library of Congress Card Number: 00-190921
ISBN: 0-9700645-8-6

Published by: Viresh Publications
               P.O. Box 2439
               Ames, IA 50010-2439

Editor: Prem Kumar
Cover design: Robin Doty

Publisher's Cataloging-in-Publication
(Provided by Quality Books, Inc.)

Prabhu, G. M.
    Anita's legacy : an inquiry into first cause /
by Gurpur M. Prabhu. — 1 st ed.
    p. cm.
    LCCN: 00-190921
    ISBN: 0-9700645-8-6

    1. Philosophy—Fiction. 2. Religion and science
—Fiction.   I. Title.

PS3566.R525A55 2000   813.6
                           QBI00-525

Printed in India by
Arc Publications
38 Castle Street
Richmond Town
Bangalore 560025

In this world, there have always been, there are, and there will always be original thinkers and those that follow. Our ancestors, both men and women, were leading original thinkers who strived hard to point us toward the Truth. But time and time again, our path to Truth is diverted by those who choose to control us, not help us out. This book is dedicated to those who rise from the ashes and help us find the Truth.

"In questions of science the authority of a thousand is not worth the humble reasoning of a single individual."
— **Galileo Galilei,** circa 1600 A.D.

Author's Note:

This book is an inquiry into *The Question: why is there something instead of nothing?* Religion believes that *The Answer* is the Supreme Being called God. Science believes that the road to *The Answer* goes exclusively through astronomy, cosmology, and physics. Not so. The road goes through several other places: through metaphysics, through philosophy, through religion, and through each and every one of us. We are all children of the cosmos and have a fundamental right to ask *The Question* and find an answer for ourselves.

The material presented in these pages is not to be confused with invaluable research being done by scientists. Nor is it to be confused with the abounding scholarly literature in philosophy and theology. Nevertheless the book deals with a fair amount of physics, metaphysics, philosophy, and spirituality.

A word or two about the narrative. The first draft was written through me at a phenomenal pace. It was written during the hours of 9:00 PM to 4:00 AM, it was written over a short span of two months, and it was my first experience with the Writing Muse. Such power she wielded over me that I obeyed her every whim in the fall of 1996. To remain faithful to her I have retained the original fiction structure of that draft as much as possible.

The book takes you on a journey that encourages you to think about an answer for yourself. My hope is that you will be a slightly different person, that you will begin to think differently, that you will challenge basic assumptions, that you will see the universe differently after you read it. If I have managed to accomplish that, I consider my effort worthwhile.

A substantive portion of this inquiry is a personal saga that consists of my father's thoughts over a period of 50 years. My only regret is that it did not get written in time for my mother to read it. I would like to believe that she would have found the story compelling and perhaps understood him a little better.

Anita's Legacy is written in loving tribute to my father, Major K.

Prologue

Thursday, May 2, 1996 was a cool day in the Twin cities. Anita did not wake up at the normal time for school in the morning. She would not wake up ever again. She had died peacefully in her sleep with a smile on her face. It was a heart-wrenching experience for her mother Meg and her father Alan to lose their only child, about two weeks short of her 16th birthday.

When Major Kay, their neighbor down the street, heard the news, he rushed over at once. Major Kay was a 71-year-old retired army officer. Gardening was his hobby, but physics and philosophy were his passion. He had been a good family friend and his grandson, Chris, was Anita's classmate. Anita used to visit their house frequently.

Nobody, not even his wife or his army buddies had seen the major cry, but on this day Major Kay's tears could not be contained. He and Anita had been soul mates for several years. They had spent hours together discussing physics, philosophy, and religion. Anita's kinship with Major Kay was even stronger than her kinship with her father.

Months ago, Anita had told her mother that when she died she was to be cremated. She wanted her ashes to be scattered around Mt. St. Helens in the state of Washington.

At the memorial service held three days later, Major Kay was the last to speak. He said: "We all know what a sweet girl Anita was. She touched our lives in different ways during her short stay on earth.

I would be remiss in my duty if I did not talk about a facet of her that is unknown to many of you.

"Since the beginning of civilization, people have wondered about the purpose of life and the origin of the universe. We ask ourselves where we came from, why we are here, and where we are going. We desperately look for answers. Science looks for answers in the quest for a single theory that describes the whole universe. Religion embraces the principle of a Supreme Being and looks for answers in the Word of God.

"Anita too was curious about many things. In the 12 years that I have been her friend, she has pestered me with lots of questions. The funny thing about her questions was that they usually altered my thinking and forced me to come up with answers. These answers have given me a totally different picture of the universe and the concept of God. Because of her probing, I believe things today that I would not have dreamed of believing a few years ago.

"Anita was fascinated by astronomy. To her, it was the queen of all the sciences. I cannot forget the gleam in her eyes when she gazed at the heavens. She would wake up before sunrise, and point her binoculars towards the summer triangle of Vega, Altair, and Deneb. Then she would eagerly wait for the constellation Andromeda to rise, wherein lies the nebula Messier 31, believed to be the twin of our galaxy.

"During the last six weeks she was transfixed by the appearance of Hyakutake. The comet is named after an amateur Japanese astronomer who discovered it less than two months before it could be viewed with the naked eye. It literally came out of the blue, surprising, and even embarrassing many respected astronomers. For us in the Northern Hemisphere it was a truly spectacular sight. Anita followed the comet with great interest as it continued to brighten along the northern byway of the sky—from Arcturus to the Big Dipper's handle, through Ursa Minor, and on into Perseus before fading away from us. I stayed awake with her a couple of nights watching the comet's mighty tail from dusk till dawn.

"Her death coincided with the day darkness descended on Hyakutake. On May 2nd, it turned around the sun and will be dark for the next two weeks, hidden by the sun's glare. Like the comets in the night sky, I pray that her soul shines forever in the far reaches of the universe.

"Anita's favorite smell was rain falling on dry sand. I recall standing outside with her during the first showers this year. As we

12

smelled the sand and became wet, she asked me, 'Major Kay, what is your legacy in life?' 'Anita, that's for others to determine after I'm gone,' I replied. 'No, Major Kay,' she said. 'You are a child of the universe and carry your own cosmic legacy. Your spiritual purpose is to find out what this legacy is before you die, not for others to describe it after you are gone.'

"It sounded strange to me the first time I heard it, but not any more. Death comes to us all, no doubt, but before it snatched her away she had figured out her purpose in life. I summarize her legacy by quoting Albert Einstein: 'Science without religion is lame, religion without science is blind,' he had said. For the last two centuries there has been an ever-widening gap between religion and science, between the mystic and the scientist. The mystic explores reality through meditation; the scientist investigates reality through scientific laws. The two camps are hopelessly separated: the scientist embraces an empirical philosophy that is not religious enough, while the mystic embraces a religious philosophy that is not empirical enough.

"From practicing the martial art of Tae Kwon Do, Anita learned the importance of possessing an indomitable spirit, a spirit that would not be vanquished as she spent her short life repairing the breach between the mystic and the scientist. Her legacy consists of the questions she raised and the answers she provided to narrow the chasm between religion and science.

"She was inspired by Werner Heisenberg, the founder of the uncertainty principle of quantum mechanics, who had once said:

It is probably true quite generally that in the history of human thinking the most fruitful developments frequently take place at those points where two different lines of thought meet. These lines may have their roots in quite different parts of human culture, in different times or different cultural environments or different religious traditions: hence if they actually meet, . . . then one may hope that new and interesting developments may follow.

"The developments have certainly been new and exciting. They have unlocked, for me, some of the mysteries of existence. I consider myself fortunate to have been her friend and gleaned her wisdom. You have all heard the saying 'Whom the Gods love die young.' The gods loved Anita very much—they sent Hyakutake—a Finger of God—to take her back. She was not of this earth.

"My feelings are best summed up in the words of a fourth century poet:

Whenever I look upon you and your words, I pay reverence . . .
For your concerns are directed at the heavens, . . .
You who are . . . the beauty of reasoning,
The immaculate star of wise learning."

WHEN the major finished talking, all one could hear was the sound of the plants blooming. After everybody had paid their last respects to the departed soul, Major Kay went over and hugged Meg and Alan. He said to them "Anita's darkest hours are over. The candle of knowledge can now burn brightly in the dawn of the light she has left behind."

As the sun set and night fell upon the crematorium a swarm of fireflies appeared from nowhere, periodically glowing as though to stoke her eternal fire.

One

Megan Hatley was the fourth daughter in a family of five girls. She grew up in the state of Washington in the Tri-Cities area of Richland, Pasco, and Kennewick. Her parents, Evelyn and Dennis, owned a fruit orchard and many of her summers were spent picking and packaging fruit. Mostly due to her mother's insistence, Meg and her sisters attended St. Joseph's Catholic school run by Franciscan nuns. At school the children were trained not to ask questions but to have faith in God. Dennis tried several times to change Evelyn's mind about sending their children to St. Joseph's, but she was adamant.

"We have to be careful with girls, Dennis. If we had boys, it would be all right for them to attend other schools."

"Why on earth would it be all right for boys but not for girls?"

"Wait till your daughters start dating. Then you'll understand the influence the school has on shaping their values."

"Honey, you talk as though sex is a sin. If it is, then you and I wouldn't be here. Everyone has to experience life and form his or her own value system. I think the Catholic school stifles the growth of our children."

"That's easy for you to say. What if one of your daughters gets pregnant before marriage? What are you going to do? Sex is not always a sin, but understanding its power is not easy when you're young. It takes responsibility and strength and sound judgment to deal with it. And I believe the school does a good job with that."

"I don't doubt you for a minute. It's the guilt feeling they lay on children that bothers me."

"Making young children feel guilty is the best way to control them. You men don't know anything about raising girls."

"Okay, honey. I'm not going to interfere with their schooling. I'll leave that to you."

So Kristin, Amy, Rachel, Meg, and Amanda attended St. Joseph's Catholic school. Meg graduated in 1978 and enrolled in Washington State University that fall. Having worked in her dad's orchard, she wanted to major in business administration. The university was located in the eastern part of the state in Pullman, a small town with a population of 7,000, which increased to 25,000 when the students came. The closest McDonald's was in Moscow, Idaho, seven miles east of there.

In Pullman, Meg felt like the *simoom*, a desert wind of North Africa that could blow wherever it wanted to. Eastern Washington was like a dust bowl, and much of the soil in the rolling hills of the Palouse and Inland empires was actually blown in from the Tri-Cities area. It had been deposited there thousands of years ago by floods that swept out Lake Missoula in northwest Montana. When the floodwaters reached Wallula Gap they left behind millions of tons of glacial silt, and the winds were blowing the silt back to where it came from. That was their ritual, day after day and night after night, relentlessly executing Nature's will.

The blustery and gritty days of late summer and early fall is the time when residents of eastern Washington take their vacation. But Meg didn't give a hoot about these hazy days—they were a small price to pay for her freedom.

Like her sisters before her, she joined the Chi Omega sorority. There were many activities to keep her busy after school and they met fraternity boys under close supervision. Evelyn was pleased with the way her three older daughters had grown up. The only scary thing that kept her awake at nights was the name Ted Bundy. Bundy had systematically raped and killed many women of Chi Omega all over the country.

DURING the summer of '78, Alan Avis completed his undergraduate program at Wazzu and decided to pursue a doctoral degree in physics. When he was not studying, Alan spent his time as a bridge bum. On Tuesday afternoons he could be found in the Union building playing bridge with Pete Pluhta, a math graduate student who had been there so many years that he deserved tenure, Alex Kuo, an English teacher, and James Whipple, a professor of psychology. Occasionally he would drive up to Spokane with Pete and Alex to play in duplicate bridge tournaments. They would stay with Bandana Dave, last name Westfall, an antique dealer who could talk for hours on Cabernet wines. Alan learned that wines had legs. Swirl the glass and watch the wine as it trickles down, he was told. The closer and thinner the legs, the more full-bodied the wine.

The arrival of students in fall was like a breath of fresh air after the long summer days. The fresh faces and chirpy voices brought a liveliness to the campus that pulsated throughout the town. Alan would spend his mornings drinking coffee and smoking and getting intoxicated by the pitter-patter of high-heeled shoes on the cobblestones in front of the Union.

"Excuse me, can you tell me where Sloan Hall is?" asked a pretty young thing.

"It's quite a ways from here," he said, putting out his cigarette. "Why don't you come with me? I'm going there myself. What's your name?"

"Meg. What's yours?"

"Alan. I have to teach a beginning math class in Sloan Hall."

"That's a strange coincidence. I have a math class in Sloan Hall too. Are you a professor?"

"No. I'm just a physics graduate student, teaching math this semester."

They soon found out that she was going to be his student for the semester. Meg sat in the second row from the front. Her tanned complexion, black hair, and beautiful eyes mesmerized him. He had to work hard to fight off the distraction and focus on his lecture.

She became a frequent visitor during his office hours for the course, asking basic questions about the homework. They could sense a chemistry silently working inside them. Their biological cells were screaming to be joined together. Others could easily tell they were in love through their body language. A

17

friendly touch now and then, a door held open for her, a C homework returned with a smile.

A month passed by and Alan gave his first mid-term exam. Meg did not fare well, barely passing it. The next time she was in Alan's office she asked him, "Aren't you going to ask me out some time?"

"I don't know what to say Meg. I find you attractive. But considering the fact that we're teacher and student, I don't think it's a good idea. It would be difficult for me to grade your work objectively. I hope you understand."

"How about dinner and a movie? I'm not here to negotiate a higher grade in the course. If I want to, I'll work harder and earn it. Maybe you can be my private tutor."

"Okay. Let's have dinner this Friday at Alex's. They have some nice Mexican food. Then we can go for a movie."

"Will you pick me up at 7 o'clock? I stay in Chi Omega."

"Sure. I know where it is. What's your phone number, just in case?"

Meg scribbled her number on a piece of paper and gave it to Alan.

"See you later," he said and took the number with him.

ALAN shared an apartment with Arjun Gupta in Chinook village. Kali, as he was popularly known, was a graduate student from India with oily black hair and brown skin. The Chinook village was named after the warm winds that originate in the Pacific Ocean and blow across the Cascade mountain ranges. Sometimes these winds can melt a foot of snow in mid-January.

Nobody, with the exception of Lord Brahma, knew how a nice name like Arjun got transmogrified to Kali. Perhaps it was a Hollywood moniker for Mr. Cool Cat's future film career.

"Kali, I need to talk to you."

"What's up doc?"

"I'm falling in love with a student in my math class. Whenever I see her, my heart goes thumpity-thump."

"Careful, bro. You know the rules well enough not to mess with your students. Let me do you a favor and take care of her this semester."

"KALI!"

"Okay, okay. Calm down now."

"We're going out for dinner to Alex's this Friday. What should I do?"

"Take it easy, man. It's only dinner. Talk to her but don't order any liquor. She's probably too young to drink. You don't want to be arrested for cradle snatching, do you?"

"Kali, you're impossible to talk to. I wonder what they taught you in India about girls and love."

AT the restaurant Meg was nervous and so was Alan. He didn't want to be seen by anyone who knew that she was his student. The waitress brought a basket of chips and salsa, and they both ordered cokes.

"Is Pepsi all right?" the waitress inquired.

"Yes," they both replied.

"You should try the fajitas here. They're excellent," suggested Alan as Meg pored over the menu.

"I'll pass on the meat today."

"It's not Lent, is it?"

"Gosh, no. I'm Catholic. I don't eat meat on Fridays."

"Okay. Where did you go to school?"

"St. Joseph's Catholic school in Kennewick."

"What did you learn there?"

"I don't know. The usual subjects I suppose. The nuns were very strict and taught us not to commit sins and to do as we were told."

"And did you?"

"Did I what?"

"Do as you were told."

"Most of the time I listened to my teachers. But I'm confused about many things I was taught."

"Like what?"

"Oh, about what's a sin and what's not."

"Gee. Everybody knows what's good and what's not good. If you didn't know what a sin was, how would you know that you committed one?"

"I'll tell you what happened one time. In sixth grade, Tommy Wilson, a small skinny boy with protruding teeth, answered Sister Jean Mary back. She grabbed him and beat him until he cried and said he was sorry. She told the class not to tell

19

our parents or anyone. I'm not sure whether beating up somebody is a sin or not."

"Incredible. If a teacher had done that in my school, she would have been in big trouble."

"That's not all. They controlled us all the time. When I was in second grade I came home crying one day. My older sister Kristin asked me what was wrong. I was crying so much that I couldn't talk. The teacher had passed out the host and told us it was the body of Christ. She said we should tell on anyone who didn't eat it. Mary Ann was sitting next to me and she took the host out of her mouth and threw it on the floor. I told on Mary Ann. Sister Patrine became so angry that she made her pick up the host and eat it. I couldn't bear to see that because the host was covered with dust. My mom never let us eat anything from the floor. Everyone in the class glared at me for telling on Mary Ann. I felt like dying right then and there."

"What is a host?"

"It's a sacred wafer signifying the body of Christ. It's made out of unleavened bread that the Jews baked when they fled Egypt. Mary Ann never talked to me after that. It's one of the few things I remember from second grade."

"It wasn't your fault. You did what you were told. We always remember things that we feel bad about. You must have felt very guilty and ashamed of yourself. Mary Ann should have listened to the teacher."

"I suppose she should have. And I suppose I should have used my judgment. Incidents like this have confused me about the nature of sin."

"Surely they taught you that drinking and gambling were sins."

"And smoking too," looking at his cigarette. "But the big sin was sex. We were always told that sex was taboo."

"They didn't tell me that in my school."

"Where did you study?"

"In a public school in Wenatchee. The apple capital of the world."

"I've been there once. For some parade in May."

"That would have been the annual Apple Blossom festival. I was there earlier this year."

"Do your parents miss you when you leave home?"

"No. They're probably glad to see me go. Dusty and Zelda keep them busy now."

"Your brother and sister?"

"No, the dog and cat. I'm an only child."

The waitress came to take their food orders. Alan asked for more chips. Meg ordered vegetarian burritos and he ordered steak fajitas.

"Tell me more about your school. I'm curious about what they taught you."

"It was a regular school like yours. They taught us math and science and history and social studies. It's just that we led very sheltered lives. No matter what we did, we had sinned against somebody or something. In addition to the Ten Commandments, there was a book that listed all the sins we could possibly commit. In confession we were told to look through the pages to see if we had committed any of those sins. Adultery and murder were the biggest sins."

"What about beating up children? Was that listed as a sin?"

"Yes, hurting somebody was a sin. Although the teachers could beat us if we did not obey them. I've been slapped across the face a few times for talking too much. Once an eraser was thrown at my head because I used my finger to rub the blackboard."

"Somebody should check into your school system. Perhaps conduct a review of its policies and methods."

"We get reviewed all the time by senior priests. I think they come from New York or somewhere. They revise the curriculum and the textbooks used in all our classes. My sisters used totally different books for many subjects."

"Not that kind of review. I meant an external review by an independent agency. From what I've heard today, I think there is a strong case for child abuse."

The waitress got their table ready for dinner. She put a plate containing guacamole, sour cream, shredded lettuce, tomatoes, and rice and beans next to Alan. She also put an empty plate in front of him and a red plastic tortilla-keeper with a lid. Meg got a plate with rice and beans. The waitress told them she would be right back with their food.

The sizzle became louder as the waitress approached them. It sounded like a steam locomotive grinding to a slow halt at a station. The smell of sautéed green peppers, onions and steak strips filled the air. For a while there was smoke all around the table. It was Meg's first introduction to a fajita. Her entrée of vegetarian burritos looked pale in comparison.

She watched Alan as he started eating. He removed a tortilla from the tortilla-keeper, meticulously spread sour cream and guacamole, added lettuce and tomatoes, and finally put on some steak strips, green peppers and onions. Then he rolled it up like a burrito and sunk his teeth into it. He performed this ritual three times, eating rice and beans on the side.

They finished dinner and went past Ricoh's, a local bar, to the movie theater where the James Bond thriller, Doctor No, was playing. After the movie they walked back to the sorority. They talked some more on the steps outside, and Alan left.

For a couple of hours after that, Meg felt the poky bristles of his beard rubbing against her chin. The smell of sautéed onions and cigarette smoke lingered in her mouth.

WHEN he reached home, Kali was waiting for him.

"Hi Alan. How did it go?"

"Pretty good. We ate at Alex's, saw Doctor No, and then I dropped her back. She is one confused chick. Went to a Catholic school you know. Short of brainwashing her, they did everything else."

"Did anything happen on the date?"

"I told you what we did."

"Not that boring stuff, man. Did you make out with her?"

"I held her hand when we walked back from the movie. I kissed her good night before I left."

"Wery cool. I once took a Catholic girl, Vilma, on a date. Her mother was with us all the time. You can never trust these religious types. Vhat was it like to kiss her?" Kali had his w's and v's mixed up.

"It was just a kiss. Why do you want to know?"

"I have to coach you for next time, don't I?"

"Her lips were thin and soft and I didn't want to stop. She kissed me back and it felt so tender. I wanted to melt in her mouth."

"Hold it buddy. Red light. One step at a time. How long did you guys kiss each other?"

"Oh, about five minutes maybe. Maybe longer. I didn't check."

"Steaming shit. You better think through this one. You don't go so far with a Catholic girl on the first date. She might take you seriously."

"I guess I'll have to roll the dice and find out."

"What did you have at Alex's? Maybe it had an effect on you."

"The usual fajitas."

"Big mistake."

"Why?"

"Don't you know they marinate their fajitas in peyote?"

"Don't bullshit me, man."

"I'm serious. Dino works there part time and told me that their new chef, Juan Carlos, started this."

"His Colombian friend?" inquired Alan.

"No. He's Mexican. Named after his father, Carlos, and his godfather, Don Juan who is a Yaqui Indian. The small amount of peyote they use in the marinade is masked by Adobada sauce. It's used to line the stomach before consuming more peyote and going on a vision quest."

"You're not kidding, are you?"

Kali bobbed his head up and down, meaning no. The shake from side to side would have meant yes.

"No, I'm not kidding. I hope they didn't lace your fajitas with too much peyote."

"Do you know how long the effect lasts?"

"Nobody but Don Juan knows. I'll check with Dino. You better stay away from Alex's on your next date. Or order something else."

Alan was a little worried when he went to sleep that night. He was attracted to Meg but not ready to get serious with her. He didn't know whether to believe Kali's story about the peyote. Kali was such a smooth operator—he could sell non-perishable ice cubes to the Bedouins in the Sahara.

THE next day Meg got a phone call from home. She exchanged pleasantries with her mom and then asked to speak to her younger sister Amanda.

23

"Guess what Amanda. I went on a date last night with my math teacher."

"Your math teacher? Isn't he too old for you?"

"No. He's not a regular professor. He's a graduate student."

"Oh. What did you do?"

"We went out for dinner to a Mexican restaurant. Then we saw Doctor No. He kissed me good night before he left."

"Uh-oh. Be careful sis."

"Don't worry about me. How's school going?"

"School's fine. Did you know that Sister Patrine has eloped?"

"Eloped? With whom?"

"Father Meeden. The rumor is that she's carrying his baby and they ran away to get married."

"No! I don't believe it. Especially after she told us many times that sex was the worst sin in the book."

"Believe it Meg. It's true. All the girls have been talking about in recess."

"You better watch what you say. They can punish you for gossiping also."

"I'll be careful. What's your boyfriend's name?"

"He's not my boyfriend. We just had one date. His name is Alan."

"Okay. Let me know what happens with you and Alan."

"He's pretty conservative. I don't know if we'll ever go out again. Unless I ask him."

"You never know. Take care now. We'll call you again next week. Bye."

Meg saw Alan the following week during his office hour. She was his most frequent visitor. When she told him about Sister Patrine, he smiled to himself.

"Looks like you've learned the eleventh commandment," he said.

"Excuse me?"

"There are the Ten Commandments they teach you, and then there are more insights you learn when you get out into the real world."

"What's the eleventh commandment?"

"Thou shalt do as I say, not as I do."

24

"That's so true. The nuns broke many of the rules they expected us to follow. No wonder I'm confused about the concept of sin."

"When I was in school, I was also confused. Fortunately for me, my parents never went to church. I was encouraged to ask questions all the time. That's what got me interested in physics. Science does not need the hypothesis of God. It bases all its conclusions on observed evidence. You ought to take the path of science to sort yourself out. We're soon going to find a theory of everything."

"Really? That'll be hard for me to understand. Math and science are not my strong subjects. When my science teacher in school was talking about Darwin's theory of evolution and survival of the species, I asked her whether fish discovered water to stay fit and ensure their survival. She shook her head and said, 'You'll never amount to anything as a biologist, so don't even think of taking science in college.' That's why I decided to major in business administration. I'm a people person and was good at dealing with customers in our orchard."

"I think women do all right in business administration."

"I'm still shocked by what Sister Patrine did. She was my favorite teacher."

The second mid-term exam was held after Halloween. Meg fared better on this one, getting a high B.

ON November 18, 1978, the whole nation was riveted by news of the mass suicide in Guyana. Bernard Shaw of ABC News reported that 914 followers of the Rev. Jim Jones had been found dead in an open field in Jonestown. Bodies of men, women, and children were lying close together. Some of the bodies overlapped each other. Those who failed to take the poison had been shot dead. Bernie was nauseated by the pungent smell of decomposed bodies. His cameraman had covered his mouth and nose and was struggling to take live shots of the ghastly scene. The pictures were burned in the nation's memory.

"How can one person kill so many others?" asked Meg when she discussed this with Alan over a cup of coffee in the union.

"It's the cult phenomenon," replied Alan. "Many people are confused about life and its purpose, and they seek spiritual guidance. They do whatever their leader tells them. A form of mass hypnosis."

"The Pope is our spiritual leader. He doesn't ask us to die like this."

"I'm not sure about that. You can be physiologically alive and still be brain dead, endlessly regurgitating the teachings of the church. It's a different kind of death. The death of your individuality and creativity. The death of your personal inquiry into truth."

"You have a strange attitude towards religion, Alan."

"Not really. The scientific community thinks like I do. By the way, are you free on Friday night?"

"Yes, I think I am. Why?"

"Kali is going to Seattle for the weekend. I thought it would be a good idea for you to have dinner at my place and play scrabble or something."

"I didn't know you could cook."

"I serve the best pizza in Pullman," boasted Alan with a straight face.

"Sounds good. I'll call you and confirm it."

Alan picked her up on Friday evening and brought her to the village. It was drizzling a little and the forecast called for rain and sleet that night. His idea of cooking was to order a large pizza, half of it topped with sausage and pepperoni and the other half with mushrooms and green peppers. He asked Meg if she wanted some wine or beer.

"No thanks. I shouldn't be drinking."

"Why don't you try a beer? A small glass won't count as a sin."

"Oh, all right. I'll have a beer." If Sister Patrine could elope, she could certainly have a small drink.

He opened a tall boy of Bud, the king of beers, and poured it into two glasses. As they drank beer and waited for the pizza, they watched a rerun of M*A*S*H. The theme song, Suicide is Painless, evoked images of Jonestown in Meg's mind. The images flickered for a while, and were swamped out by the stupidity of Frank Burns and the laugh track.

Meg liked the beer and drank it rather fast. She asked for a refill. Alan told her to go easy on the pace. The pizza, as usual, was delicious to tuck into a hungry stomach. Meg went to the bathroom for her first beer release. When she returned, Alan

26

noticed that her blouse was loose. He could see her bra and if he gazed harder, her nipples. He had been in a state of inaction with her and perhaps the time had come to taste the fruit of action.

She sat on the couch after dinner, drinking beer and watching TV. Alan dimmed the lights and sat next to her. They watched an episode of *Hart to Hart*. The sexy voice of Stefanie Powers expunged all his inhibitions. He got another beer, turned off the TV, put on some music by Abba, and snuggled up to Meg with his arm around her. He kissed her on the cheek first, then tasted her malty lips. His hand slid inside her blouse. It moved up and down and made further adventures across her body. It struggled for a while near the bra strap on her back.

"What are you doing?" she asked.

"Nothing."

"It opens from the front. Let me do it."

And then the hand was in heaven, feeling the pointed tip of a juicy tangelo. With one hand threading her tresses, his lips\ glued to hers, the other kneaded the softest bread dough in the universe. Their passion propelled itself into the bedroom. A crack of thunder rumbled outside.

"Enough, Alan. Let's stop now."

"Just a little more. Please."

His naked body touched hers and sparked a sizzle, quite different from a fajita. Their atoms collided with each other, but it was not the time to ponder the spin of the electron. Doctor No became Mister Yes.

As the thunderstorm passed over, the union of lightning and thunder produced a heavy downpour that lasted for about seven minutes. The front moved through quickly causing the rain to change into a gentle trickle at the tail end of the storm.

Meg lay still on the bed as Alan lit up a cigarette. A part of her wondered what Sister Patrine must have gone through. Another part was guilt-ridden at what she had done. When the sun came up in the morning it caressed the virgin clouds with a crimson hue, the same color as the stain now showing on the bedspread.

THE next week was Thanksgiving and they didn't see each other until after the break. When Kali heard what had happened, he cautioned Alan and wished him good luck. Meg was behaving

27

strangely towards him in class. At the end of the week, he could stand it no longer and asked her to see him that day during his office hour.

"Is everything all right with you?" he asked nervously.

"How can it be after what happened?" she retorted.

"It was natural. We were attracted to each other and nature took its course."

"You have to be married before doing that sort of thing. And I committed the biggest sin of all." She started crying. "I hope I'm not pregnant."

"Have you told anyone about this?"

"No. I dare not. I belong to you now."

"What the hell does that mean?" exclaimed Alan, his voice a little louder.

"It means we have to get married."

Tears gushed down her face and Alan gave her a Kleenex. He hugged her and said, "Meg, listen to me. I like you very much. But marriage is a big step. Both of us are so young. Let's think it over during the Christmas break. I promise you everything will be all right. Trust me."

Two

Meg left Pullman after her last exam. Alan had to stay behind and grade papers. Kali had nowhere to go for Christmas, so Alan asked him to come to Wenatchee. On a frosty morning, they started out in Alan's Volkswagen Bug. First on HWY 195 north to Colfax, then west on HWY 26, and north again near Saddle Mountains, hugging the Columbia River all the way into Wenatchee.

"What should I do with Meg?" asked Alan.

"I warned you about these religious girls. Why don't you get some advice from your parents?" replied Kali.

"Bad idea. I don't relate to them at all."

"How come? You're an only child. You should have favored child status all the time."

"Nah. Not me. My parents are victims of the beat generation, Kali. Flower people. A couple of *dharma* bums."

"I don't understand. Isn't *dharma* something from Hindu religion?"

"Yeah. Yeah. Whatever. In the 1950s the young and the restless were dissatisfied with the teachings of the Judeo-Christian culture. They took trips to your country and the Far East, looking for gurus to tell them what absolute truth was. My parents have been lost in this quest, trying to integrate life and nature."

"That's all right, I suppose. But why do you call them *dharma* bums? What's *dharma* got to do with anything?"

"I don't know. That's what Uncle Jack calls them. And I do the same. They live in an abstract world, not in ordinary reality."

"Have they been to India?"

"No. But others have, and they influenced my parents. You'll get a chance to see their act."

"What got them started on this trip?"

"I don't know how the beat mentality started. It was quite a hip thing in their time. Men like Alan Watts, Jack Kerouac, and Allen Ginsberg were some of the key advocates. And spiritual-hungry people like my parents devoured their message. These days they kowtow to a new kid on the block, Robert Pirsig. He wrote some shit about Zen and motorcycles."

They stopped at Dusty for gas and a beer piddle. Kali reloaded on the beer, and bought some cigarettes and potato chips.

"Way to go, Kali. More junk food."

"Lays are good for you. *You* ought to know that."

"Yeah. Right. Let's get going. We need to be home in time for dinner. Wanna hear a bridge hand I botched up?"

"No thanks. Not right now. Tell me more about your parents."

"What can I say? You'll see them soon enough. They find it amusing to answer a question with a question."

"We all do that sometimes."

"Not like they do it. I'll tell you something I remember. I once asked them 'What is the difference between Christianity and what you believe?' And my mother replied, 'What is the difference between the way of the cat and the way of the monkey?' They both broke out in cackles when they saw my dazed look.

"It's things like this that piss me off. I dare not follow any of their advice. What I've learned over the years is to do the exact opposite of what they tell me. That way my decisions turn out sensible."

"I think you're too hard on them, Alan. I'll reserve judgment till later."

At dusk on a summer day, they would have been in raptures over the majestic rolling hills of the Palouse empire. The winter days were much shorter though, hiding that spectacular view, and it was already dark by the time they reached Washtucna. Meg would have turned south to catch Highway 395 into Kennewick.

"Did your parents go to church?" asked Kali.

30

"No. They stopped believing in the church. Thank God for that. I haven't been programmed by the Judeo-Christian morality."

"Perhaps Meg can learn something from your parents."

"Nah. She is much too young and innocent. Still swayed heavily by the premises of the Catholic church.

"Kali, you're the only one who can help me sort out this mess. Women. Damned if you mess with them, damned if you don't."

"Take it easy, Alan. You seem to be protecting Meg from your parents. I think you love her."

"Maybe I do."

"Why don't you follow your heart? She seems interested in you. I think she won't handle it well if you dump her now. She might turn into a mental wreck. And you don't want that on your conscience."

"I'm not planning to dump her. I don't want to commit myself to marriage right now. I couldn't afford it. Unlike you, I don't depend financially on my parents. Besides, I've been losing money lately to the old fart Whipple. He can't even play the cards. He's just a lucky bastard."

"What are you going to tell Meg after the break?"

"I don't know. Maybe she will come up with some ideas. Maybe she will get over it."

"Uh-huh-huh. I don't think so. The ball's in your court. She told you she wants to get married."

"I know. I know. If people have to get married because they sleep with each other, the line for marriage licenses would reach the sun. About 93 million miles."

"She's really a sweet girl, Alan. She'll be good for you."

There was a long pause before Alan spoke again.

"I kind of like her. Her raspy voice and slender figure, ample in the right places. The mole on the left cheek. The coy smile."

"Cut out the poetry, asshole. Leave Meg's theme to Zhivago."

"I'm just trying to sort myself out by going over the pluses and minuses. The pluses are her beauty and sweetness. The minuses are my financial woes."

"This is a matter of the heart, Alan. You can't analyze her and arrive at some kind of bottom line. You have to go with your feelings."

31

"Yes, I can. I have to approach it from a practical viewpoint. Besides love and fresh air, we have to eat and pay bills."

"I understand what you are saying. Your heart says yes, your head says no."

"Precisely."

THEY passed Royal City and the road gradually turned north. For a brief while they headed east on Interstate 90, then north again, climbing into the Big Dipper which had risen from the darkness. The Columbia River was to their left and they would follow it upstream for another hour.

Memories of fishing trips Alan had taken with his grandfather came back to him. One of their favorite places was Chelan Falls, a little north of Wenatchee. His grandfather was an outdoor person and loved nature. Alan recalled what his grandfather had once told him, 'Rivers are like roads that carry us to our destination. And everyone has to go down the river of life. What makes the journey bearable is the company we take on the trip.'

As he reminisced about the river, he turned to Kali, "Too bad you can't see the river at night. We'll get a chance to catch the view on the way back."

Kali opened up the last beer can, took a couple of sips, and said, "I've been thinking about you and Meg. I know your concerns about money. Marriage is a big venture. But please do yourself a favor, Alan. Listen to your heart, not your head. The only regrets you have in life are the risks you don't take."

"Speaking from experience, eh?"

"Somewhat. I left behind a girl in India when I came to the U.S. Her memories have haunted me for a couple of years."

"Why don't you ask her to join you?"

"It's not easy. Nitya is happy over there. Besides, her parents are too strict. They wouldn't allow it. The only news they read about the United States is from newspapers: murder, robbery, rape, and government scandals. They are terrified of what might happen to their daughter in this society."

"They ought to know better than to trust the media for God's sake. The media will do whatever it takes to sell a story."

"The written word has a power of its own, Alan. Many people believe what they read."

32

"Why don't you go back to her?"

"I have to sort out my own life too. It hasn't been easy."

They drove in silence till they approached Rock Island dam. From there it was 10 minutes to Alan's house.

"There is a magic about Meg that I fell for the very first time we met," said Alan.

"Yes, my friend. No question about it. Perhaps she can get a job to help out with the money situation."

"I really wouldn't like that. But it maybe the only option till I graduate and find a real job."

"Does that mean yes? Do I hear wedding bells ringing?" asked Kali smiling. "And do I see you changing diapers?"

"Not diapers. That's the last thing you'll see me doing."

Kali gulped down his beer just as Alan pulled into the driveway. His dad met them at the door.

"Dad, this is Kali, my roommate. He's from India. An expert on *dharma*."

"Really? Very good. We'll get a chance to discuss that after dinner. Why don't you boys come on in?"

They washed up and sat down to eat. Kali was shocked to see Ken's appearance: braided hair tied in a ponytail and an earring in his left ear. Sharon's hair was cut very short, her ears were bare, and she was wearing a shawl cluttered with beads. In India, thought Kali to himself, the man wore the pants in the house.

The meal was simple—a stew consisting of chicken stock and cornstarch with tomatoes, corn, and cubes of chicken thrown in. Salad and bread rolls completed the dinner fare.

"Pass the black pepper to Kali, Mom. His taste buds are from a different world. At school he uses Tabasco sauce with all his food."

"So, what is your religion Kali?" asked Ken.

"Hinduism, sir. But I don't know much about it," he replied respectfully. "It is a way of life with endless rituals and ceremonies. Most of these have no meaning at all. At least I don't know what they mean."

"You can cut out the sir in this house. Just call me Ken."

"Okay sir."

"Surely you know something about your religion? Alan told us you were an expert."

"He's kidding. I once mentioned to him that I was very confused about Hinduism. It taught me that everything was an illusion, called *maya*."

"*Maya?* I think I've heard the term."

"It's a difficult concept to understand. Too abstract. If you asked a Hindu priest to explain the deaths in Jonestown, he would say that it was *maya*. I find that so far removed from ordinary reality."

"I think your wedding ceremonies are pretty interesting," said Sharon.

"Hardly how I would describe them. They make you jump through all sorts of hoops for two days. When my time comes, it'll be my worst nightmare. I find *your* weddings simple and interesting."

"Like the way of the cat and the way of the monkey," giggled Sharon.

"Excuse us, Mother. We don't understand those kind of analogies," said Alan, a little miffed at his mom for dumping her crap on Kali.

"It's simple, Son. The way of the cat is effortless—the kitten just cries 'meow' and the mother carries it in her mouth hither and thither. The way of the monkey is difficult—the young monkey, with great exertion, somehow clings to its mother's hair for dear life." Sharon and Ken both laughed out loud, as if it was a private joke between them.

"Very funny, Mom," said Alan sarcastically.

AFTER dinner they retired to the family room. Alan got the bags out of the car and took them upstairs.

"Honey, why don't you give Kali some ouzo?" suggested Sharon.

"Good idea," said Ken and poured out some ouzo for everyone.

"Hmmm. Tastes good. A bit sweet," said Kali. "Where's it from? It contains some Indian spice."

"It's a Greek liqueur," said Ken.

"It tastes like something we call *saunf* in India. It's eaten after meals and good for digestion."

"This stuff's good for digestion too. I first drank it when I was in Turkey. Ever been there?"

"No sir."

"Turkey is a fascinating country. Istanbul, or Constantinople as it was called, was the cradle of civilization. It served as the rest stop for European travelers as they trekked from Macedonia, through the Ottoman empire, to Mesopotamia, and to Egypt and beyond. I was stationed there for two years in my army days."

"Dad, do we have to listen to your Turkish stories again?"

"For Kali, Son. He hasn't been there."

Alan excused himself. "I'm going to take a shower. I'll be back soon."

Ken and Kali refilled their ouzo.

Ken continued with his tour of Turkey. "My army base was in Izmir on the western shore bordering the Aegean sea. I visited Istanbul in the north, Ankara in the middle, and Efes to our south. The food was great. They make a tremendous dish out of lamb—it's called Iskender kebab."

"Iskender? That's close to what we call Alexander the Great in India—Sikandar."

"The dish is probably named after him. There were other good dishes too: shish kebab, eggplant, and lentil soups. The best soup I had was at a truck stop called Ikbal in Afyon, south of Ankara. Further south is Antalya, a glorious place to spend the summer. We sat on the beaches, drank beer, cruised chicks, and lost ourselves in the deep blue color of the Mediterranean sea. My favorite drinks in Turkey were beer and tea. Tea was served in small cups, chai they called it."

"That's what we call it in India."

"I'm sure the Persian influence rubbed off on your languages and customs. They constantly invaded your country, didn't they?"

"Yes. Right from the time of Sikandar. But it's probably Indian languages that rubbed off on the Persians. Sanskrit is the oldest language known to man."

"Some day Sharon and I are going to visit India. We've heard so much about it."

"You have to be careful, though. The map is not the territory."

"So true Dr. Schweitzer," exclaimed Ken, laughing. "Listen to what happened to me in Efes. I was visiting The Grand Theater, a structure with stone pillars and stone seats that has withstood the ravages of time, perhaps since the days of Aristotle.

"I stood on a small boulder near the stage area of the theater and spoke out loud. My buddies told me that my voice reached the farthest rows in the back. I jumped on another rock close by and tried the same thing. This time my buddies in the back row couldn't hear me at all. I tried speaking from two other rocks and they couldn't hear me. When I spoke again from the first boulder, it was as if the sound system had been turned on. My voice resonated into the wilderness and beyond. My spirit felt as though it had stood there centuries ago, lecturing on something.

"You see Kali, even in the territory, things don't always appear to be what they are. They differ, based on your viewpoints."

ALAN joined them after his shower. They all filled up their ouzo glasses.

"Go easy on the stuff, Kali. It tastes sweet but it's 90 proof. I see that my dad has been unloading his Turkish episodes on you."

"It's all right, Alan. It was interesting."

"Alan doesn't believe what happened to me in Efes."

"Of course, I don't Dad," snapped Alan, his hands in the air. "Your buddies must have been kidding you. Anyone who has studied sound waves knows that it shouldn't make a difference which rock you were standing on."

"It did make a difference to me Son."

"Let's not get into this again, you guys," said Sharon. "Talk about something else for a change."

"Okay Mom. I have something I want to tell you. I'm probably getting married soon."

There was complete silence for about five minutes.

"To whom?" asked Sharon.

"To a student at the university."

"A girl student?"

"Yes Mother. A girl student. What did you think? Her name is Meg."

"Does Kali approve of the girl?" asked Ken.

"Yes sir. She's a very sweet girl."

"Is she also in graduate school?"

"No, Mom. She's an undergraduate freshman."

"How did you meet her?"

"She was a student in my math class."

36

"You might want to give it more time, Son. Why don't you date her for a while and then decide on marriage?" said Ken.

"That's what he intended to do, sir. But Meg is a Catholic girl and wants to get married," blurted Kali.

"Oooooh. CATH-O-LIC," said Ken facetiously.

"Honey, stop it," said Sharon. "Do you love her, Son?"

"I think so."

"Well, let's propose a toast. Ken, give me some more ouzo please."

They raised their glasses in a toast to Alan and Meg's future. Sharon put on some music and wanted to dance. Kali was pretty sloshed by this time and joined them in a Turkish-Greek dance as they went in snake-like fashion all over the house. Ken was the leader, followed by Kali, then Sharon, and finally Alan.

"What does *dharma* mean?" hollered Ken to Kali, over the sound of the music.

"I think it means duty or purpose in life."

"What's your *dharma?* "

"I don't know. Probably to make lots of money. What's yours?"

"Right now, my *dharma* is the same as that of the sun—to wake up tomorrow," replied a plastered Ken, barely able to control his laughter.

Kali looked at him weirdly. Alan was right, he told himself. His parents were truly over the edge. Soon they got tired of dancing and went to bed. It was 2:00 A.M.

IN Kennewick, Meg celebrated a traditional Christmas at her house. On Christmas eve, her mother's family came over for dinner at six o'clock. The following day they would visit her father's folks in Walla Walla. Evelyn loved to cook, and she had prepared for days to get the meal ready. Dennis had put up a real Christmas tree a week after Thanksgiving. It had been neatly decorated with colorful lights. The floor area beneath the tree began filling up with presents, wrapped in the seasonal red and green paper. There were ribbons around the tree and hanging from the branches were letters of the first names of each of the girls. They had made these in preschool and Evelyn had mummified them.

Dinner started with Dennis saying grace. The soup was cream of tomato with croutons. Salad with an oily Italian dressing followed. Then came the main course: lasagna, beef Wellington, and a chicken salad with crunchy noodles, garnished with slivered almonds. The cordon bleu was salmon, baked in a French sauce with a strong flavor of garlic.

The food was washed down with wine, for everyone except Meg and Amanda. The sound of Christmas carols bounced off the walls: *Joy to the World, Jingle Bells, The First Noel, Silent Night,* and many others. After dinner, the family caught up with each others' lives.

Meg dared not reveal what had actually happened between Alan and her. Amanda was her only confidante, and she had advised Meg not to bring the matter up even in confession. It was not safe, Amanda said, because they would easily recognize Meg's voice and then tell her parents. Neither of them wanted fireworks until July 4th. When they attended midnight mass, Meg prayed, "God, please make Alan marry me. All my problems will be solved."

The drive to Walla Walla the next day took an hour. For lunch, they had sandwiches with cold cuts of meat, and settled down to play bingo. Everyone had pooled in, bringing gifts for the prizes. The challenge, for the winner, was to find out which present Billy had brought and avoid that till the very end. Uncle Billy was a cheapskate. One Christmas he had brought a bicycle water bottle, probably from K-mart. Meg had cried when she won this, much to Billy's surprise. He was the only one who didn't know what was going on, and nobody had the heart to tell him.

TO say that Christmas at Alan's house was not traditional would have been an understatement. There was a Christmas tree without any lights. Sharon and Ken believed that one ought to be able to see the light always, not just during the season.

They had planned a small party, inviting a few of their friends for dinner—John the clown and Jill, Lila Mohan, and Bob and Julie Snyder. The crackle of the fireplace seemed to produce its own music, blending in nicely with George Winston's *December* in the background. There were no presents exchanged at all. The only ritual was to hug everyone. The quality time they spent with each other could not be wrapped as a gift. An hour of the lively repartee in the house could easily have chased away the winter blues. Kali capitalized on every opportunity to be near Lila, an innocent-looking girl with large bright eyes.

The meal was Chinese home style cooking. Egg drop soup, vegetable egg rolls, soft rice noodles with asparagus and celery, a stir-fry chicken with broccoli, and mixed vegetables in an oyster sauce. Served with plain rice.

"Kali, this is not normal Christmas food," whispered Alan apologetically. "You can see that my parents are really into this Zen shit. Totally out of reality."

"Like TV commercials, huh? To be honest with you, I prefer this food over the turkey I had at Thanksgiving. Tell me what you know about Lila. She's really cute."

"Lila's dad is a doctor in Yakima. I think she's taking some classes at the community college here. Why don't you ask her out if you're interested?"

"I might do that."

Kali found out Lila was planning to transfer to Wazzu the next fall. That opened the door for a lot of conversation about the campus and what it had to offer. The Christmas ritual took on a different turn after they ate. Everyone had to tell a funny after-dinner story. Ken went first.

A Zen master took three of his American disciples to the stream. A horse was standing near by. The master said, 'I will give you all a challenge. I want each of you to try to make the horse drink water from the stream.' The first disciple was a college student from the Midwest. He played some rock and roll music he had brought along. Unfortunately, Michael Jackson's Beat It didn't succeed in moving the horse. The second disciple was a computer geek from California. He began loudly chanting some Unix mantras. The horse stared at him, grunted back a few of his own, but didn't budge. The third disciple was a senior editor from a publishing house in New York. He asked the master, 'Has this horse been certified by a literary agent?' The master replied, 'I do not understand you my son. It's only a horse.' 'Oh well, if it hasn't been certified, I'm not going to mess with it.' The master asked them, 'You all give up then?' 'Yes,' they said. 'Why don't you show us how it's done?' The master approached the horse, mounted it, and rode for about 15 minutes. Then he brought the horse to the stream. As soon as he got down, the horse started drinking. 'See, my sons. You have to learn to focus. You focused on methods to make the horse drink the water. I focused on making it thirsty, so it would drink by itself.'

In this manner, they passed the time, taking turns in story telling. Invariably there was laughter after each story. Sharon went last.

"I'm not going to tell a story. I'm going to play a question-answer game. The question is, 'What kind of music do you like?' Those who don't give the right answer get to clean the dishes." She went around the room, recording the answers.

John the clown said, "Country western."

Jill answered, "Soft rock."

Lila said, "Rock and roll."

Kali uttered, "Same as her," pointing to Lila.

Bob, who thought it was a trick question gave a Zen-like answer. "Nothing," he exclaimed. "I don't like music. I like talk radio."

Julie answered, "Western classical."

Ken said, "Turkish music."

And Alan ended with, "Bach."

"I'm afraid none of you came up with the right answer," said Sharon. "It's dish-washing time."

"But what is the right answer?" asked an incredulous Kali.

"The right answer is *good* music."

"What makes that right?" persisted Kali.

"Well, don't you like different kinds of music? Perhaps some music from your country?"

"Yes," he replied. "I like a few tunes from Indian movies."

"See, then it's not easy to classify what you like, is it? You could have used a combination classification like Rock and roll-cum-Indian film music-cum-whatever. Or you could have said good music. Education has trained us to babble like Aristotelian parrots, neatly classifying everything. Makes it near impossible to think differently."

"That was smooth, honey," said Ken. "You got us all, that time."

Kali could not handle what Sharon had said. "How can you insult Aristotle like that? He's one of the greatest philosophers of all time."

"I'm just the messenger, Kali. The person who gave Aristotle a good bashing was GARP. It appears you haven't read *Zen and the Art of Motorcycle Maintenance,* or have you?"

"No, I haven't. What did Garp say in his book?"

"GARP is short for Great Author Robert Pirsig. He went hunting for absolute truth; in fact he spent 10 years in your country studying philosophy. He was mighty irritated by the dualistic subject-object classification of Aristotle, and introduced the notion of Quality which was the source of all things. Quality contained both subjects *and* objects. It could not be defined, yet everyone understood it."

"What's that got to do with motorcycle maintenance?"

"He got a little obsessive about motorcycles in his book. The motorcycle is a prop, a metaphor, for the individual who journeys into truth. It is a dangerous path, and such an individual must take care of himself, maintain himself if you will, lest he fall sick. Pirsig had a mental breakdown during his quest, you know."

"Mom would rather believe a loony than Aristotle," chimed in Alan.

"Is Pirsig normal now?" asked Kali.

"Maybe you should ask him that. I don't know who's normal and who's not. People think that Ken and I are not normal. Even Alan has problems identifying with us."

Three

Kali and Alan left Wenatchee after the new year. They drove north for a while and then east on HWY 2 towards Spokane. Alan was joining Pete and Alex for a duplicate bridge tournament and Kali, who had played some bridge but not at Alan's level, was going to kibitz them.

"If you think you've had culture shock meeting my parents, you will have one more jolt with the bridge crowd," said Alan. "We're staying at Dave's place. He's quite a wild nut at the bridge table. Overbids like a maniac, but plays the cards well."

"What does he do for a living?" asked Kali.

"He's a bum like many other bridge players. Owns an antique business and knows a lot about wine. Likes spicy Indian food. Tandoori chicken is one of his favorites."

"Has he been to India?"

"I don't think so."

"Are you playing with him?"

"In the team event, yes. His regular partner is Pete. I played with Dave once and my blood pressure shot up. There's a lot of action at his table. No doubled contracts."

"Why not? Are the opponents afraid of him?"

"He intimidates them easily just by his persona. Pete and he pull out long cigars to scare off the little old ladies. The opponents do double him, but by partnership agreement a redouble is automatic. Once we had a mix up and I was playing five clubs redoubled for

42

down eight and minus 4600. I don't know how we went on to win the match. After the event, I told Pete that it would be better if I didn't play with Dave."

"Hey, look, we just passed through Coulee City. In India, *coolie* means porter."

"That's where one of Dave's friends stays. Miles Adkins. We might run into him in Spokane."

"Another bridge bum?"

"Yes. A rich one. He owns a few farms and is pretty well off. Let's take a detour and go past Grand Coulee Dam. You'll enjoy the view."

"I'm sure I will. It's been a fantastic trip so far. Lila is really a cute chick."

"How was your date with her? Did you check her out?"

"We went out for dinner and then to a movie. She's of Indian origin, but not like Nitya at all."

"Is that good or bad?"

"Nitya would be very conscious if I touched her in public. A quiet soft-spoken girl with conservative values. Lila is the exact opposite. We held hands in the theater and she talked nonstop even during the movie. I wish I knew where her off button was located."

"What happened after the movie?"

"Nothing. Indian girls are more conservative than Catholics. At least I got her phone number. She's thinking of transferring to Wazzu in fall."

"Give me the bottom line. Is there any chemistry or not?"

"It's too early to tell."

WHEN they reached Spokane, Kali met Dave Westfall for the first time. With a band around his head and shoulder-length hair, it would have been difficult for Kali to tell whether Dave was a man or a woman. Another hip guy like Ken, thought Kali to himself. The bridge arena was buzzing with voices. Kali understood a little bridge, but the players spoke a strange language that was difficult for him to follow. Phrases like *stiff ace, king-queen tight, jack third, six clubs cracked, negative double, splinter,* and many more permeated the playing area. Kali kibitzed Alan for a while and then moved to Dave's table.

43

A pair of little old ladies showed up and the cigars came out. Pete asked Kali for a match and joked for a while about lighting up his cigar. When one of the ladies protested that she was allergic to smoke, they glared at her and started chewing their cigars. Dave doubled every bid made by the lady on his right. Whether it was nervousness on her part or general fatigue or Dave's intimidation is not known, but during the bidding on the next hand, the lady on Dave's right fainted. She had to be rushed to a hospital and many people in the room knew that Dave had done her in. With his headband, a glass of red wine, a cigar, and long hair, most juries would have found him guilty by appearance alone. Kali understood what Alan had meant by action at Dave's table.

After the bridge game, they hung out with Dave for a day and headed back to Pullman. Alan's squad had lost the team game by a narrow margin. Much to his surprise, in their private conversations with him, Kali found everybody on the team blaming the loss on everybody else except themselves.

THE spring semester started in the third week of January. A week passed by before Alan got a phone call from Meg.

"Have you forgotten me?" she asked, a little apprehensive.

"Not at all. I didn't want to call you at home. Kali and I spent Christmas at my parent's home in Wenatchee. How does your schedule look this semester?"

"Pretty busy. I'm taking 15 credits."

"Let's have coffee one of these days. Why don't you tell me when you are free."

"How about Tuesday afternoon?"

"That's not a good time. Unless you want to come and watch me play bridge."

"Okay. I'll see if I can be there."

The Tuesday afternoon bridge club met at 2 o'clock in the Union building. When Alan saw Meg, she appeared nervous, biting her nails often, something he hadn't noticed before. He introduced her to everyone at the table. Alex was visibly distracted by her presence and offered her a cigarette.

"No thanks. I don't smoke. I've been telling Alan that it's not good for him.".

"It's an old habit, and old habits die hard," replied Alex.

44

They played for two hours, after which Alan and Meg left for his office. His door had barely closed before she started crying.

"What's the matter, Meg?"

"I don't know. I don't know what's going to happen to me. I don't want to rot in hell."

"Everything will be fine. Did you think about our situation over the break?"

"There's nothing to think about now. What's done is done," she blurted, sobbing a little more.

"Okay, okay. Will you stop crying please? What happened between us wasn't all that bad. It was completely natural."

"I've been back for a whole week and you haven't even called me. I think you don't care for me any more."

"That's because the first week of the semester is always hectic. I was going to call you when you called me."

"Aren't you worried at all that I might be pregnant?"

"Are you?"

"No. Thank God I'm not. My mom would kill me if I was. Did you know that you were the first one?" She had an embarrassed look when she said that.

"That can't be true. Not a pretty girl like you."

"Yes, it's true. I didn't go out on many dates in school. Most guys thought that I would get asked out by others and didn't even bother calling me. There were many days when I used to sit by the phone and wait for it to ring, while my friends went out and had a good time. The guys I dated turned out to be creeps."

Alan, who didn't have the faintest clue that Meg had been a virgin, understood what she was going through and why she appeared so nervous about the whole affair. He hugged her tight and consoled her.

"Please stop crying. Why don't you have dinner with Kali and me on Saturday? Then the three of us can discuss the matter. Kali knows about our situation."

They ordered pizza on Saturday night and Meg succeeded in taking Kali's breath away. The entire evening she got the distinct impression that he was constantly staring at her breasts. Kali assured Meg that Alan was concerned about her.

"I told him to listen to his heart, not his head," he told Meg when Alan had stepped outside for a smoke.

"I hope he has something in both places to listen to," she replied.

"Don't you worry about him. I know he will do the right thing. It's just that he has to figure everything out first. In Spokane he was the slowest player at the bridge table—very deliberate, thinking before every card he played."

After dropping Meg that night, Kali and Alan hung out at Ricoh's. They ordered a pitcher of beer and shot some pool. Kali suggested to Alan that if he got married, he could move into Fairway—inexpensive family quarters that were subsidized by the university. These quarters were used as barracks during World War II and home to many international students with families.

"Kali, did you know that I was the first one to make love to her?"

"You cradle snatcher. I'm not surprised. Catholic girls are pretty conservative."

"In your country, perhaps. But I didn't think it would be so here."

"You better do the right thing and marry her now."

"She would certainly like me to propose to her. I sense that."

"I have an idea. Propose to her on Valentine's day. Set up a date and take her out to dinner. After dinner, give her a red rose and a ring, and ask her to marry you. That would be the romantic way to do it."

"I can't afford an expensive ring right now."

"The ring is a token of your love for her. It doesn't have to be expensive. It has to be something special, that's all. I can help you look for one."

ON Valentine's day, a nervous Alan followed Kali's advice and proposed to Meg in his apartment. She smiled at him and said yes. It was something she had badly wanted to happen and it brought tears to her eyes.

"Why do you always cry for everything?"

"This time I'm crying because I'm happy."

She was delighted with the idea of being engaged to Alan, but afraid to tell her parents. The best way, she thought to herself, would be to tell her sister, and have Amanda break the news to her parents.

When Evelyn found out about Meg's engagement, she insisted that she get married as soon as possible. Dennis thought otherwise, saying that she was too young to take on marital responsibilities. They debated about it for a while and Evelyn convinced Meg to get married in June that year. Alan was a little taken aback at being rushed into it but he went along with the plan. When Meg told him that it would be a church wedding, he hesitated for a while and told her that he would have to check with his parents. Sharon and Ken agreed to it and told him that they would definitely be present, church or no church.

The wedding date was set for June 23, 1979 at St. Joseph's Catholic church in Kennewick. Alan's parents came on Thursday and, being the groom's parents, took Meg's family out to dinner. Alan was most insistent that it should be a steak house and not a Chinese restaurant. Meg had warned her parents that Alan's folks were not church-going people. The tension was heightened by Ken's appearance, which sent shock waves through Dennis and Evelyn.

"Oh my God," she whispered to Dennis. "Look at him. What will everyone say at the wedding? I'm embarrassed already. I hope Meg is marrying into the right family."

"Take it easy, honey. Appearances are deceptive. It's a bit too late to do anything now. We have to go on with the ceremony."

"What do you do for a living, Ken?" asked Dennis, as they sat down at the table.

"This and that."

"And what else?"

"Ken used to be in the army," butted in Sharon. "He's retired now and does several odd jobs. Drywalling, wallpapering and painting."

"I also take photographs and try to sell them," added Ken sheepishly.

"Photographs of what?" asked Dennis.

"Oh, almost anything."

Evelyn whispered to Dennis, "I knew there was something fishy about him. He must be taking dirty girlie pictures."

Ken continued describing his hobby. "One of my pictures won third prize at a show. It's a black and white photograph of a car, called Smitty. The award mentioned the nice chiaroscuro effect that was produced."

"What effect?" queried Dennis.

"A chiaroscuro effect. It's the distribution of black and white in a picture. Like the photographs Ansel Adams took of Yosemite."

"Your life must be peaceful, now that Alan is in college," said Evelyn, turning to Sharon.

"I wish it was. But my days are hectic. I volunteer my time to the Red Cross."

The waitress came to get their drink orders.

"Please order whatever you want. Sharon and I are drinking martinis. Make mine a double," said Ken to the waitress. "My son's getting married."

Dennis and Evelyn didn't drink hard liquor. About the only thing they drank at home was wine, and champagne for special occasions. Their family ordered two carafes of red wine, with Meg and Amanda ordering apple juice. Alan ordered a pitcher of beer and two glasses, one for himself and one to empty Meg's apple juice into and give her some beer which would pass off easily as apple juice. It was a Kali-designed game plan which had the potential to succeed because Alan's parents were doing such a great job distracting Dennis and Evelyn and keeping them occupied.

The drinks arrived in a little while, and they ordered food. Everyone opted for prime rib except Ken and Sharon. They ordered vegetarian food in a steak house. Ken took a sip of his martini and summoned the waitress.

"It's not dry enough for me. Can you take this back and ask the bartender to mix mine with sake instead of vermouth?"

"I beg your pardon, sir. Could you repeat that?"

"Sake. It's a Japanese rice wine. I hope you have it."

As they waited for the food to arrive, Dennis continued the conversation with Ken.

"What was your army career like? Did you serve overseas?"

"The army was nice to me. A bit monotonous, but nice on the whole. I spent two years in Turkey."

"That must have been exciting. What was it like?"

"I promised Alan that I would not tell any Turkish stories tonight."

"Your son looks so smart and intelligent. How did you two manage to steer him into a scientific career?" inquired Evelyn.

"We didn't. I think this is what happened. When he was in high school, he came to us for advice on his career path. His classmates were talking about majoring in medicine, law, and

48

science. We told him that traditional careers taught many things, but did not teach you how to live life. 'We want you to follow a career where you learn how to live life,' we said.

'What on earth do you mean, Dad?' he asked. 'Why don't you talk straight with me just this once?'

"We replied, 'Son, in college, and in life after that, your mother and I will be happy if you are ordinary, not special. Eat when you're hungry, pass urine and stool, and sleep when you're tired. And remember to breathe once in a while.'

"Alan was so angry with that answer that he did not talk to us for a whole year. I guess he wanted to be special. That's why he took up physics."

Evelyn was sorry that she ever asked the question. She could not believe that anyone could talk like that at the dinner table. She hadn't seen the likes of Ken and Sharon before and hoped that she wouldn't have to see them again.

The wedding ceremony took place without much incident. Meg was 19 and Alan was 23. Kali was the best man and proposed a toast during dinner.

"To the bride and groom—may they enjoy many happy years together."

For the honeymoon they drove to Vancouver, British Columbia. They had planned to stay there a week but their money ran out in four days.

THE reality in Pullman was a far cry from the luxurious hotel in Vancouver. The Fairway barrack with its aluminum siding looked decrepit from the outside and spooky from the inside. At $80 a month, however, it was a no-brainer. There was a heater, a range, electricity, running water, and an air-conditioning system that worked when you kept the windows open in front and back.

With Alan's research assistantship they were able to make ends meet. They spent the summer settling in their new home, furnished largely with stuff bought at garage sales. Meg was a good cook and Alan ate some delicious meals at home. Stew with fresh tomatoes tasted so different from the canned products that Kali and Alan used in their apartment.

Within three weeks after fall semester started, Meg found out that she was expecting a baby. The news shocked Alan. He was not ready to support a wife and a child on his research stipend.

"How could you be so foolish?" he asked. "I thought you would be careful enough not to get pregnant. We don't need more problems now."

"What do you mean by that?"

"Don't you take the pill or something? All women take care of themselves."

"I'm not supposed to practice any form of contraception. It's against my religion."

"You're not serious, are you?"

"Yes I am. Catholics use only the rhythm method."

"What the hell is that?" he asked, wondering to himself what other method could be used to make babies.

"I don't know how exactly it works. There are some days when it's safe to have sex and some days when it's not."

"It's always safe to have sex."

"I didn't mean that. What I meant was that I could get pregnant on some days but not on other days."

"Didn't your mom ever tell you about the birds and the bees?"

"She never discussed sex with me at all. All I know is what they told me in school. And they didn't go into specifics about it because sex was considered a sin."

"Didn't your older sisters ever tell you about contraception?"

"Kristin explained to me what Sister Jean Mary had told her. Right after sex, she had said, a girl should jump up and down 100 times to dislodge the sperm. That way you could avoid becoming pregnant."

"Get out of here," said Alan laughing. "I haven't heard such baloney in my entire life. Except from my parents."

"It's true. That's what Kristin told me. It's added protection because the rhythm method is not accurate all the time."

"I don't think we can afford to have a baby."

"You mean financially?"

"Yes."

"We could save some money if you stopped smoking."

There was a moment of silence. Alan stood up from his chair. "NEVER TELL ME WHAT TO DO," he screamed. "You're the one who screwed up. I'll decide WHAT I want to do and WHEN I want to do it."

He slammed the door and went outside to light up a cigarette.

"Damn bitch," he muttered to himself. "Telling ME what to do."

AFTER a couple more cigarettes, he went over to see Kali. Lila was at Kali's place, watching a football game with Dino. Alan took Kali aside and told him what had happened and how he had reacted to the situation.

"Proves that you're only human," said Kali. "I think she has a point. Perhaps you could save money if you stopped playing bridge instead. After all, you're the one who's always worried about making ends meet."

"I'll have to think about it," replied Alan to Kali's suggestion.

They joined the others and Alan stayed on to watch the football game. After a few beers he returned home. Meg had just finished fixing dinner.

"I'm sorry for screaming like that," he said. "What I'll do is give up playing bridge for a while. That will save us some money. Lately, my luck hasn't been good at the card table."

The financial concerns that Alan had raised made sense to Meg, but deep inside, she had a moral dilemma about an abortion. Did humans understand enough about life and their role in the bigger scheme of things? From all that she had read, she was not convinced that people understood life and its origins. There were plenty of theories and there was a lot of preaching from the Catholic church, but the simplest and most puzzling questions were never clearly answered.

She conveyed to Alan her desire to have the baby, telling him that she would work part time in the mall in Moscow, Idaho. The baby was due in the beginning of June. Both her parents and in-laws wished her a safe pregnancy. She found a job at J C Penney, working some evenings and weekends. It was time for Meg and Alan to stay focused, get through the winter and complete the fall and spring semesters. Fall passed by quickly and winter as usual passed by very slowly. In the northern tier of states, the perfumed hint of new mown grass in April is a sure sign of spring in the air. People rarely go by what Phil the groundhog says in Pennsylvania on February 2nd.

Meg had not experienced much morning sickness in the first trimester, and had put on 30 pounds by early April. The baby was showing and she was mighty proud of it. Alan and she used to take long walks in mid-April and there was about a month left before spring semester would be over.

On the last Saturday in April, Kali invited them for dinner to his place, which he was now sharing with Dino. While Alan and Dino drank beer and discussed the peyote-marinated fajitas at Alex's, Meg and Lila talked about the baby.

"What's up Meg? How's the baby doing?" asked Lila.

"She's started kicking my insides. The doctor tells me that everything is all right."

"How are things with you?"

"Pretty good. I'm waiting for the semester to get over. Alan's parents have invited Kali and me for the Apple Blossom festival next week. Why don't you join us? It'll be fun."

"I don't think we'll be able to go. It's too close to my due date."

"But that's only in June," answered Lila.

"It's risky for me to travel right now. Besides, spending time with the in-laws is not on my list of fun things to do. They're a bit weird. Don't you think so?"

"No. They are certainly different from the mainstream, but not weird."

"My mother told me that my in-laws were being punished by God. That's why He didn't give them the gift of faith."

"Maybe they have some bad karma, that's all."

"What's karma?"

"It's a Hindu belief that states that we are the sum of all we have done, thought or desired in our past lives. Until we liberate ourselves from the bondage of existence we continue to be reincarnated. Good deeds lead to good karma in future lives, bad deeds lead to bad karma."

"I don't believe in reincarnation. Lord Jesus Christ, our Savior, sacrificed Himself and died for our sins. But what you said about bad karma for my in-laws makes sense to me. There's no other explanation for their behavior."

They walked over to watch what Kali was fixing for dinner.

"What are you cooking, Kali?" asked Meg. "It smells yummy."

"It's a chicken curry with the spice toned down."

"How do you make it?"

"Here's my recipe, Meg. It's best if eaten with plain rice or *roti*, a kind of wheat bread. You won't find this recipe in cookbooks. It's a family secret from the Gupta dynasty."

Kali's Recipe

Buy six boneless, skinless thigh pieces of chicken. Buy a can of coconut milk from Don's Chinese grocery store on Oak Street. Cut the chicken right away when you get back from the store, each thigh into six pieces, discarding any fat that might be present. Wash the chicken pieces and put them in a bowl. Sprinkle one teaspoon salt, half a teaspoon concentrated lime juice, and one teaspoon paprika. Mix well and store in the refrigerator.

Peel the skin of two medium-sized red potatoes, cut them into cubes roughly the size of the cut chicken pieces, wash and keep aside. Heat the coconut milk in a small pot till it boils and turn it off to cool. Chop one small onion, a couple of pods of garlic, and a quarter-inch piece of ginger. Grate these in a blender using some of the coconut milk to obtain a thick sauce-like consistency.

Cut another onion into very thin long pieces. Sauté them at medium heat for 5 minutes using one tablespoon oil in a medium non-stick pot with a lid in which the dish will be cooked. Add 3 Roma tomatoes cut into small pieces (or 3 tablespoons tomato paste). Add one flat teaspoon paprika, a quarter teaspoon ground cinnamon, one flat teaspoon garam masala and the contents of the blender and cook for another 5 minutes. Add the potatoes, half a teaspoon turmeric powder, half a teaspoon salt, a little coconut milk and cook with the pot covered for 15 minutes.

Sauté the chicken separately till the pieces lose their pink color and add them to the pot with the rest of the coconut milk. Add one teaspoon salt, stir a little, and simmer with the pot covered for about 45 minutes. Taste, and add salt as needed.

"My mouth's watering already," said Meg. "I'm ready to eat. I'll have to try it one of these days."

FINAL exams were to take place during the last week of May and Meg and Alan both hoped that their semesters would be over before the baby was born. In situations like this, however, Murphy's law takes over your life and you just have to go with the flow.

On Sunday, May 18, 1980, Alan and Meg woke up in the morning and had their first cup of coffee around 8:00 A.M. Meg was concerned about getting too much caffeine, so their coffee was not strong. Around 8:30 A.M. she went to the bathroom.

"I think I've wet my panties," she said when she came out.

"It's about time you got toilet trained," replied Alan smiling.

"You men don't know what it's like to carry a baby."

"Yes, we do. But fortunately we don't have to do it."

"Alan," she said, as if remembering something the doctor had told her, "maybe it's my water bag that has burst. I think I'll call the nurse and find out what to do."

When she called the hospital, the nurse asked her to get there right away. Couples expecting a baby are supposed to have a bag packed and ready to go, so they do not have to waste time in emergency situations. Since their baby was not due for two more weeks they hadn't worried about it. Meg quickly packed some clothes and Alan took her to the hospital.

The doctor ran some tests and determined that it was indeed the water bag, and told them to get ready for the baby. The contractions started around 11:00 A.M. and Meg was beginning to feel the pain. It was her first baby and the contractions were painful—as if someone had stuffed a tennis ball up her nostril.

At 3:52 P.M. Meg gave birth to a baby girl, weighing six pounds and 15 ounces. It was a normal delivery but she was quite exhausted. Neither Meg nor Alan knew what was going on outside the hospital.

They would find out later that at 8:32 A.M. that very morning, Mt. St. Helens had erupted with a huge cloud of volcanic ash. It was in the southwest portion of the state, about a five-hour drive west of Pullman. Prior to the eruption it was a beautiful volcano covered by old-growth trees. The blast killed about 60 people and destroyed all life in the near vicinity of the mountain. A huge cloud of volcanic ash spread east-northeast across the state, and around 2:30 P.M. Pullman became pitch dark—it was like nighttime, street lights had to be turned on, and it was 'ashing' like dusty, powdery, dry snow. An inch or two fell on the town. The university was closed the next day and people had to move about with gas masks covering their faces.

And so Anita was born in pitch black darkness without a single star in the sky to witness her birth, not even the sun. Was this an omen from the Gods? Would darkness surround her life? Meg was worried about these things when they got home, but Alan assured her that it was pure coincidence that Mt. St. Helens erupted that day, and that Anita was a healthy baby and that she would be all right.

Four

Anita came home from the hospital after a couple of days. Alan and Meg could not sense it at the time, but their sleeping pattern was soon going to change. They had taken Incompletes in their courses for spring semester and, except for some grading that Alan had to do in the course he was assisting, they both had ample time to take care of the baby.

Meg was nursing Anita and planned to do it as long as she could. For about three to four months, milk would be Anita's only food. Evelyn and Dennis visited them over the Memorial Day weekend.

"She looks just like me," said Evelyn, beaming with pride when she picked up Anita. "So sweet and tiny. An absolute little darling. What do you think, Dennis?"

"Yes, dear. She does look like you. She's very cute. I see some resemblance to Ken also. Especially the forehead."

"Oh no! Not him. We don't want our granddaughter to be influenced in any way by that piece of trash. His own son can't put up with his antics," she uttered, out of Alan's earshot.

Evelyn showed Meg how to hold the baby and how to burp her after every meal by putting her on the shoulder and gently patting her on the back.

"That's going to be your job for a few months," she told Alan.

"What if she spews out icky saliva on my clothes?" he asked.

"All babies do that. Soon she'll put her hand in her mouth. You should use a receiving blanket to wipe her from time to time." "How do I bathe her, Mom?" asked Meg.

"For the first two weeks, just use a sponge and clean her very gently. Then you can put her in a baby tub and wash her with water. Let me show you how it's done. After a few times, it'll be easy."

Evelyn showed Meg how to bathe Anita and gave her a few more motherly tips on what to do in various situations. Her last bit of advice was, "Remember to put on a new diaper as soon as you notice it needs changing. If she stays too long in a soiled diaper, she will get diaper rash which is quite painful."

SHARON and Ken visited them over the Father's Day weekend. By that time Alan's eyes had taken on a reddish tinge from sleeping in four-hour intervals at night. As soon as Ken held Anita, she started crying, apparently irritated by something. He handed Anita back to Meg but the crying persisted for a while.

"Does she have colic?" asked Sharon.

"I don't know," replied Meg. "If she does, then it's something that just happened."

"Alan was also colicky at this age and Ken could not deal with it all," said Sharon. "I recall he once told me to use his martini remedy for colic—shake the baby but do not stir. Even in jest that was not very funny. Little babies are so fragile and can die if you shake them. You need lots of patience for a couple of months. As soon as Anita eats solid food, the colic will stop by itself."

"Who does she look like, Dad?" asked Alan.

"She looks like me," interjected Sharon. "I ought to show you some of my baby pictures."

"I think she looks like herself, dear," answered Ken. "A baby is a gift from God, and every baby has different talents. I'm sure Anita will find a way to express her uniqueness."

"What do you think about her birth coinciding with the eruption of Mt. St. Helens?" said Meg to Ken.

"I think that's very mysterious. I don't know what significance it has. The force of the volcano was equivalent to that of an atomic bomb exploding every second for 16 hours straight. Scientists are not sure how so much energy is generated. Anita must be a special baby. Don't you agree, Son?"

"How can you say that, Dad? All babies are special to their kith and kin. You can't prove any scientific causality between the volcano's eruption and Anita's birth. You'd better leave that stuff to astrologers. Maybe the moon was in the volcano's seventh house. There are no coincidences in life. Mystics like you folks always try to believe in some mumbo-jumbo." He threw his arms up in despair, more in disgust, and went outside for a smoke.

"You better get used to this when Anita grows up," said Ken to Meg. Pointing to Anita he continued, "Small kids, small problems." Pointing to Alan who was outside, he added, "Big kids, big problems."

"I heard that, Dad. You make some smart-ass remark when you can't answer things scientifically."

"No, Son. The medical community has established what I just said. By a Dr. Spock I believe. I read his book and got the impression that good parenting was easy with easy kids and bad parenting was easy with difficult kids."

"Come on, Dad. You know it's easy to write books on how to take care of other people's kids but not your own."

AFTER Sharon and Ken left, the grim realities of parenting slowly began to set in for Alan and Meg. Alan had a summer job as an instructor and Meg had given up her part-time job in Moscow. They didn't go out for movies together any more—they would take turns—Meg seeing a movie all by herself while Alan was at home with Anita—and Alan doing likewise. It was a change in their social lifestyle dictated by financial necessity, as they barely managed to keep the proverbial wolf away from the door. The only times they went out together was when Kali and Lila offered to baby-sit Anita. That wasn't often as Kali was busy with schoolwork. He had changed majors from physics to computer science.

At the age of four months, Anita was introduced to solid food. Her colicky crying stopped and she turned into a peaceful and serene baby. By Thanksgiving of that year, she started sleeping through the night and Meg and Alan felt that they were the best parents in the world. Meg was getting very restless staying at home with Anita and told Alan that she wanted to get back to school and resume her part-time job.

Spring semester was hectic at their home. Meg worked some evenings and weekends and their schedules had to be adjusted so that one of them could stay with Anita while the other was busy. Tempers flared and the tension mounted along with endless household chores. Laundry was done once in three days at a nearby Laundromat, and grocery shopping was done on Saturday mornings. Meg cooked on the days she was not working at nights and they ate leftovers on the other days. Once in a while they all went out to a pizza place. The dishes had to be done everyday, especially Anita's bottles and nipples. When Anita turned nine months she began to spit out food that she didn't like. Meg tried hard, but could not force any meat products or applesauce down her throat. If she did, it came out very quickly—in a time interval shorter than the Planck time of 10^{-43} seconds—one of Alan's jokes during that phase of Anita's growth. The Planck time, 1 divided by the number 1 followed by 43 zeros, is believed by physicists to be the smallest duration of time.

THE thing that worried Meg the most was Alan's attitude towards changing Anita's diaper. Before she took up her job, she was the one always doing it. Alan was never interested in learning how to change Anita. One day when Meg came back from work on the weekend, Anita was crying persistently.

"What's the matter, Alan? Did she get hurt?"

"I don't know, honey. Babies cry all the time. If you ignore them the crying usually stops."

"When did you change her diaper last?"

"I didn't. I don't know how to do that."

"Has she been in the same diaper all day since I left in the morning?"

"I guess so," he replied, shrugging his shoulder.

"How can you take such a casual attitude about changing her diaper? She's crying because she probably has diaper rash."

Meg quickly removed Anita's diaper and cleaned her nicely. Then she bathed her with some warm water. Anita cried throughout the bath. The diaper rash was severe and Meg applied some Desitin cream that her mother had given her.

"Do you realize what you have done to her?" she asked Alan, a little angrily.

59

"LOOK," said Alan, "I don't change diapers. Period. I'm not habituated to looking after small children. I have more important scientific things to worry about. My father didn't change diapers and my grandfather didn't change diapers. I'm not about to change that family tradition."

"But she's your own daughter! Don't you care about her well being at all? I know some dads who don't mind changing diapers. That way they're sure their kids are eating well and not constipated. If I have to continue to work, I need you to assure me that her diaper is changed. Otherwise, I'll never have peace of mind." Meg wiped away tears from her eyes.

"Okay, honey. Will you stop crying, Puh-LEASE? I've heard enough crying for one day. I'll do my best to change her. How do I know when to do it?"

"You can smell her or you can change her once every four hours."

As the year progressed Alan started changing Anita. On many occasions, as if she knew how to train her father, Anita would wait for Alan to change her, and then stink up the place in her new diaper. Alan really got lots of practice in changing her.

FOR her first birthday, Anita got a child walker from Meg's parents and a huge stuffed monkey from Alan's parents.

"I wonder why your parents didn't give her a teddy bear?" asked Meg.

"Beats me," replied Alan. "I'll ask them about it."

When Sharon called them for their wedding anniversary Alan inquired about Anita's birthday present.

"What's with the monkey you gave Anita, Mom? Is that another one of those cat and monkey things?"

"No, Son. Anita was born in the Chinese year of the Monkey. Unlike the Western Zodiac signs, the Chinese follow a lunar calendar. Like the monkey, she will grow up to be a captivating and mischievous child."

"Are you serious?"

"Yes. Don't you know that when we got independence on July 4, 1776, it was the year of the Monkey too? That's probably why our country is so resourceful."

"Whatever you say, Mother."

ANITA'S second year passed by faster than her first. Alan had cleared his qualifying exams and established himself as a doctoral candidate. Meg had adjusted her schedule remarkably, between looking after Anita, her job, and her studies. Anita was beginning to walk and talk and soak in input about the world. She loved books and loved stories at bedtime. Every day Meg would read her a couple of stories.

The first word that Anita said was "mama," the second one was "moon"—she was fascinated by the moon and would point to it and say "moon" several times. A little later she learned to say "dada."

By her second birthday, Anita had memorized a few of her favorite books and would read these by herself. She enjoyed the Cookie Monster on Sesame Street and would count numbers along with the Count. She had a book on animals and the chicken was her favorite animal—you could make her laugh by saying "cluck cluck goes the chicken." Although she loved books very much there was an incident when Anita was two years old that Meg found hard to explain.

On a warm summer day Meg had taken Anita to the public library to return some books and borrow new ones. A few dark clouds lingered in the sky and there was a small chance for rain on Anita's first trip to the library. As Meg parked the car and walked towards the entrance, a crack of thunder roared from above. When they reached the library steps, for some inexplicable reason, Anita burst into tears just as the rain started coming down. The scorched concrete, heated by the sun and as if about to catch fire, seemed to quench itself with the raindrops. Meg tried her best to convince her daughter to go inside but did not succeed. Anita threw a temper tantrum and decided to get wet staying outside, rather than take shelter inside the library. Frustrated and wet, Meg dropped off her books in the book return and ran quickly to the car. As soon as they left the library the rain subsided and Anita stopped crying.

The library incident was not the only thing that Meg did not understand. Anita was turning out to be a very picky eater. She disliked the smell of any kind of meat and this made it difficult for Meg to prepare food for the family. While Meg and Alan ate regular meals, Anita would get a separate plate with plain bread, carrots, celery, and red grapes. On meatloaf days Anita would not even sit at the dinner table with her parents. "Yuck yuck," she would say. On pizza days, the cheese and toppings would have to come off the pizza before Anita ate it. She didn't like the smell of cheese and wouldn't even eat macaroni and cheese—something that all kids were supposed to like. Her parents were surprised at her eating habits but thankful that she drank milk. When they brought the subject of Anita's food before the pediatrician, he laughed and said, "All children are picky eaters at this age. Don't you worry. She'll change soon. I am concerned, however, that she's not eating any meat. Please give her a daily vitamin—one with an iron supplement."

BY Thanksgiving of that year, Alan had made good progress on his research. His academic advisor told him that it was time to write up his dissertation and prepare to graduate the following spring. Kali was planning to graduate in summer 1983 with a masters degree in computer science and Meg would be getting her bachelors degree in business administration. Both Alan and Kali were excited as they started applying for jobs early in the spring semester of 1983.

"What are your plans, Alan?" asked Kali.

"I want to get a position at a good research university. Perhaps do some teaching also. What about you?"

"I'm applying for an industry job."

"That's probably good for you. Sometimes the things that happen in academia are just atrocious."

"I think it's the same in industry. Did something happen to you that I don't know about?"

"Three papers have been published from my research work. But I'm not listed as the first author on all of them."

"Why not?"

"I don't know. On two of the papers that are of reasonable quality, my name is listed first. On the third one, which is based on an excellent idea, my advisor, Prof. Dennis Lake, decided to put his name first because he felt that he had made numerous editorial changes to improve its presentation. The idea, of course, was mine, and so also was the work."

"Can't you tell him that it was your idea and that the names should be listed in alphabetical order? You told me that he was just a paper tiger."

"That's what I thought. A tiger that ate grass. Now I think he likes meat. What I've heard from other students is that he can make your life miserable and even fail you in the final exam."

"Uh-oh. Then you better not fight it, man. Remember that every place has its politics. One person cannot change the system. Unless you are Mahatma Gandhi. And he too didn't do it by himself. Better to be quiet, get your degree, and don't do the same thing to your students."

"Have you got any interviews lined up?"

"Not yet. It's a little hard for me because of my visa status."

"Why? Have you done something illegal?"

"Only to Lila. No, it's just that I need a work permit from Immigration to accept a job outside a university campus."

"That should be easy to get."

"Sometimes it is and sometimes it's not. The company that hires me has to sponsor me for a work permit. Many foreigners look for companies that will sponsor them to be permanent residents."

"Does it cost them money to do it?"

"Yes. Attorney's fees and other filing fees. But they'll get it from me by hiring me for lower wages until the process is completed and I become a resident alien."

"Resident alien? Sounds very Trekkie."

"That's the official name. The card that I finally receive is called a green card."

"No kidding. Green like the color of money, eh?"

"Yes. A very capitalist green."

By April of that year, Alan had a job offer from a Midwestern university. The University of Illinois at Urbana-Champaign was a good school and he accepted their offer to be a tenure-track assistant professor in the fall of 1983. Kali had applied for many jobs but hadn't been called for any interviews. Finally he got an interview from a fledgling company in Seattle called Microsoft. Unlike his other classmates who were flown to Silicon Valley in California, Microsoft was paying his round-trip Greyhound bus fare to Seattle.

Alan poked fun at him and said, "Are you sure you want to work for a company that won't even fly you in for an interview?"

"It's the only choice I have, man. I haven't been called for an interview by anyone else. I'd better not get picky. Besides, the job involves writing system-level code that I enjoy."

ANITA'S favorite bedtime companions were her *blanky* and a stuffed cow. She had learned to read by this time and her favorite book was *Green Eggs and Ham* by Dr. Seuss. She was also fascinated with numbers and could count up to 100 and add numbers up to 10. And she had learned all this on her own. She hated to be taught by anyone, exhibiting a stubbornness that left her parents depressed on many occasions.

When Meg graduated in August, Kali received a job offer from Microsoft. Both Alan and Kali decided to drive to their new jobs—Kali across the state to Seattle, and Alan across the country to Illinois. Lila had another year left at Wazzu and Kali was glad to be close to her. Alan sold his Volkswagen Bug to Kali who, for a change, knew all the problems about the used car he was buying. He and Alan had spent many hours fixing the air-cooled engine of the VW.

Alan rented a U-Haul truck, packed their belongings into it, and headed east. They passed through Idaho and through Big Sky country—the state of Montana where Robert Pirsig had spent a few years. At the end of the first day they stayed overnight at Mammoth Hot Springs. The next day they saw Old Faithful, the famous geyser of Yellowstone National Park. From there they went past West Thumb and Cody catching Interstate 90 near Sheridan and on into Rapid City, South Dakota where they stayed the night. They visited the Mt. Rushmore National Memorial and headed east on I–90. Of course, they had to stop at Wall—Anita had counted 96 signs to Wall Drug store on their trip from Pullman and was curious to see it. Since Mt. Rushmore was not advertised much at all, she was under the mistaken impression that Wall was the birthplace of the four presidents. The marketing god was already wielding his influence on her tender mind. On the drive through South Dakota they witnessed the most spectacular lightning they had ever seen. Fortunately it was in the distance and the thunderstorm did not affect their journey.

When they entered Iowa, the state sign read 'Iowa, A Place to Grow.' Meg wondered whether it was a statement about corn and soybeans that the governor had intended or whether it was a statement about personal growth. In interacting with her in-laws she had begun to question the Christian value system that she had been brought up to believe. She was asking herself questions about her growth as an individual and about the purpose of existence. During the last few years she had been undergoing a terrible feeling of guilt—about her Catholic upbringing, about sex, and about marrying Alan because she had slept with him. Perhaps he wasn't the right person for her. Perhaps she should have waited a little longer instead of rushing into marriage. Only time would tell.

They stayed overnight with one of Kali's friends in Ames, Iowa, a small university town where the first digital computer had been invented in 1939 by a physics professor, John Vincent Atanasoff. His ideas were usurped by some East-coast suits from Princeton who continue to take credit for the historic invention.

THE long drive from Pullman ended late in the afternoon the next day as they checked into a Motel 6 just outside Urbana. Like Washington State University, the University of Illinois is a Land Grant school. It is located in the twin cities of Urbana and Champaign, partly in Champaign but mostly in Urbana, with a combined population of 90,000. The metropolis of Chicago is two and a half hours northeast of Champaign along Interstate 57. The endless flat terrain of the Central Plains was quite different from the rolling hills of the Palouse and Inland empires of Washington. If your dog ever ran away from home in Illinois, you would be able to see it till the edge of the world.

Within a couple of days Meg and Alan found a two-bedroom duplex in Urbana with a one-car garage. They unpacked their things from the U-Haul and started the process of settling in their new home. Anita was excited because their new home was bigger than their old one in Pullman and she could run around and play in the backyard. The fenced backyard was a comforting feature to Meg, as she would not have to worry about Anita playing there by herself. From a neighborhood moving sale they bought a swing set with a slide and a sandbox and Alan fixed both of them in the backyard. Anita was very happy with the sandbox and soon forgot her friends in Pullman.

After a week or so Alan bought a used car, a two-door Honda Accord. The university was an unpleasant walking distance away, and Meg dropped Alan off at work everyday and kept the car for herself. She found a nice child-care facility for Anita, operated by a woman in her own home. The child-care provider, Mary Mathis, had two small children of her own and Anita started going to Mary's

65

place for 3 hours each afternoon as Meg ran various errands around town.

"Is there anything I should know about her?" inquired Mary of Meg.

"Not really. I hope she adjusts well. She hasn't been to any child-care at all. My husband and I have been taking turns looking after her. She doesn't eat any meat or cheese. Peanut butter sandwiches without jelly and the crust cut off. Oh, and one more thing. If you take the children to the library, watch out for her. For some strange reason, she always cries when I take her there, as if not wanting to go inside."

After a month or so, as Anita began to like Mary's place, Meg decided that she should also work. She sent out applications for jobs in the area and found one as a store manager at the mall in Champaign. Her work hours were between 9:00 A.M. to 6:00 P.M. on weekdays. Alan had to drop Anita off at Mary's place, drop Meg off at work, pick Anita up in the evening and then pick Meg up at 6 o'clock. Fixing dinner became a tiring chore and tensions ran pretty high. Meg had to abandon her notions of cooking quality meals with fresh vegetables because that took time and everyone was famished and tired in the evening. She made a partial food schedule for the week: Monday nights were leftovers, Wednesday nights they would use a coupon for pizza, and Friday nights would be take-out from a Chinese restaurant. Anita, after being at Mary's house and watching other children eat, was finally willing to try new foods, but not meat.

This went on for a month until Meg's job kept her later than 6:00 P.M. some nights. She asked Alan if they could buy a second car so that Anita could maintain an evening schedule of dinner at 6:30, followed by a bath, and bed time at half past eight. Alan exploded when he heard this idea.

"I don't think it's a good idea for you to work," he screamed.

"Why not? I haven't got my degree to stay at home all day long. I want to put my education to some use."

"Being a business major, you ought to know that it's foolish to spend dollars to save pennies."

"What do you mean? I don't get it."

"It's quite simple. Would you drive 10 miles to buy a box of cereal using a 50 cent store coupon?"

"Many people use coupons to buy groceries. My mom always uses coupons."

66

"Honey, you don't get it, do you? The cost of gas to travel 20 miles exceeds the savings you get from the coupon. You are better off buying the cereal from a nearby store without the coupon."

"What does that have to do with my job?"

"When you factor in the cost of the second car we will end up spending dollars and saving pennies. That's why I'm not sure it is a good idea for you to work outside the house."

Meg was stubborn and wanted to be independent. It was the last piece of advice her father had given her before she left Pullman.

"If you think it's a bad idea for both of us to work, why don't you stay at home?"

"Don't make me angry now. We both know that that doesn't make sense. Let's discuss this some other time." He went outside for a smoke.

In his graduate student days, Alan had, on many occasions, worn socks with holes in the toes. On cold winter days, he would wear two pairs of socks to keep warm, but sometimes his toes would still stick out. Spending money on cigarettes took higher priority over new socks. During the winter, when he had to walk back home at 3:00 A.M. after finishing an experiment, he would tell himself that once he got a real job, he would be able to afford a decent pair of socks. Both Meg and he had real jobs now, but even with two paychecks their monthly savings were meager. Between the house rent, utility bills, two cars, health and car insurance—especially one for Meg that had a high premium since she was under 25, federal and state taxes, and social security payments, he felt like he was going to have to wear socks with holes for the rest of his life.

The winter of 1983, their first one in the Midwest, was a hellish experience. The wind kept howling through the shingles. They were used to cold temperatures in Washington—the temperature in Pullman dipped below zero degrees Fahrenheit but the wind was blocked by the Cascade Mountains. In Illinois and the Central Plains the wind chill factor made winters uncomfortable. The only way to stay warm was to cover yourself with layers of clothing, especially cover the head, and wear woolen gloves inside a leather mitt. An exterior of leather was about the only thing that would stop the wind from penetrating through to your skin. Winterizing a car meant that you simply had to carry jump-start cables, a bag of sand, a gallon of gas, as well as heavy boots and a thick blanket.

And two pairs of socks without holes in them.

ONE evening in mid-March the following year, Anita surprised Alan by asking for an egg at dinner time. She had seen another child at Mary's house eat an egg and decided she was going to try one herself.

"How do you want it cooked, Anita?"

"Just the white part, Papa. I don't like the yellow. It looks yucky."

"Okay. One white egg coming up."

Since Meg was working late in the evenings, Alan was in charge of Anita's supper. He decided to fry the egg without the yolk. He could make a few things by himself—toast, eggs, coffee, tea, and sandwiches. He also knew how to order pizza.

"Papa, I know something that Mary doesn't."

"What's that dear?"

"I know where eggs come from."

"From the grocery store?" exclaimed Alan.

"No, Papa. That's what Mary said. Eggs come from chickens."

"Correct, correct. Your egg is ready. Time to eat now. Would you like a piece of bread with it?"

"Yes. And also a fork."

Alan quietly watched her eat her first egg at home. By this time Anita had trained her parents to leave her alone while eating. She didn't like any comments at all about her food and how she was eating it.

"Papa, where do chickens come from?"

"From eggs. Chickens lay eggs and baby chicks are born from the eggs. Do you remember what sound the chicken makes?"

"Cluck cluck goes the chicken. Papa, where did I come from?"

"Hmmm. Let's wait for mom to answer that one," replied a stumped Alan.

That night when Meg came home, Alan told her about the egg and Anita's question.

"What should I tell her next time she asks it?" he said.

"Tell her whatever feels right. I'm beginning to ask the same question myself. I don't know where I came from and I don't know where I'm going."

A couple of days later, Anita asked her dad for an egg again, white like the last time.

"Papa, where did I come from?"

"Honey, you came from mommy's stomach."

"Was I born from an egg, Papa?"

"Well, yes. But then you grew in mommy's stomach before you were born. Time to eat now."

"Papa, is mommy a chicken?"

"Don't be silly now. Mommy is not a chicken."

Later that night after her bath, Anita asked her dad to read the book on animals. When Alan came to the part about the chicken, Anita interrupted him.

"Papa, are baby chicks born from eggs?"

"Yes."

"Papa, how was the first chicken born? Which egg did that chicken come from?"

Now Alan was flabbergasted. His four-year old daughter had just asked him to explain the celebrated cause-and-effect tangle that had defied explanation for centuries.

Which came first, the chicken or the egg?

While he was thinking for what seemed to be a long time, Anita repeated her question.

"Papa, which egg did the first chicken come from?"

"Honey, this is not something that *you* should worry about. You're just a girl. Play with Barbie and leave this question to a few important men. When these specialists find the answer, they will tell the whole world."

"Papa, you always answer my questions. Can't you answer this one, please?"

"I'm afraid not. I don't know all the answers."

"Papa, do you know all the questions?"

"Bed time, Anita. Nite-nite."

Five

Anita turned four in May and would begin preschool in the fall. The following year she would attend half-day kindergarten.

Alan was busy writing up his research work for publication. Academia worked under the tenure system and he had to publish his work in scientific journals. The unwritten and unspoken rule of the tenure process was the number of publications that one had when being considered for tenure. This was an easy measure, easy for people to count, but did not truly represent the quality of one's research. Whatever dislikes one had of the tenure system, if you were in it and wanted tenure, you realized that the system could not be changed by one individual.

Alan, like many others in academia, fell into the rut of publishing papers and using the number of papers as "collateral" in applying for research funding from agencies such as the National Science Foundation. Funding agencies solicit proposals from scientific investigators, have them evaluated by their peers on the strength of the ideas and the credentials of the investigator, and make awards to the successful ones. The credentials of an investigator are measured by the number of published papers. An investigator with a large number of publications and good contacts easily obtains funding awards that are not entirely based on creative ideas. An investigator with creative ideas but few publications is not so fortunate. Funding and proposal writing operate more like a business venture with publication count being the measure of creativity.

After a while, it becomes easy for an individual caught up in the publishing game to actually consider himself or herself a good researcher based on the number of published papers. You start evaluating other people in a very quantitative manner by counting their publications, not pausing to ask whether any of the research work is being read by others, whether any of it is useful to society, whether any of it is disseminated to students, or whether any of it is useful in advancing the cause of science. If you do so, then you are in danger of admitting to yourself and to others the shallowness of your own research. Publication count in academia is *the* important aspect of one's credentials.

Being a physics major, it would not be easy for Alan to get other jobs and so he worked hard at his academic career. He became interested in using computers to solve some problems in physics, and sat in on an advanced course in computer programming. With a teaching load of two courses per semester, this took up a lot of time. There were some weeks when he would work 60 or 70 hours including weekends.

MEG was busy with her career too. Any ideas she had entertained about spending more time with Alan slowly disappeared. Life, for them, passed by one day at a time. On some days they would not even see each other. They barely managed to run the home, take care of their daughter, and take care of their jobs. Late nights were ruled out for Meg because Anita was an early riser. Alan was the one who got to sleep in late on weekends.

Partly because of the tension and partly due to the pressure of getting to work on time, Meg was involved in an accident. Her car was hit broadside at a four-way stop sign by a guy in a pick-up truck. Fortunately, the bodily injury was not severe.

When Alan heard about the accident, he was furious. "When are you going to learn to drive properly?" he screamed, not worried in the least bit about any injury to her.

"I know how to drive properly. I have a driver's license."

"Don't you know the rules at a four-way stop sign?"

"Yes I do. It wasn't my fault. I reached the intersection first. Whoever comes first gets right of way. Isn't that true?"

Alan shook his head from side to side in disbelief and said, "Uh-huh-huh. There are rules they teach you in driving school, and

71

there are rules you learn from experience. When a man and a woman arrive at a four-way stop sign at roughly the same time, the man always gets the right of way. Remember that in the future."

"But that's not fair. How do you know it's a rule?"

"From experience. Lots of women have learned this rule. It shouldn't be hard for you to learn it also. Believe me, it'll be a lot safer if you follow it. What's the guy's side of the story?"

"He claimed that I wasn't paying attention to the road but was beautifying myself in the rear-view mirror. I was not. I was just checking to see whether my bangs needed trimming. I knew I had reached the intersection before him. He wasn't even at the line. He had stopped way behind the line."

"It doesn't matter where you stop, but when you stop. Besides, I've seen you many times using the rear-view mirror for putting on makeup. Was there an accident report filed at the scene?"

"Yes. The male police officer asked me how old I was, and held me accountable for the accident."

"Shit. Our insurance premium is going to get bumped up. Is there anything at all you can do without getting into trouble?"

The rift between them widened as Meg replied, "Okay, okay. I'll do my best not to have any more accidents."

IN August of that year, just three weeks before school started for Alan and Anita, Mary Mathis dropped a bombshell on them. Her husband, Dan, was getting transferred. Dan worked for the Federal Highway Administration, and they would be moving to Sacramento, California. In the Federal government, getting transferred was one way of getting promoted. The move was planned during the first week of September around Labor Day.

Mary had worked out so well for them the previous year. She was an amazing woman and knew how to look after young children. Anita was so comfortable with her and Mary always had a genuine smile in the morning when Anita was dropped off and an equally genuine smile in the evening when Anita was picked up. Alan jokingly called her superwoman Mary.

As luck would have it, Anita's child-care problem was soon solved. A new family had moved into their neighborhood from Chicago. It was a single parent family, a mother and son, Rebecca and Chris. Chris was born in November 1979, and would be attending the same preschool as Anita. Rebecca, Becky for short, was divorced and had been on welfare for a year until she found a job in Urbana.

For all practical purposes, Chris was a normal child. The only problem with him was that he had not spoken a single word in his life. Becky was a little concerned when he didn't speak at age two and panicky when he remained silent at age three. The pediatrician had comforted her, "Don't worry. Chris is a healthy boy. Even Albert Einstein started talking quite late in life." At age four, however, when Chris still didn't talk, Becky was in despair. Could her son be retarded like his grandfather? Was he autistic? She asked the pediatrician to conduct a psychiatric evaluation. It turned out that there was nothing wrong with Chris. He just didn't want to talk.

About the time Becky got separated from her husband, her mother had died of complications from breast cancer. Her father, Major Norman Kay, was a retired army officer staying in Florida. When she got the job in Urbana, Becky requested that her father come and help her out with Chris until she was settled down. Her father agreed and took full charge of Chris. It was no problem for him to also take care of Anita after preschool was over. The plan was for the major to pick Anita up at 8:45 in the morning and drop her to preschool along with his grandson. At 11:30 he would pick them up. Despite the ugly scar on his face from an old motorcycle accident, the preschool teachers, who were in their fifties, found him very handsome. At least that's what he told Becky.

Meg was worried that Major Kay might impose some kind of military drill on her daughter and spoke to him at length about Anita's eating habits so he would know in advance not to force her to eat. Somewhat to her surprise, Meg found him a very likable man. The only condition he insisted on was that she not even think of paying him. Maybe $5 a week would be enough to cover Anita's lunch and snacks. That was all. Meg was confident that Anita would be in good hands. To return the favor, she invited Becky's family for dinner on the weekends when she was not working, and sent over a casserole or pie to them now and then. Chris and Anita became very good friends and so did Becky and Meg. Chris would show Anita how to fix Legos and Anita would read books to Chris. Becky and Meg would do things together like shopping or the movies, leaving the kids with Norm.

Norm taught Anita to count up to 100, to add and subtract numbers and multiplication. She recited the multiplication tables from 2 times 2 to 2 times 10 all the way to 10 times 10. Anita was fascinated with books, numbers, and the night sky. The planet Venus, the goddess of dusk in the western horizon, was her favorite. Norm was amazed by her abilities that far exceeded those of his grandson.

THE preschool they attended arranged field trips from time to time and on one occasion the teachers decided to take the children to the local library. It was November 17, 1984, Chris's fifth birthday. As they were about to enter the library, Anita burst out into uncontrollable tears and refused to go inside. Her favorite teacher, Mrs. Lang, had to be with her while the other children completed their field trip. Between sobs Anita kept asking for Major Kay, and Mrs. Lang just could not understand her fear about entering a harmless library. She knew that Anita loved books and had observed that her reading skills were well above the level expected of a preschooler.

Chris rushed over to her side. "Are you all right?" he asked. Both Anita and Mrs. Lang were shocked but overjoyed to hear him speak.

"He can talk, he can talk," yelled Anita, as her crying subsided.

"Why were you crying?" asked Chris.

"I don't know. I'm afraid to go inside the library."

Mrs. Lang hugged Chris, a bit unusual for her, and told him, "You are going to be all right. It's so wonderful to hear you talk."

Major Kay was delighted when he came to pick up the kids after school.

"Give me five, my man," he told his grandson, and Chris knew exactly what to do.

He telephoned Becky and she came home right away, taking the day off from work. It was a time to celebrate after many years of vexation.

"It's a trauma he had to overcome," said Major Kay to his daughter. "Sometimes when you die a terrible death in your past life, it requires an equally traumatic incident like Anita's fear of libraries to overcome it."

"Whatever you say, Dad. Thank God he's talking normally now."

That same day, Anita asked Major Kay to fix her an egg for lunch.

"Just the white part," she told him.

Major Kay fried the egg without the yolk like Meg had told him to do. Chris decided he wanted the same thing. As she was eating, Anita said, "Major Kay, do you know that my dad can't answer all the questions?"

"Really?"

"Yes, he told me so himself."

"That's very gracious of him to admit. Most people think they know the answers to all questions."

"I once asked him a question, and he did not know the answer."

"What question was that?"

"He told me that eggs come from chickens and chickens come from eggs. Then I asked him which egg the first chicken came from. And he said he did not know the answer."

A smile lit up the major's face as he asked her, "What did he say to you?"

"He said that some special men would find the answer and tell the whole world. He told me I was just a girl and asked me to play with my Barbie doll."

The smile turned into a frown. He couldn't believe the manner in which Alan had summarily snuffed his daughter's curiosity. Here she was, an innocent child, raising a fundamental issue in the philosophy of science.

First Cause. Big Bang. Supreme Being Principle.

Major Kay was very well read on these subjects. He had a passion for physics and metaphysics. For the last thirty years he had studied the writings of Albert Einstein, Carl Sagan, Stephen Hawking and others. In his opinion, nobody had answered her question satisfactorily.

In fact, it was not even a compelling question in modern times. Anybody who has gone into it in depth knows that it is hard to answer and quite complex to analyze. Civilization seems to have reached such a comfort zone with material goods and luxuries provided by technology that a question like this is simply not relevant any more. What has become important is the pursuit of success in terms of fame, personal wealth, and the steamy substance of the marketplace that changes direction whenever the wind changes direction.

Fortunately for us, there are a few soldiers in the Temple of Truth who are in vigorous pursuit of this question. Although, some of them pay a stiff personal price for haunting the inner confines of the temple's corridors. Robert Pirsig was one such soldier who experienced a mental breakdown during his pursuit of the Truth, he called Quality. There have been others before him and there will be others after him until a satisfactory answer is found.

As Major Kay picked Anita up and brushed her curly black hair back from her forehead, he kissed her brown eyes and told her, "Don't worry about what your father said, Anita. You are as much a part of the universe as anyone else. You have as much of a right to ask this question and find the answer. The next time you have such questions, you come and ask me. I will help you find the answers."

"Major Kay, do *you* know which egg the first chicken came from?"

"Yes, Anita. It is a very special egg that is hidden in the Easter Bunny's basket. It is at the bottom, it is dark black, and it is hard to notice among the other colorful eggs in the basket. We have to go on a treasure hunt to find that egg. Many people have hunted for that egg but have not found it. Maybe we will get lucky and find that egg someday."

"Holy kullolee. An Easter egg hunt! Can I join too, Grandpa?" asked Chris.

"Sure, sure. The three of us will go on an Easter egg hunt in spring. Okay?"

"Thank you Grandpa."

Major Kay could not believe that four-year old Anita would ask such a fundamental question, but it seemed to be appropriate. He wondered whether there were other fundamental questions that children would naturally ask but not get the right answers to. Anita would soon prove to him that that was indeed the case.

He decided to help Anita and Chris find the answer to her question. In order to do that, though, he would have to find a way to bring scientific discoveries and religious writings to a level that the children would understand. It would be a challenge, yet he was excited about meeting this particular challenge. Anita's question had stoked a fire that had been smoldering inside him for many years.

Six

\

Back in the year 1925, on Wednesday, March 18, a man named Christopher was having a hard day. He owned a small service station in Murphysboro, Illinois, seven miles northwest of Carbondale. That day he had received several complaints about the quality of his automotive repair work. In the small town of 4,000 people he had to personally attend to every complaint. Little did he know that after putting out the customer fires, his day would become even harder. The trailing edge of a thunderstorm, filled with flashes of lightning, passed overhead around noon and it seemed as though the weather would become sunnier.

He decided to go home early for lunch and check on his wife, Kitty, who was nine months pregnant with their second child and ready to deliver any day soon. Their eldest daughter, Dawn, was barely three years old.

"Honey, can you take the afternoon off today?" asked Kitty.

"Sure. Are you all right?" replied Christopher.

"I'm feeling very weak and my labor pains have begun. I'll probably deliver the baby today. Dawn was terribly scared during the thunderstorm this morning and clung on to me the whole time."

"Why don't I take you to the hospital now?"

"There's still time. Let's go after you have lunch."

Christopher had a simple lunch of bread and chicken-noodle soup in their one-story farmhouse. Kitty didn't feel like eating or drinking anything. After clearing the dishes, he gave Dawn some milk and made some coffee for himself. He telephoned the service shop and told Mel, his senior mechanic, to take charge for the rest of the day.

Reading the newspaper while sipping coffee on the porch was a ritual for him. In the distance he heard a muffled roar. He put out his cigarette and looked towards the southwest sky. Dark masses of clouds were moving in his direction.

"Come quick, honey," shrieked Kitty as he finished his coffee.

"What's the matter?" asked Christopher, rushing inside.

"We had better go to the hospital now."

"All right dear."

KITTY'S contractions were becoming more painful as she got her bag ready for the hospital. Christopher went outside to bring the car close to the house. Looking up, he saw the clouds becoming darker and heard a peculiar whistling noise that sounded like the buzzing of a million bees. At his next glance towards the sky, he saw swirling mists of clouds that were beginning to shape into thin funnels. The mists were changing to a solid brown mass, and as the hissing sound became louder Kitty's contractions occurred closer together.

Christopher left his car, ran full speed towards the house, and yelled to Kitty above the loud whistling noise, "There's a cyclone approaching us. We can't go to the hospital now. Can you manage till it's over?"

"Please take Dawn and go to the cellar. I can't move at all. But I'll be all right."

He kissed her and said, "We'll be back soon. Hold tight to the easy chair. I love you honey."

As Christopher grabbed Dawn and headed for the root cellar which was 50 yards from the house, the hissing sound changed to a terrible deafening roar that swamped out the noise of the warning sirens. They reached the cellar and got inside just as the house began vibrating and ripping apart.

"Oh my God! A big one," he yelled. The last thing he remembered hearing before closing the cellar door was the roar of a thousand freight trains.

The deafening sound continued for what seemed to him like an eternity. When it died down after 15 minutes, he got out into a torrential downpour. He located Kitty about 100 yards from the house and rushed to her side.

She had been thrown from her chair and was lying unconscious with a broken piece of the dining table close to her head. He didn't notice any bleeding from her body. Nearby he heard a baby crying. He couldn't believe his ears. He found the baby, picked it up, and ran to the cellar.

"Dawn, dearie, please stay here until I get back. You will be fine. I have to get some help for mommy. Okay?"

"Mommy, mommy," cried Dawn.

"She'll be all right. You stay here and wait for papa to come back. Don't touch the baby and don't leave the cellar."

He bundled up the baby in a blanket, sprinted to the car, and drove to his service shop. Fortunately it had not been damaged much.

"I need help," he screamed, as he rushed inside. "Mel, you and Joe come home with me right now. I'll explain on the way. Joe, you drive."

Christopher told them what had happened. They carried Kitty into the back seat of the car, and dropped Mel and Dawn at the service station.

"Take care of her till I get back," said Christopher.

Joe drove as fast as he could to Carbondale. Christopher was in the back seat, holding on to Kitty and the baby. When they reached the hospital, Christopher darted inside and said, "My wife needs help right away. She's unconscious. Can one of you please take care of this baby? It was born a few minutes ago when the cyclone slammed into our house. I don't know what to do with it."

He handed the baby to one of the nurses and he and Joe carried Kitty into the hospital. The nurse could not feel her pulse and immediately summoned a doctor. They tried hard to revive her, but Kitty's lifeless body did not respond to anything. After a while, the doctor said, "We've tried everything. There's nothing more we can do now. I'm terribly sorry."

THE tornado had done extensive damage to the town. Several houses were unroofed, walls blown down, trees uprooted, and debris scattered all over the place. Twenty-five children who had taken shelter in the school gymnasium had died. Small animals were killed and horses were carried distances ranging from a quarter- to a half-mile, some still tied to their broken fence posts. A grain silo near their house was miraculously standing upright. The kidney-shaped coffee table in the living room was in its exact same spot, as if glued to the floor.

The twister, called the Tri-State tornado, formed in southeast Missouri, cut a swath across southern Illinois, and ended 219 miles away in Indiana. It killed a total of 689 people, injured 1,980, and caused about $17 million in damage. On the Fujita scale for classifying the intensity of tornadoes, this one was rated as F5—an incredible tornado with wind speeds exceeding 250 mph.

Christopher was deeply saddened at the circumstances surrounding his wife's death, wondering to himself why on earth he had not taken her to the hospital before lunch. The only solace for his guilt was the child she had delivered unto him. When he went to check on the baby, the nurse told him that it was a healthy boy.

That was how Norman Kay entered the world. The hospital recorded his time of birth as 1:37 P.M. His mother had paid the ultimate price to give him the gift of life.

IT was very hard for Christopher to manage two small children and despite the help and support he got from his parents and Kitty's parents, he thought it best to get remarried. His second wife, Beverly, was a good woman but not used to dealing with small children. It would be a learning experience for her.

While Dawn was an easy child to raise, Norm was the exact opposite. He was an extremely independent and stubborn child. It was hard for Beverly to discipline Norm, and on some occasions she would find herself spanking him into obedience. She certainly would have been guilty of child abuse by today's standards but in those days it was all right to spank a child who misbehaved. When it comes to raising stepchildren, it is much easier to love a child who is well behaved than one who isn't. Norm's temperament made it very hard for Beverly to love him. She was as nice to him as she could possibly be as a mother, but did not love him as a true mother would. So during his childhood years, Norm did not experience the true feeling of motherly love.

They lived through the Great Depression that began in 1929 and ended when World War II broke out. Dawn graduated from school and got married at the age of 18. Norm went on to pick up his undergraduate degree in physics from the University of Pittsburgh. Then, in 1947 he decided to enlist in the army at the age of 22. By that time the horror of the war had taken its toll on many people's lives. Joining the armed forces was the last thing that came to one's mind. Norm, however, thought it best for him to take a break from school, and he liked the disciplined life in the army. A totally different Norm from his childhood years.

IN the army there was a routine to be followed, duties assigned to everybody, and a strict chain of command. Outside of the armed forces, people talk about leadership and what it means to be a good leader. They do not think that being a good follower is a necessary condition for being a good leader. Leader and follower are considered exclusive opposites of each other. There are many who would claim that the world has not produced a great leader in the last 30 years, and they would be right. Except for leaders with a background in the armed forces. Such people make good leaders because they have learned how to be good followers, a necessary experience in being an effective leader.

There was another reason that Norm wanted a break from education. He had been disillusioned by some of the answers he received during his study of physics. In his sophomore year, his professor had quoted a passage from Lord Kelvin's writings:

> *"...if you can measure that of which you speak and can express it by a number, you know something of your subject. But if you cannot measure it, your knowledge is meager and unsatisfactory."*

It made perfect sense to him as he conducted experiments and measured quantities to test scientific hypotheses. Then in his senior year in a course in quantum mechanics, he was taught the uncertainty principle of Werner Heisenberg, which stated that one could not simultaneously measure both the position and the speed, actually momentum, of a fundamental particle such as the electron. If you tried to measure the position accurately, then the speed would not be accurate and vice versa. And why would you want to measure both the position and the speed? Would one of them not be enough, and couldn't they be measured one at a time? You could first measure the speed and then measure the position. These questions were easily answered. A theory should be able to predict future states of particles based on their present state. Since the particle is in motion, its present state is captured by two quantities—its position and its speed. With the knowledge of *both* these quantities, one could then use the theory to make predictions about the future state of the particle.

The uncertainty principle has been discussed by many physicists and philosophers and is still the subject of a lot of controversy. It introduced unpredictability and randomness into physics. When Norm questioned the professor as to why one should believe this principle, he was told that many scientists had accepted it because it agreed with experimental results.

Norm was disturbed by that answer. The principle stated that you could accurately measure either the speed or the position of a particle but not both. Assume that for a given particle, its speed was accurately measured but not its position. Since the particle was in motion and always had a position, how could one argue that the uncertainty principle agreed with experimental results when there was no way to measure the position of a moving object? Was it, in fact, the inability of science to make simultaneous accurate measurements of position and speed that led to the uncertainty principle? What was the goal of science? Certainly not limited to formulating principles and theories that could *only* be confirmed by experimental observations, he thought. Or was it?

Later on Norm would find out that Einstein had objected to the randomness introduced into physics by quantum mechanics, but for now, he wanted to take time off and discover for himself the answers to some of his questions. The army was a good place to drift for a while and ponder such matters. He took all his books with him and, unlike the other cadets, spent a lot of his free time studying physics. His interest in science and scientific inquiry was not superficial; he had a true desire to get to the bottom of things. He believed that there was some basic underlying truth that governed the universe and the goal of science was to determine a theory that described it.

NORM'S initial posting was at Letterkenny Army Depot located in south central Pennsylvania near Chambersburg. The primary mission of the army installation there was maintenance. Norm's army training was intense for the first month but after that he got used to it. Within a couple of years he was transferred to Oakland Army Base in California. By that time he had saved enough money to afford a motorcycle. He bought a nice used one that needed a little work, but he fixed it and it ran just fine. On weekends, he would ride up north with his best friend, Bill Kaplan, to a place off San Pablo Bay called Lone Tree Point. There, they would sit with their books, smoke at least a pack of cigarettes, and read for most of the day. Norm had turned from physics to metaphysics as he pursued his quest for some sort of basic truth.

Bill, however, was more mystical in his approach to enlightenment. According to him, the universe was like an energy field that flowed between the negative pole of the Chinese *yin* and the positive pole of *yang*. To be at one with the universe, therefore, was not a static condition but a dynamic one. His favorite poets were Omar Khayyam and Jalal-ud-din Rumi and to break the monotony of their day Bill would recite loudly from their poems:

The Worldly Hope men set their Hearts upon
Turns Ashes — or it prospers; and anon,
Like Snow upon the Desert's dusty Face
Lighting a little Hour or two — is gone.

Think in this batter'd Caravanserai
Whose Doorways are alternate Night and Day,
How Sultan after Sultan with his Pomp
Abode his Hour or two, and went his way.
                                                    —Khayyam

Physical senses are the ladder for this world;
Religious senses are the ladder for heaven.

The man of God is a treasure in the ruins.
The man of God is an ocean without limits.
The man of God is made wise by Supreme Truth.
The man of God is beyond faith and godlessness.
                                                    —Rumi

AS Norm started reading metaphysics, the branch of philosophy that addresses the ultimate nature of existence, reality and experience, he began to understand that there had been a different approach to science in the last century. Theories were based on scientific materialism whose basic tenet was that all reality consisted of matter. Matter existed and all things were explicable in terms of matter alone. Thus, free choice was considered to be an illusion since matter could not act freely. Norm wondered about this for a while. Did a thought in one's head exist or not? Was it composed of matter? And when a professor explained something in the classroom did the professor's thoughts get transferred from his head to your head during the process of understanding? He couldn't believe that a thought consisted of matter and could move from one place to another. What he did believe was that some process took place when knowledge was imparted in the classroom as one tried to understand something. When you understood something it was as if something clicked inside your head. What that process was or how it worked was not clear to him.

In the 20th century, physics was turning science away from the materialistic trend it had in the 19th century. Atomic physics introduced a duality aspect to matter—it could sometimes be viewed as a particle and it could sometimes be viewed as a wave. Maybe it was a wave all the time and when you tried to "measure" the wave in terms of position and speed, you could not do both accurately. That might have been why the uncertainty principle established a boundary for physics—a sort of limitation as to what could and could not be measured.

ABOUT that time there was trouble brewing in the Korean peninsula in the Far East. The peninsula was under Japanese control from 1910 and when World War II ended in 1945, the Soviet Union helped establish a government in North Korea and the United States helped establish a government in South Korea. When the United States withdrew its forces from South Korea in January 1950, North Korea invaded South Korea in June 1950. The attack consisted of North Korean troops, which were much better trained and equipped than those in the South that crossed the 38th parallel and occupied Seoul, the capital of South Korea. President Harry Truman, without a congressional declaration of war, committed U.S. involvement in

Korea and moved the U.S. Seventh Fleet into the Formosa Strait off Taiwan, a show of strength to intimidate China and prevent them from getting involved. He appointed General Douglas MacArthur as American commander in East Asian theater of operations. General MacArthur committed his ground, air, and naval forces against North Korea. Thus started the Korean War or as some would call it, the Korean conflict, depending on your point of view.

Norm's unit was commissioned to go to Korea in July 1950. His job was to perform maintenance and repair work on tanks and other equipment. The United States had contributed most of the air and sea power and about half of the ground troops with the remaining troops coming from the ranks of the South Koreans and UN forces. Within a couple of months the North Koreans were pushed out of South Korea. But the Chinese got involved in the war and by year's end the Chinese army struck with full force. MacArthur was caught by surprise at the extent of the Chinese involvement, and American and South Korean units had to retreat south of the 38th parallel. The city of Seoul was once again in the hands of the North Koreans.

During this attack, the United States had to muster up all the reserves and send them to the front lines. It was Norm's first experience holding a gun in an actual war. The training he had received in the army did not prepare him for what he experienced. It never does. He *actually* shot and killed other human beings—those were his orders and he was carrying them out. The bloodshed that he witnessed, the injuries to his colleagues, and the acrid melange of scorched metal, melted rubber and decomposed bodies would linger in his memory for a long time. Norm got through the fighting by reminding himself that he was a soldier and that he was doing his duty, and this gave him the strength to carry on.

The South Koreans were friendly to the American troops. Some of them spoke a little English and Norm would talk to them to find out more about their culture. The Korean language was so different from English—the alphabet set, the grammar, and the phonemes had no connection whatsoever with Latin. English was funny in its own way too. A word like phoneme, which represents the sound of a given letter, should itself be one of the easy ones to sound out. It would be if it were spelled 'fohnemes' rather than 'phonemes.' All very phony. The Koreans had a strange body language when it came to answering no to a question. Whenever they answered no, they would nod their heads up and down which to Norm would mean yes. It took a little getting used to at first. Life in Korea was totally different from what he had seen in the United States. People got by on less and expected far less than what was expected as the standard of living in the United States.

IN April 1952, Norm got his orders to return stateside. Negotiations for a cease-fire had been going on for some time but the talks were frequently suspended and no firm agreements had been reached. He was happy to leave Korea and as he lay down on a canvas bunk in the troopship going back home, he thought about the war and what it had done to him. Bill Kaplan had become a war statistic. Norm would never be able to forget him—he was the one by Bill's side as he took his last breath in the 43rd MASH unit, a group of 100 soldiers who staffed a 36-bed hospital. The doctors had done their best, but Bill would not come back. His last words to Norm were, " Read Khayyam my friend. You will find the answers you are looking for. The Moving Finger writes; and, having writ, Moves on: . . ."

Being neither a celebrity nor a hero, except to his family and friends, Bill would soon be forgotten. This was the fate of many soldiers on both sides who had walked the Korean hills, crossed its rivers, and proudly fought for their country. As the odor of death passed through his nostrils, Norm's thoughts drifted towards the meaning of existence and the purpose of life.

He recalled something he had read in Oakland about the old story of science. About matter being the only thing that existed. That nothing in man could survive death. That if thinking was an activity of the brain, then it could not continue after the brain was destroyed. That every part of man was matter and every part was mortal.

His experience with death in the war was having an effect on him and his beliefs about life and death. He recited a verse from a poem that he had read in high school, *Elegy Written in a Country Churchyard* by Thomas Gray:

> *Can storied urn or animated bust*
> *Back to its mansion call the fleeting breath?*
> *Can Honour's voice provoke the silent dust,*
> *Or Flatt'ry soothe the dull cold ear of death?*

He could remember as a child being told stories of God and the soul of human beings. What was the nature of the soul? Did it consist of matter? If so, then how could the soul exist after one died? If the soul consisted of matter and could somehow exist in the universe after one's death, then it would defy the laws of physics that he had learned. He wondered whether there was a reason for humans to believe in God. Perhaps humans had a basic internal need to deny their non-existence and thus establish for themselves a permanence in the universe. Maybe that was why one's soul was considered sacred and permanent.

The troopship reached California and after spending a couple of months at his base in Oakland, he was transferred to Fort Knox, Kentucky.

Seven

Joann Larson was born and brought up in Iowa. Her family owned two farms and as she grew up she helped out with her share of the chores. After graduating from high school she found a job as a nanny for a family with two small children in Louisville, Kentucky. She worked there for a year and then decided to earn a college degree at the University of Louisville. The money she had saved in her nanny's job was not enough, so she worked part time as a waitress to pay her way through college. That's how she met Norm. On weekends, he would ride his motorcycle 25 miles to the café where she worked and spend a lot of time drinking coffee and reading. There were times when she refilled his cup a dozen times. Joann was a pretty girl and everyone noticed her, including Norm. To him, Joann's face looked like the face of kindness itself. There was no single feature that stood out but the total effect was magic. With a vivacious nature and svelte figure, she put her full being into whatever she did, including waitressing.

Joann saw that Norm was in the army, but she could not believe that an army man would read that much. Especially the kinds of books on physics and philosophy that Norm was reading. She found that somewhat strange and mostly out of curiosity, she asked him to take her to a movie. That was a very forward thing to do at the time, but Norm didn't mind.

They rode on his 350cc Bullet Roadster made by Royal Enfield in India. It had four gears, one down and three up. The gearbox was bolted to the crankcase and it was a two-valve pushrod design. The gold lines on the gas tank and mudguard were hand-painted by an artist at the factory in Tiruvottiyur, Madras, an art form that continues to this day. Norm had bought the used bike from a British gentleman. The single-cylinder thumper needed a little work, but after fixing it the bike cruised at a maximum speed of 50 mph.

For the first date, Norm had primped himself and looked immaculate from the outside. Joann had dressed more casually in jeans and a jacket as this would be her first motorcycle ride. After the movie they went to an ice cream shop. Norm discovered that Joann was very good-hearted, volunteering her time to many community activities, and as pretty, if not more, on the inside as she was on the outside. Maybe some of it came from her Midwestern values. Slowly but surely he began to fall in love with her.

They started dating each other once a week. The feeling of being considered very special by someone else was something Norm had not felt before in his life.

Joann found out why Norm was reading so much. He told her about his experiences in Korea and about Bill Kaplan's death. She had never wondered about any of the questions that Norm was asking. She was raised by her parents to attend church every Sunday and she believed in the Lord Jesus Christ. He was the savior of humanity who sacrificed Himself so others could live. In their conversations, Norm asked Joann several questions about the New Testament. Were Matthew, Mark, and Luke the actual authors of the Gospels? Had they really listened to Jesus Christ or had they merely scribed the Lord's sayings from others who had actually listened to Him? Joann's view was that the Bible contained the Word of God and that one was not supposed to question it. Norm, of course, disagreed. He had a difficult time understanding Joann's strong faith in Christianity.

IN May 1953, Norm proposed to Joann and they got married in the fall of that year. The wedding date had been set for August 29th. Norm's father, Christopher, had undergone heart surgery in the beginning of August and was recuperating in a hospital. A couple of days before his wedding, Christopher's condition worsened and Norm was asked to come immediately to Murphysboro. Like a dutiful son, he rushed to his father's bedside and was in time to hold his father's hand as he died in the hospital on August 29th. Joann was with him throughout the ordeal. Of course, the wedding had to be postponed and they got married on September 26th that year.

Both he and Joann insisted that Norm's stepmother, Beverly, come and live with them in Kentucky for a few months. After politely turning down their initial invitation, Beverly could not refuse repeated requests to come and visit them. She decided to spend a couple of months at their home. Joann made Beverly feel so comfortable in their home and treated her as her own mother. Norm also spent a lot of time with Beverly who couldn't help thinking to herself that he was a totally different person than the one she remembered. He was very much like his father in his pursuit of philosophy and religion. When talking to Beverly, Norm found out some things about his dad that he never knew before. He discovered that his dad had an avid interest in philosophy and religion. Beverly recalled a brief conversation she had some years ago with Norm's dad.

"Do you believe in reincarnation?" Christopher had asked her.

"No. That's not described in the Bible," Beverly had replied.

"Do you believe that everyone has a soul?"

"I think so."

"Do you think the soul is eternal and existence merely a human manifestation of the spirit?"

"I don't know. Only heaven and hell are eternal. That's what I've been taught."

Norm was very curious about his dad's question and asked Beverly to tell him more. But she did not remember any more than that. Christopher was a quiet man and rarely talked much about anything to anybody. He probably knew that Beverly did not share his beliefs and did not pursue the matter with her. Norm asked her whether his father had written down some of his beliefs in philosophy. Beverly replied that she didn't know but would look through the house and send over anything she found to Norm.

BEFORE Beverly returned to her home in Illinois, she suggested to Norm that he write down his questions and thoughts in a private diary as he went along lest he forget them later on. He thought it was a great idea. Perhaps in the process of writing them down he would be able to determine whether some of his questions were dumb. Perhaps he would find answers to some of his questions. From that day on, Norm kept a journal recording all his questions and thoughts. He wrote down the following questions:

• *Does the soul consist of matter?*

• *Is the soul eternal, and is human existence only a manifestation of the soul?*

• *What existence test would one apply to determine if the soul exists after death?*

• *As humans, do we have a basic need to deny our non-existence? Is the reason we believe in God and soul a selfish reason—to establish for ourselves a permanence in the universe?*

• *What exactly happens when one dies?*

• *Is the goal of science limited to formulating principles and theories that can only be confirmed by experimental observations and validated by mathematical reasoning?*

• *What is the basis for the uncertainty principle of quantum mechanics?*

• *If everything that exists consists of matter, does a thought in one's head exist or not?*

He first thought of classifying these questions into categories. A category for philosophy, a category for religion, and one for physics. But then he convinced himself that all three branches had to be in pursuit of the truth. He was sure of physics but not so sure about philosophy and religion. For the time being he decided to leave the questions as they were and to write more as they occurred to him.

91

IN mid-August that year, Joann told Norm that she was expecting a baby. The baby was due in late April the following year. It was very good news for Norm. He had been pondering questions related to death in the last couple of years after returning from the war. Now, he would have a chance to witness the birth of a life.

After marriage, Joann had requested Norm to attend church every Sunday. While Norm did believe in a concept of God, he didn't think that the church would provide any real answers as to who or what God was. The priest would give a weekly sermon from the New Testament and they would sing some hymns in praise of the Lord. As long as that was what Joann wanted to do every Sunday, Norm just did it. He added another question to his journal.

• *If there is a God, did this God leave behind His Word so that humans could find out the meaning and purpose of life? Is this Word of God contained in the Bible?*

He decided to study the origins of the Bible. Going to church had awakened his inner curiosity. He first read about the origins of the Old Testament, or the Hebrew Bible. Around the 3rd century B.C. there was a large Jewish community living in the city of Alexandria in Egypt. Their religious texts were written in Hebrew but the common language spoken at the time was Greek. King Ptolemy I of Egypt, who succeeded Alexander the Great, decided that as sacred as Hebrew was, it was more important that people read the religious writings than to preserve them in the Hebrew language. The message, he felt, was so important that one had to be able to read it. So he hired 72 Jewish scholars to translate the religious texts into Greek. The translation that they produced was originally called the Septuagint. The scholars had to consult several books, and selectively chose some portions that they felt would be useful to pass on. The books that they consulted, the notes they made during the selection process, and the original copy of the Septuagint were kept in a library in Alexandria. The Alexandrian library was founded by Ptolemy I and supported under the rule of the Ptolemys of Egypt. They attracted scholars from all over the world by funding and housing them in the Library, and it became the literary and scientific center of the Hellenistic and Roman eras. The Ptolemys valued original scrolls of manuscripts and went to great lengths to get original works from Persia, India, and other parts of the world. There were many fires associated with the destruction of portions of the library, especially its apocryphal burning during Julius Caesar's entry into Alexandria in 48 B.C. and some time during the 5th century A.D. the library was eventually destroyed by a fire. At the time it must have contained a million handwritten papyrus scrolls from many cultures and in many languages of the world. Civilization had permanently lost not only the original ancient writings from which the Old Testament was derived, but also important scientific and mathematical writings gathered over a period of seven centuries. Lost in that fire were writings of Jews in the Persian period, the writings of Josephus who had believed in reincarnation, and numerous books that were referred to in the Hebrew Bible. Biblical scholars would never know about the selection process that the scholars used in choosing from some books and not others—in closing the canon for the Old Testament.

AS he read the Old Testament in some detail, Norm could not find answers to any of his questions. He did not find anything that he felt could explain to him some basic truths about the universe in scientific terms that he could understand. He added some more questions to his journal.

• *Does the Old Testament shed any light on existence and our purpose in the universe?*

• *Does anybody else besides me have doubts about the accuracy of the Old Testament? Is it possible that in closing the canon the scholars may have missed out some important early writings?*

• *Is there an uncertainty principle that applies to religion— that one cannot know the Word of God and write it down or explain it clearly to someone else at the same time?*

This last question was based, in part, on his dialogue with some priests. When asked to explain what exactly the Bible said about the truth in the universe, they frequently resorted to answers like, "He is Omnipotent—He is Omniscient—and He knows the purpose—it is not clear to you now, but one day He will enlighten you. Just pray to Him, believe in Him, and follow the Gospel of the kingdom of God."

When he heard answers like that Norm felt that either the priests did not know the answers themselves, or they could not satisfactorily explain it to him.

NEXT, Norm started reading the New Testament. It was divided into four main parts. The first part contained the four Gospels according to Matthew, Mark, Luke and John. The second part contained the Acts of the Apostles. The third part contained the Epistles of Paul— letters by him and others as they spread the Christian Church in the Roman empire and established Christianity as a new world religion. The fourth part contained the Book of Revelation. The New Testament was originally written in Greek. The Gospels themselves were anonymous books and neither the original authors nor the original manuscripts of the four Gospels have been found. The sands of the Middle East have been guarding them for centuries, occasionally giving up a few secrets in the form of fragments of ancient manuscripts. The dry heat in Asia Minor helps in preserving papyri and in 1920 a tiny tattered piece of papyrus about the size of a hand was found in Egypt. It was a fragment from the Gospel of John, and the writing had a single question: "What is truth?"

The surrounding text was from John 18:38, and it is perhaps the oldest original fragment of the New Testament ever found.

. One night when Norm was reading the Gospel of Luke, he came across a passage that he thought he had read before.

But Jesus called unto him, and said, suffer little children to come unto me, and forbid them not for of such is the kingdom of heaven. — Luke 18:16.

He was reading Luke for the first time, and yet this passage sounded familiar. He flipped back the pages to the writings of Matthew and Mark, and to his surprise found passages that were similar to the one he had read in Luke.

But Jesus said, suffer little children, and forbid them not to come unto me: for of such is the kingdom of heaven. — Matthew 19:14.

94

But when Jesus saw it, he was much displeased, and said
unto them, suffer little children to come unto me, and forbid
them not: for such is the kingdom of heaven. — Mark 10:14.

IT was no coincidence that Norm had found passages that were similar. Biblical scholars have referred to the Gospels of Matthew, Mark, and Luke as the synoptic Gospels. The prevalent belief is that the Gospel of Mark, which is presumed to be the one that was written first, and another mysterious document called Q were used as sources by Matthew and Luke in writing their Gospels. That is, Matthew and Luke, who wrote their Gospels 15 or 20 years after Mark wrote his, had in front of them two sources that they scribed from: one was Q and the other was the Gospel of Mark.

But John's Gospel was different. It was the last of the four Gospels to be written, and John who was a beloved disciple of Jesus was one of the original twelve apostles. Before the New Testament was put together in its present form, John's Gospel was kept in a church in Ephesus, known as Efes in modern day Turkey.

As he studied the origins of the New Testament, Norm was somewhat mystified by what he had read. Mark was a friend of the apostle Peter and Luke was a friend of the apostle Paul. Actually, Paul was not one of the original twelve apostles. He was a persecutor of the followers of Jesus Christ until one day, on the road to Damascus, a vision of Jesus appeared before him. That vision transformed Paul into a dedicated missionary for Christianity and the title of apostle was extended to him by later writers. Matthew was one of the original twelve apostles, a tax collector and not a laborer like the other apostles. Excluding the writings of Matthew and John, where were the writings of the other ten original apostles? By this time Norm was suspicious about the accuracy of the New Testament and whether or not the four Gospels contained the Word of God.

His suspicions were confirmed when he read how the present day Bible was put together. The process by which the canon of the New Testament was formed began in the 2nd century with a collection of some of the letters of Paul. There were debates among the scholars of that period as to what should go in the canon and what should not. About that time, the Emperor Constantine wanted 50 Bibles and was willing to pay a nice price for them. There was no choice for the scholars but to obey the Emperor's orders, especially as he was willing to fund the production of the Bibles. So the debates were cut short, the canon was closed, and the New Testament came into being.

In 1945 the sands of the Middle East revealed another of their secrets—the Nag Hammadi papyri which contained many ancient writings, one among those being the Gospel of Thomas who was one of the original twelve apostles of Jesus Christ. None of Thomas's writings are included in the canonized version of the Bible. The Gospel of Thomas is not as organized as the other Gospels in the New Testament and it is mostly in question and answer form—as though the living Jesus was directly speaking to him.

From what he had read so far, Norm was convinced of one thing—that the religious writings in the Old and New Testaments were not complete. That they did not contain the *total* preaching of the Gospel of God. That they were not presented from a scientific viewpoint. They were writings of faith, and described covenants and laws and had great rhetorical power. They were not writings that would be useful to him in his inquiry into truth.

ALL this reading and studying took up so much of his spare time that he neglected Joann completely. One day she lost her temper and exploded.

"Nobody in my family ever questions the Bible like you've been doing. Several members of our church and millions of Christians around the world believe in the Lord Jesus Christ. There comes a point in your life when you ought to have faith."

"Yeah, yeah. That's what the Bible thumpers in Iowa have told you. How do you know it's true?"

"How dare you talk to me like that?" Her face became the color of a ripe tomato. "Don't you have any respect for anything? Has science been able to create life? Isn't that a mystery of God? How can so many people who believe in Him be wrong?

"What gives you the right to question the authority of the church? Can your science and logic explain everything, you damn bastard?"

Now there were tears in her eyes. Norm kept his mouth shut. This was not the right time for him to answer any questions. As he hugged her and held her tight, he thought to himself that religion had a tremendous grip over people. It appeared to him as a close-knit cult seeking power and control over the masses. He decided to close his books for a while, spend time with Joann, and await the birth of their first child.

Eight

In January 1984 Kali and Lila decided to get married. Kali's parents wanted the ceremony to be held in New Delhi and they promised to do all the planning. The first step was to choose an auspicious time based on the horoscopes of the bride and groom. The astrologers came back with a date of June 2. In traditional families the wedding would be the first time the bride and groom would meet, but that was not the case with Kali and Lila.

Vivaha or the marriage ceremony is one of the oldest and most important rites of passage of Hindu religion. *Grahastha Ashram,* or the householder stage, is rich in symbolism and viewed not as a concession to human weakness but as a means for spiritual growth. Man and woman are soul mates who, through the sacred covenant of marriage, embark on a spiritual journey. Hindu marriage is a life-long commitment of one wife and one husband, and is the strongest social bond that takes place between a man and a woman and their families. Although there are differences in the way the ceremony is performed from region to region and caste to caste, the final aim is Eternal Unity.

A day before the wedding Kali's female relatives and their friends and Lila got together at Kali's aunt's house for the *Mehendi* ceremony. The young people decorated their palms and feet with henna and Lila was teased with music and dance about her soon-to-be husband and in-laws.

On the wedding morning both Kali and Lila found out what it meant to be really clean. Lila was given an oil bath by applying oil to her feet, hands, knees, and shoulders five times. She refused to allow them to apply oil to her hair, which was so accustomed to shampoos and conditioners. Kali was scrubbed with turmeric powder applied in the same way.

Traditionally the groom's family and friends go to the bride's home in a procession called a *barat*. The groom sits on a decorated horse and is in the center of the procession accompanied by a live band that provides music for dancing by the *baratis*. Since the wedding was held at Kali's home, he was so thankful to have missed this exciting part of the ceremony.

Lila was bedecked with jewelry and wore an intricately embroidered pink wedding dress. *Mehendi* on her hands and feet, *bindi* on her forehead and bangles completed the necessary accessories. Kali wore the traditional churidar-pyjama and a turban.

For the wedding ceremony they were escorted to a *mandup,* a wooden frame whose posts were draped with flowers. They were seated before *Agni,* a sacred fire, separated by a screen.

In Hindu marriages the bride and groom are likened to Indian goddesses and gods: Shakti and Shiva, or Lakshmi and Vishnu. The priest acts as Brahma. As the priest invokes the god with Vedic mantras and reads the holy book, the screen is removed and the bride and groom finally see each other.

Lila's father first symbolically gave her to Lord Vishnu. Then he took her hand and placed them in Kali's, transferring his responsibility for her to Kali.

Kali tied a sacred thread around Lila's neck. The ritual of agni pradakshina followed in which they walked around the fire seven times. For the first three rounds Lila walked ahead of Kali, for the next four Kali led the way. The priest elucidated obligations they would have towards each other and to each responsibility they answered, "I accept."

As they finished circling the fire, rose petals and rice were thrown from the priest, their parents, and well wishers to bless them with happiness and good luck.

The rituals and ceremonies came to an end but the long journey of practicing their symbolic significance was ahead of them.

The marriage ceremony did not prepare them for events that could happen on their spiritual path in life. Any questions they had about the meaning of love would persist inside them. Any questions they had about morality would persist inside them. Any questions they had about whether or not they would love just each other and no one else would persist inside them.

If, for example, they found people on their path whose cells wanted to unite with their cells, would they deny fulfillment of their desires by taking a moral stance? Or would they view such encounters as expressions of Divine Love?

The answers would not be easy. Nothing would train them to be tested in this manner. If the answers existed, they would be found within the deepest recesses of their souls and would most likely not have any rational or moral basis.

The only thing that would be clear to them was that if they wanted peace of mind they would have to look at their own faults and not anybody else's faults.

THE Midwestern United States typically experiences four seasons: fall, winter, spring, and summer. Some, of course, would argue whether spring was actually a season or whether it lasted just a couple of weeks in the transition from winter to summer. If the winter was long and cold like the one in 1983-84, they would be right. The shift from fall to winter is marked by three events—colorful leaves falling from the trees, trick or treat night on Halloween, and freezing rain. The last of these poses the deadliest driving conditions. The temperature is around the freezing point of water and when it rains, the rain freezes on the ground, on car windshields, and on all surfaces it falls on producing a sheet of ice. Driving on snow is less dangerous than on ice.

Anita and Chris were excited about Halloween that year. Chris was dressed as a pirate and Anita wore a witch's costume with a small broom. Norm and Alan accompanied them as they went from door to door. Some houses would have parties where the adults could go inside and sip hot cider. Meg took them to the mall in Champaign where she worked—each store in the mall celebrated Halloween and handed out treats. After the children returned to Anita's house, Norm stayed on for a while to have a cup of coffee.

Anita asked her dad, "Papa what is Halloween?"

"It's something we celebrate on October 31st each year."

"But why do we celebrate it, Papa?"

100

Alan was embarrassed that he did not know the answer. Norm noticed him squirming and came to his rescue.

"Anita, Halloween is the night before All Saints' Day. It used to be known as All Hallows' Day earlier and the night before it was known as All Hallows' Eve, which became Halloween."

"What happened on this night, Major Kay?"

"People used to believe that ghosts and spirits flew around on this night, and the Celtics used to celebrate it as a festival for the dead."

"The Celtics from Boston?" quipped Alan.

"No, no. The Celtics were ancient Europeans who settled in Britain before the Romans."

"Where did they come from?" asked Chris.

"That's still a mystery. They had a lot in common with warrior groups of the Indus Valley Civilization, around 2000 B.C. They may even have come from Vedic India."

"What are spirits, Major Kay and what happens when you die?" asked Anita.

Alan cut short Norm by telling Anita that it was late, and that she had to go to bed soon. Perhaps they could talk another day. He didn't want his daughter to know about death, not yet anyway. As Norm and Chris walked back home, Norm was awestruck by Anita's curiosity. She was asking some deep questions and not getting the proper answers.

ON the next day when Anita came back from preschool, Chris pursued the question about death with his grandpa.

"Grandpa, why did Grandma die?"

"Do you children know why you get shots at the doctor's office?" asked the major.

"No. Mom takes us there and makes us get them," replied Chris and Anita together. "And after the shot we get a sucker."

"Well, let me tell you the reason. You get shots to stay healthy. But sometimes your body gets germs that make you sick. That's what happened to Grandma Joann. She fell sick and got a germ called cancer. The doctors could not give her any shots to get rid of it."

"Holy kullolee. What happened when she died, Grandpa?"

"When she died, she could not breathe, she could not laugh or talk or cry, and she could not move her arms and legs. It was like she was in a deep sleep, and her body was then buried in a coffin."

"Is she going to wake up again, Major Kay?"

"No, Anita. Once you die, your body turns into dust and you don't live again. But your spirit lives on."

"What is spirit?" asked Chris.

"Many people believe that every person has two parts—a body and a spirit or soul. The spirit is different from the body and does not die when the body dies."

"Can I see my spirit, Major Kay?"

"Some people can and some cannot. As Chris's grandma used to say, you just have to believe that it is there."

Norm was now being pushed to the limits of his ignorance. He had read somewhere that knowledge could be defined by the boundary where one's ignorance commenced. He could understand some of Meg's and Alan's frustrations in answering the kinds of questions that Anita was asking. Fortunately for him, it was time for "Sesame Street" on TV and he would get a breather, for a while at least. He knew that these questions would not stop and decided to have a talk with Anita's parents as to how he should answer them in future.

FOR Thanksgiving that year, Meg and Alan invited Becky, Chris, and Norm over to their place. Meg planned to serve turkey with a stuffing, mashed potatoes and gravy, green beans, corn bread, and cranberry sauce. Becky was bringing over wine and pumpkin pie. Anita spent Thanksgiving morning at Chris's house. She did not like meat and could not stand the smell in the house when the turkey was being roasted. Norm told Chris and Anita the story of Thanksgiving. It was an annual holiday celebrated on the fourth Thursday in November. The early settlers observed Thanksgiving as three days of prayer and feasting after the harvesting of the crops.

"What day is it today, Major Kay?" asked Anita.

"It's Thanksgiving, Anita." replied Norm.

"No, no. What number is today?"

"Oh, today is November 22nd."

"What day is Halloween?"

"Halloween is on October 31st."

"And what day is Christmas?"

"Christmas is on December 25th."

"I know, first comes Halloween, then comes Thanksgiving, and then comes Christmas."

"Now, both of you run along and play outside for a while. Make sure you wear your jackets, hats, and mittens."

The Thanksgiving supper was excellent. Meg's turkey stuffing was made from a family recipe handed down by her mother. While the women were clearing up after the meal, Norm and Alan had their second glass of wine.

"I've been observing Anita quite a bit," said Norm. "She's a very curious child."

"Ain't that the truth?" replied Alan.

"She told me about her chicken-and-egg question. Why did you discourage her from pursuing the answer?"

"I don't think she's cut out for science. I want her to be a normal and successful girl."

"What do you mean by that?"

"You know, to get a good husband and raise a good family."

"Alan," said Norm, shaking his head with an expression of disbelief, "it never works that way in life. You can't find good things for your daughter. Goodness will have to find her when she's ready for it."

"What do you mean by goodness will have to find her?"

"It's an American Indian way of interpreting good. You wouldn't understand it. Let Anita be herself. You should encourage her curiosity, not quell it. By the way, have scientists found an answer to First Cause?"

"No. But we are getting close. The road to the answer goes through astronomy, cosmology, and physics. I think you should leave it to us specialists to find the answer and tell the whole world. We are at a point in the history of civilization where we know all the important aspects of nature. We're going to put an end to science soon. It's best for people like you to lead a practical life and not worry about such deep matters."

Norm's ire was visibly evoked by Alan's tone. "What kind of brain fart is that?" he retorted.

"Excuse me?" said Alan.

"You heard me right. The history of civilization has always given rise to surprises, right from the days of Aristotle, Newton, and

Einstein. The road to First Cause is not the exclusive domain of astronomy, cosmology, and physics. It goes through several places. Through metaphysics, through philosophy, and through religion. What makes you scientists so special? If it were the sole domain of physicists, then intellectual giants like Einstein, Sagan, and Hawking would have found the answer by now. All you specialists do is hide behind principles and postulates that the common man is unaware of and afraid to question.

"No, Alan. First Cause is civilization's problem. Each one of us is a child of the cosmos and we have a fundamental right to ask this question and find an answer. Perhaps the reason physicists have come up empty on an answer is because their search has not been broad enough."

"That's simply not true. We have the most powerful telescopes and have seen billions of galaxies."

"Yes. And you have classified the galaxies as spiral, elliptic, and irregular. What the hell is an irregular galaxy? To me it's a cop out—it's another way of saying that we don't know what we are doing, but if you give us more money we will figure it out. There's too much emphasis placed on observed evidence."

"Isn't that an obvious thing? How else would we verify the answer to a question?"

"Maybe there are other ways of verifying, Alan. Maybe you can start first with an answer and then ask the right question. But that will take us into a long philosophical discussion. Let's talk about your area of research and what you work on."

"Okay. I work in the area of fundamental particles—the subject of what matter is composed of."

"Well, what is it composed of?"

"All kinds of good stuff. Atoms, their nuclei, orbiting electrons, protons, neutrons, matter particles called quarks, and force-carrying particles called gluons."

"Why does matter have mass, Alan?" asked Norm.

"Ask me a harder question. There's plenty of evidence to prove that it has mass. Haven't you stood on a weighing scale?"

Norm was disappointed with Alan's answer. He was surprised that Alan was not aware of basic questions in his own field. The question of why matter had mass was a central unanswered question in fundamental particle physics. Alan's ignorance probably had to do with the fact that he was busy publishing research papers and had lost track of the important questions.

"Okay. I will ask you something harder," said Norm. "How does the tenure system work nowadays?"

"You're expected to publish papers, but nobody has told me how many," replied Alan.

Norm laughed loudly. "Same old game. The rules haven't changed at all."

"Well, they need some measure of productivity, don't they?"

"I suppose they do. Tell me, do you know what percentage of research papers is actually read? Not just in physics, but overall."

"I would guess maybe half of them."

"Far from it, Alan, far from it. I read an article stating that the number of papers read by people other than the authors and their friends is close to 5%. Many of them gather dust in library shelves. Everybody is in such a rat race to publish papers and there is not much quality control anymore. There are some people who publish a dozen papers a year."

"Well, I published 10 papers last year," remarked Alan.

"Don't you think a paper ought to contain at least one good idea? I can't imagine people getting a dozen good ideas every year. Einstein himself would be happy if he got one good idea every five or 10 years."

"It's not fair to compare everybody with Einstein."

Meg and Becky joined them after clearing up the table.

"Haven't you heard of Einstein's speech in which he talks about the temple of science and the kinds of people who have entered the temple?" continued Norm.

"Oh, Dad. Are you asking those questions of yours again? Please don't mind him, Alan. He has been asking such questions for many years now. Oftentimes, my mom would tell me that she was tired of my dad's maniacal persistence in asking questions," said Becky.

"It's okay," shrugged Alan, and told Norm, "No, I haven't heard of this speech of Einstein."

"I think I read this speech in a book that your mom gave me," said Meg to Alan. "It was Robert Pirsig's *Zen and the Art of Motorcycle Maintenance.*"

"That's right, Meg," remarked Norm, sipping his wine. Turning to Alan, he continued, "What Einstein was actually questioning was the goal of science and the role of scientists in realizing that goal. Science is not an intellectual sport whose goal is to publish papers. Nor is its goal to advance technology. Those are just the side effects. The goal of science is to find out a theory to describe the universe, and explain some of the mysteries of Nature.

"What is happening currently is that scientists are publishing papers for the sake of publishing them, or for getting tenure, or for building credentials to obtain funding. There seem to be few people who are making a real contribution to the goal of science. And in the process it is difficult for someone to read and keep track of the real progress that has been made. There are volumes and volumes of papers, and I don't know which ones are worthwhile reading and which ones are not. On some days when I visit the library, I get the feeling that there are more published papers than stars in the universe."

"Are you trying to redefine how scientific research should be done, Norm?" asked Alan, somewhat miffed.

"Well, maybe I am saying that. What frustrates me most is the posturing that scientists engage in when evaluating their work. If you ask me it's nothing more than intellectual jostling."

"I beg your pardon?" says Alan.

"Masturbation. Pure intellectual masturbation. Nothing more than that. I'll tell you what will improve the system. Let's say that after your doctoral degree you were hired as a full professor with tenure at a full professor's salary. The extra money would really come in handy when starting your career. Every time you felt the need to publish a paper that you thought was worthwhile, then you took a professional hit. If you published five papers or got five proposals funded, then you got demoted to associate professor with a salary cut. Five more would push you down to the rank of assistant professor without tenure. Administrators would be happy because they always feel the pressure of having to assign full professors to teach the introductory undergraduate courses. That would be easy now because the full professors would be the ones who published the least amount of creative research work. Under this system, you would get papers published by people who *really* believed what they were doing, who *really* wanted to advance the cause of science. The rest of the researchers in the temple of science could continue their research and perhaps write some position papers that got limited circulation. This would save time for people like me who pay taxes and want to read about scientific progress, especially as it relates to the true goal of science."

Now it was Alan's turn to laugh. "But nobody would publish any papers at all under this system," said Alan. Both Alan and Meg had not seen this side of Norm before. They didn't know that he was so opinionated about the nature of scientific research. Meg, who was silently gleeful over Alan's bashing by Norm, asked, "Would everyone like some coffee and pumpkin pie?" They all thought it was a good idea.

"I'm not sure that there would not be any papers published at all," continued Norm. "Don't you think you would read about Newton's laws and calculus, about the Michelson-Morley experiment, about Einstein's theory of relativity, about Heisenberg's uncertainty principle, and about Gödel's incompleteness theorem in logic? Not to mention the theories of Copernicus and Kepler published at great risk to their lives.

"These ideas have changed the direction of physics and mathematics. I will stop short of saying that it has advanced science itself, because I don't believe that some of them are correct. I think science has a boundary beyond which its ignorance commences."

ALAN could not believe his ears. He was amazed that a retired army man would dispute the findings of famous people like Einstein, Newton, and Heisenberg. Perhaps he had had one drink too many.

Meg brought out the coffee and pie and the discussion changed into formalities and pleasantries. They talked about the onset of winter, whether or not there would be a white Christmas that year, and about the children. Norm asked Alan and Meg whether it was all right for him to answer some of Anita's difficult questions. Meg thought it was all right, but Alan remained quiet. He was not sure if his daughter should associate with a dangerous radical like Norm.

Before he left, Norm told Alan, "I'll give you some advice. In your pre-tenure years, it is best for you to publish papers and do the things that are expected of you to get tenure. But after tenure, you have to listen to your inner voice and ask yourself why you got interested in science. Let that voice be your driving force. In the long run the search for truth is more important than the number of papers you publish."

Nine

After the move to Urbana, Meg started going to church every week. It was something she hadn't done in Pullman because of her busy schedule. Alan's job was to cook waffles for breakfast on Sunday mornings. Anita loved waffles and maple syrup. Alan would cut the waffle into small pieces for her and Anita would eat them with a fork. On many occasions Alan would forget the syrup and Meg would have to dash to the grocery store at the last minute to pick it up. Alan did not attend church. He spent the morning doing research work in his office.

When church was over, they would sometimes invite Becky's family over for lunch to their place. It was a gesture in return for what Norm was doing for them, baby-sitting Anita, mowing their lawn, and taking care of their yard. Gardening was one of Norm's hobbies. He would sharpen the mower blade once a month, so the grass looked really sharp when he cut it. Both of their lawns were the envy of the neighborhood. Yard work was done only between April and October after which it started getting cold. In late October, Norm would plant some tulip bulbs, which bloomed the following spring.

ONE Sunday in the first week of December when Becky's family had come over for lunch, Anita asked her dad, "Papa, who is God?"

Alan replied, "The God you pray to in church is Jesus Christ."

"Papa, why is God a boy and not a girl?"

"I don't know, honey. Ask your mother. She's the religious expert."

"That's what the Bible tells us, Anita, that Jesus Christ was a boy. He was born on Christmas eve and we celebrate Christmas to remember his birth," said Meg.

"Allow me to add to your answer," said Norm. "Anita, everybody does not think that God is a boy. There are many people who live in this world, and all of them are not Christians like us. They believe in their own gods. Gods who are girls are called goddesses. The Hindus of India believe in both boy gods and girl goddesses. For some Hindus, the Divine Mother Kali is believed to be the mother-force of the universe. The Celts also worshipped an Earth Mother."

"Why do we pray to God, Major Kay?"

This time Norm was caught without an answer. Over the years he had maintained a journal that contained many questions. Surprisingly enough, this simple question had not occurred to him and he hadn't thought about it enough. He looked pleadingly at Meg to help him out, and she replied, "Honey, people pray to God for all kinds of reasons. Some people pray to God so that they don't go hungry, some people pray to God so that they get lots of money, others pray to God so that they become famous."

"Why do you pray to God, Mom?"

"I pray to God so that our family gets His blessings."

"What are blessings, Mom?"

"I have a good idea, Anita. Next time we go to church, we will talk to Father Anthony. He can answer your questions. Okay?"

Norm wondered whether this was how people got conditioned and controlled by religion into believing who God was. It must have started at a very young age. Your parents could not answer questions about God for you, and you then slowly began to accept the authority of the church or synagogue or temple or mosque to answer your questions. At a young age, it is difficult to determine that you don't get the correct answers from the priests either. You just accept their answers and stop asking questions. Then you fall into a pattern of conforming to *proper religious behavior* and engage in all sorts of rites and rituals as ordained by the high priests of the religion you are introduced to. Norm and Joann had not forced Becky into following any particular religion—she was free to believe whatever she wanted to, and Becky was bringing Chris up in the same way. Named after his great-grandfather Christopher, Chris was still very young but he was not going to be molded into some particular faith.

AFTER lunch, Anita decided she wanted to play with Chris at his house. Norm said he would take care of them and told Becky that she could stay and visit with Meg for a while. Anita asked Major Kay to tell them the story of Christmas. Christmas was coming soon, and she was excited about the presents she would be getting.

"Christmas," Major Kay said, "is the feast to celebrate the birth of the God Jesus Christ. He was born in Bethlehem many years ago and we celebrate his birthday on December 25th. Some celebrate his birthday in January. His mother's name was Mary."

"I had a baby-sitter once whose name was Mary," said Anita.

"Is that the end of the story?" asked Chris. "What about Santa Claus, Grandpa? And what about all the presents we get?"

"The baby Jesus had lots of magical powers. He liked small children very much. On his birthday, he wanted to make small children happy. So, he went to the North Pole, and found Santa Claus. He told him that every year, on his birthday, Santa should make presents and give them to all the children."

"Does Santa go all over the world, Grandpa?"

"Yes. He rides in his sleigh all over but he's known by different names in different parts of the world. Father Christmas, Saint Nick, and Noel Baba."

"Does Santa visit all the stars?"

"I don't know, Anita. Your dad might know the answer to that. Scientists like him write research papers on stars they have never been to. Have you been good children this year?" asked Norm.

"Yes, yes. We both have been very good," said Anita.

"Then there's no reason to believe that you will not get presents, is there?"

"What if Santa forgets us, Major Kay? What if he gets stuck in the chimney this year?"

"Did he forget you last year?" asked Norm.

"No, he didn't," she replied.

110

"Well, then he remembers where you live, and you will surely get your presents."

"But what about Chris? He just moved from Chicago, and Santa might forget him."

"Yes, Grandpa. What if Santa forgets me?" asked Chris.

"Let's make sure that doesn't happen. We'll send Santa a postcard telling him that you have moved, and give him your new address. That way he won't forget you."

The children were relieved to hear that and they played happily for a while.

KEN and Sharon visited Urbana over Christmas. Meg was slowly beginning to appreciate their approach to life. After reading Robert Pirsig's book which they had given her, she understood the attitude of Eastern mystics towards Nature—it was one of reverence, which was so different from a Western viewpoint. People like her needed to take a holistic view of the universe to resolve the discord between humanity and Nature. This, however, would require nothing less than a major upheaval of her values.

Her attitude towards her in-laws had changed since she first met them in Washington. She decided to follow their tradition of celebrating Christmas but with regular food, not Chinese. Norm hit it off very well with Ken and Sharon. The three of them were from the beat generation and exchanged many stories. After dinner, it was time for the story-telling ritual.

"Okay everybody, it's story time," said Meg. "Me first."

When I was growing up, we had an orchard with many trees. During the fall, the trees would shed their leaves and make quite a mess. Once my dad asked me to clean the gutters. I was afraid to use the ladder and climbed onto the roof from my bedroom window. I cleaned the gutters and tried to climb back in, but I couldn't. No one was at home to help me climb back in and it was too far to jump off the roof. I was stuck there for two hours till my dad came and rescued me. Luckily I was wearing shoes—it was so hot up there that I just couldn't sit down.

"I have a better one than that," said Becky.

As a little girl I always wanted to help my dad in the garden. Once when I was in high school I decided to get rid of a small silly tree in our yard. So I started to saw its trunk. I sawed and sawed and sawed and nothing happened. It took me forever to saw through the trunk and eventually the tree started to fall. It was then that I realized that the tree was 20 feet high and was about to fall on the neighbor's house. I rushed over to their house, screaming for help. My neighbor hurried out to help me just as the tree missed his house by inches.

"I have one for you beat-generation types," said Alan, looking mockingly at his parents and Norm. "It was told to me by Kali Gupta, my roommate from Pullman who recently got married to Lila."

When Meg was pregnant with Anita, we were all trying to guess the sex of the baby. Kali told us that ultrasound, which was used by parents who wished to know the baby's sex beforehand, had a probability of success associated with it. It was not 100% accurate, but close to it. In India, said Kali, religious priests used advanced technology to determine with 100% accuracy the sex of an unborn baby. It was called 'black book methodology,' still used by some Indian priests to this day. It worked as follows. During the seventh month of pregnancy, the priest was invited to an expectant mother's house. There would be a feast in his honor, usually a nice filling lunch. After eating to his heart's content and complimenting the meal, the priest would meditate for fifteen minutes looking in an easterly direction. Then he would tell the mother the sex of her baby. At the same time he would take out a black book and record the date, time, and purpose of his visit. If he turned out to be right, the priest would have his praises sung to everyone who visited the house. Free word-of-mouth marketing for his abilities. If he turned out to be wrong, he would be summoned at once by the angry mother. At this time, the priest would take out his black book and go over the documented record that had been made, asserting that he had been correct all along. You see, with generations of the priest's family in this business, his biological circuits were automatically wired to write down in his black book, in indelible ink, the exact opposite of what he had told the expectant mother. There you have it, folks, the power of religion over the masses.

Norm looked irritated by Alan's mockery. "Wait till you hear my story," he said. "I'll show you the power that science has over the masses."

This is a story about field mice in a farm in Madison County, Iowa, as told to me by an army buddy, Bill. The mice slept by day and observed the sky by night. They could easily see the planets Venus and Jupiter and Alpha Centauri, the closest star to our sun. They would frequently ride in the farmer's pick-up truck whose speedometer indicated a maximum value of 60 mph.

One summer the farmer took his two children to the state fair in Des Moines. Strange things happened when the farmer was gone. The farmer's wife was seen driving with someone else in the pick-up truck. One field mouse named Harp, who was a rebellious little brat, found himself in the back of the pick-up and saw the stranger kissing the farmer's wife. When the truck reached the entrance to the farm, he jumped out. This was a distance he had traveled many times before. When he measured the time for his trip, he was amazed. His watch indicated that the truck had to travel at a speed higher than 60 mph. He reported this at once to the academic council of field mice.

What happened to Harp is obvious to us—the stranger drove faster than the farmer did. But it wasn't obvious to the other field mice. In the world of field mice in Madison County, Ebert was the high priest of the academic council. He had won a Blone prize for discovering that nothing could ever travel faster than 60 mph, which was the maximum value marked on the speedometer. 'There seem to be some strange goings-on,' he told the academic council. 'Harp tells me that he took a ride on the pick-up, which traveled faster than 60 mph. What Harp does not realize and

113

what I want you all to know, is that any time such a discrepancy takes place, you should apply a correction factor to your watch. That way the speed can be adjusted so as not to exceed 60 mph. There is absolutely nothing wrong with the speedometer on the truck. I've stated many times, as a postulate, that nothing can move faster than 60 mph.'

He took Harp aside and told him, 'Son, what happened to you is indeed strange. But I have an explanation for it. When you were traveling in the truck, small jets of waves were being hurled at you. These waves have put you under an illusion regarding the speed of the truck.'

'In all honesty,' replied Harp, 'I couldn't feel these waves at all.'

'Of course you couldn't. Your watch was feeling these waves, not you. That is why your watch needs a correction factor.'

'Ebert, what if the truck was on Alpha Centauri? Would its speed still be the same? What if the stranger was some kind of God? The way he messed with the farmer's wife was something else. Maybe he could have driven the truck faster than 60 mph.'

'Calm down, Harp. You're forgetting what the speedometer says.'

'Maybe the old speedometer needs re-calibration.'

'No, Harp. It's you who need re-calibration. All that stuff you've been reading lately about Colonel T.E. Lawrence is affecting you. I think you're beginning to dream by night when you're supposed to be awake, instead of by day when you're supposed to be asleep.'

'Ebert, if you're so sure of the maximum speed, why is it a postulate? Is it useful because it is true, or is it true because it is useful?'

'Because it is true, it is a postulate in our world. Trust me.'

Harp was not convinced by Ebert's weak explanation. What he had observed on the truck was very real. He looked at Ebert in disbelief shaking his head from side to side. Ebert figured out from his gaze that Harp was going to be a troublemaker. The next day he assigned Harp to basement duty. Harp was not allowed to see the outside

114

world anymore—the price he paid for questioning Ebert's authority.

"What a strange story, Norm," said Meg. "The farmer's wife had an affair that was witnessed by a field mouse. So what else is new in Iowa?"

"How do you like that, Alan?" said Norm. "That's the power of science over the masses. You start questioning their postulates and they ground you."

ALAN'S face by this time had turned red, and he went out for a smoke. He was the only one who saw the connection between Norm's story and Einstein's special theory of relativity. Unfortunately, he could not answer Norm back because he had no answer. Scientists had not measured the speed of light, even on the moon, and the special theory of relativity rested on the postulate that the speed of light was a universal constant. Reputed astronomers like Halton Arp, whose work on quasars implied that some of them were moving with velocities ten times that of light, did not find favor with influential specialists in the field who promptly denied him telescope time at the Palomar Observatory. Primarily because his results violated the known laws of physics, laws that were accepted by the specialists at the time.

Ken and Sharon were in awe of Norm's knowledge of science. Their outlook on life was totally mystical, firmly embedded in Taoism and Zen Buddhism. They hadn't seen anyone humiliate their son on his own turf before, and absolutely loved it.

"How do you know so much about science, Norm?" asked Sharon. "We thought you were a mystic like us."

"I am neither a mystic nor a scientist. I am just an ordinary soldier looking for answers. The true scientist is a mystic at heart and the true mystic is a scientist at heart. All of us need to get together to resolve the conflict between humanity and nature which continues to plague the world."

"I'm so glad that someone is dishing it back to Alan," Meg confided to Becky. "He's too cocky and arrogant. He always puts me down."

"You don't need to take that from him," said Becky. "Personally, I think you are better off without him. I've noticed how

115

he likes to control everybody all the time. Thank god you've got a job and don't have to depend financially on him."

"I think you're right. I don't even like him anymore."

ON Christmas day, Anita and Chris made a snowman with Norm's help and were happy to open their presents. Norm usually got a bit philosophical at Christmas time. As he looked around during the Christmas season at all the external lights in commercial and residential areas, he would find the spirit of the season reflected so warmly in the multi-colored displays, truly depicting harmony and peace. But after the season was over and people removed their lights, this spirit of harmony and peace disappeared—it was not reflected through people's internal lights. Their differences seemed to reappear and there were always problems that needed fixing. In his married life with Joann, she had demonstrated to him on many occasions that it was your internal light, your internal beauty, which was more important than what you externally portrayed about yourself.

The winter of 1984 was not as cold or as long as the previous winter. There was the usual snowfall but not many arctic blasts of cold air from Canada. On February 2nd, Phil Punxsutawney, the venerable groundhog came out of his hole and did not see his shadow. That meant four more weeks of winter instead of six. Phil proved to be right that year. The winter was relatively mild, and temperatures were climbing into the 50s by early March.

Chris and Anita were eagerly waiting for Easter. Norm had promised to take them on an Easter egg hunt to search for a dark black egg, the egg from which the very first chicken was born. Easter fell on Sunday, April 7, 1985, and Norm was stuck as to what to do. Should he paint one of the eggs dark black in color and hide them with the other eggs? That way the children would not be disappointed. As he thought about it some more, it struck him that Anita was different from other four-year-olds that he knew. The kinds of questions she was asking gave him the impression that she really wanted to find out the answers. And if she found out that the dark black egg was a fake, she would lose faith in him. So he stuck to his position and hid several colorful toy eggs, each with a candy inside, but no black one.

The children went out with their Easter egg pails, looking for eggs. They found many of the eggs that Norm had hidden. Chris was excited about the candy in each egg. Anita was happy, too, as she went on the hunt but a little disappointed that she did not find the egg she really wanted. Norm could sense her disappointment and consoled her when she came back.

"Anita, don't worry about not finding the dark black egg. I know somebody who has spent 30 years searching for that egg and he hasn't found it yet. We'll try again next year. Maybe we will get lucky."

The next month Anita turned five. She and Chris would be attending half-day kindergarten starting in late August. Chris was beginning to learn his ABCs and they could both write their own names. Anita could read many books by this time but Chris could not. After school, Norm would pick them up and Anita would play with Chris till her parents came back. Norm would give them lunch, read a few stories, and play some games. In the late afternoon they were allowed to watch TV for an hour and a half— "Mister Rogers Neighborhood" and "Sesame Street." Both these shows were made for kids and highly educational. Chris was beginning to recognize and read a few *sight* words—the days of the week and the months of the year. They would all play a game in which they took turns saying out the months of the year. Norm would start with January, Anita would say February, and Chris would say March; Norm would say April, Anita would say May, and Chris would say June; and so on till Chris would end up with December.

When the game was over, Anita had a question. "Major Kay, is Halloween on October 31st, Thanksgiving on November 22nd, and Christmas on December 25th?"

"You're almost right, Anita. Halloween is on October 31st and Christmas is on December 25th. But this year Thanksgiving is on November 28th."

"But last year you told us that Thanksgiving was on November 22nd. Remember?"

"Yes, last year it was on November 22nd. Thanksgiving is celebrated on the fourth Thursday in November. Last year the fourth Thursday was on 22nd. This year the fourth Thursday is on 28th."

"Why is Thanksgiving not on the same day every year?"

"I don't know the answer to that. I think Congress passed a law that said when Thanksgiving should be celebrated every year. They chose the fourth Thursday in November. I remember when I was young, it was sometimes celebrated on the third Thursday in November. When Franklin Roosevelt was president."

"Isn't that confusing?" asked Anita.

"Yes, it is confusing. There are many such things that are confusing in life. I don't know why they have to be that way. People just accept them as they grow up. It's called tradition."

Ten

That night after Anita had gone home and Chris was tucked into bed, Norm sat up late sipping his usual evening drink, scotch whiskey, Johnnie Walker Black Label. There are quite a variety of scotch whiskeys, some blends and some single malts, some aged 12 or more years and others aged less than that, but Norm liked the taste of Johnnie Walker Black Label, aged 12 years. The popular way to serve scotch in a bar was on the rocks, which meant scotch with lots of ice in it. Norm didn't like that. All he tasted was the cold ice and it drowned the flavor of the scotch. He would pour out some scotch in a glass and add an equal amount of water, sometimes soda, maybe an ice cube or two, and he would sip it very slowly. After his motorcycle accident in 1962, the doctor had advised him not to drink too much. A couple of drinks a day, single shots, was all he was allowed. Norm followed the doctor's advice although he would occasionally have four drinks.

Tradition. The very word bothered him. It gnawed at his innards. While reminiscing about the past, he went back 30 years up to the time that Becky was born in 1955. In those days he had thought a lot about tradition—religious tradition, traditions within society, scientific tradition, and mathematical tradition. They were all trying to condition him into believing a particular point of view and did not give him the freedom to think for himself and arrive at the truth. In the education that he had had, the focus was more on *what* to think and believe and not *how* to think for himself. Norm had gotten into a

119

lot of trouble with his persistent questions about many things. He was viewed by many of his teachers as a rebel.

He could see how religious tradition was working in Anita's case. She was asking questions about God to satisfy her curiosity and not being given the correct answers. When your own parents don't give you answers at a young age and send you to priests who presume they know the answers, you are bound to get conditioned and controlled into believing something without any firm basis. Nobody could give good answers to First Cause, not your parents, not science and not philosophy. This gave religions a basis to invoke the Supreme Being Principle to explain First Cause, and convince everyone of their wisdom in interpreting the scriptures and telling people about the mind of God.

TAKE, for example, another tradition that got so quickly, yet so firmly, rooted in society — television. By the 1980s, people had become conditioned by the television media and commercials into believing what they saw on the screen. Many companies spent huge amounts of money on marketing and the hope or rather certainty was that customers would line up to buy their products because of the images they saw on TV. It was massive control driven by corporate greed with the help of Madison Avenue. Norm wondered if there ever would be a President who would ask Congress to pass a law banning the watching of television for one day every week. It amused him to think of production crews and news anchors putting on shows that were not being watched by anyone except those in the studio producing it. He knew of people who watched the news and formed their opinions by listening to the news anchors. They would not read and analyze information for themselves. They either didn't have time or were too lazy to think for themselves. Their opinions of events in the world were being formed by television productions.

The sad part was that if the truth ever stared them in the face, if the truth was ever told to them by somebody who was not on TV, then it wasn't considered the truth. The message became less important in modern society. What became more important was the credentials of who said it, and whether or not it appeared on TV, whatever *it* was.

It could have been so far from the truth, yet there would be an audience you could reach who would believe *it* simply because *it* appeared on the medium. The medium had become the message as well as the messenger.

A popular message, a byproduct of television, was the first amendment that gave a person the right to free speech. The advocates of this amendment are always on the lookout for situations that potentially violate its intent. If they ponder some more, they would realize that the boundary of free speech stops with free thought. If you think of something you ought to be able to express it. Was there any amendment to guarantee free thought? In *Zen and the Art of Motorcycle Maintenance,* Robert Pirsig's philosopher-hero, Phaedrus, had realized that the entire body of Western thought had been conditioned by the Aristotelian tradition of neatly classifying everything into subjects and objects. This tradition had got rid of free thought altogether and anyone who didn't conform to its pattern was in danger of being classified as abnormal.

IN the scientific world, scientists were grappling with their own traditions. Let's say you were interested in studying a physical process that started in state A and ended in state B. Perhaps this process involved the motion of particles. You would have to use a mathematical model and reasoning to explain how state A changed into state B. The reasoning would have a basis in the physical principles that governed the process. The mathematical model would have to track the process as it progressed from A to B. Moving from state A to state B takes a finite amount of time. In predicting the intermediate state changes from A to B, one would have to determine the time steps at which to track the state of the process. Would it be every second, every millisecond, or was it possible to track the state continuously?

Open sesame to the scientific tradition of calculus. Invented by Sir Isaac Newton in the 1600s, it is a branch of mathematics that deals with infinitesimal changes. With the help of calculus one can track the state continuously. Norm was puzzled about Newton's calculus, especially the part about things that could change in zero amount of time. Even if calculus could predict the intermediate states of the process, it was not at all obvious to him that the physical process was aware of calculus and accurately followed the mathematical model. Norm made an important distinction between a real-world process and its mathematical representation.

Newton defined two laws of motion and a law to describe the force of gravity. These marked a shift in tradition from the existing beliefs ascribed to Aristotle. Aristotle had believed that the earth was at the center of the universe and that the sun, the moon, the planets, and the stars moved around the earth. He said that the natural state of a body was to be at rest and that it could move only if driven by a force. So according to Aristotle, force was that which changed the state of rest or inertia of matter. Newton's theory was different. From Newton's first law, force is the rate of change of momentum of a particle in uniform motion. A direct implication was that there was no absolute standard of rest as in Aristotle's theory. One place where both Aristotle and Newton agreed was in the concept of absolute time, that one could accurately measure the time interval between two events with a good clock, and time was independent of space.

Newton's theory was accepted until the early 1900s. At that time a young German scientist questioned the concept of absolute time for objects that moved at very high speeds, like the speed of light. His name was Albert Einstein. Einstein proposed his theory of relativity in which the speed of light is constant. Let's assume a pulse of light is sent from a lighthouse to a ship at sea. Let's assume that many people are observing this event, some at land, some at sea, and some in the air. In Newton's theory, all observers have to agree on the time taken by the pulse of light. They would not necessarily agree on the distance traveled by the light pulse. So if they measured the speed of light, which is the distance traveled divided by the time taken, each observer would measure a different speed for the light pulse. In Einstein's theory, the speed of light is constant—that is, everybody agrees on how fast light travels. They still would not agree on the distance traveled by the light pulse, so now they would have to make an adjustment to the time taken by the light pulse to obtain the same speed for light. In essence, Einstein was saying that the people at land observing this event, those at sea, and those in the air, would have their own measure of time even if they were using identical clocks. And so scientific tradition was changed once more with Einstein's theory of relativity.

In the scientific world, tradition was being modified as time passed on. Norm recalled an amusing incident he had read about Einstein. When Einstein had once given a physics exam to his students, one conscientious student raised his hand in class before taking the exam and said, "Professor Einstein, is there a mistake in giving us this exam? It is the same one that was given last year." No doubt the student caught several glares from his classmates. Professor Einstein smiled as he replied to the student, "No, there is no mistake in giving you this exam. The answers this year, however, may be different from last year."

It was not clear to Norm which tradition he should accept. Should he believe in absolute space and absolute time, or should he believe in relative time? The very nature of scientific work required that one had to select from among many hypotheses to arrive at a reasonable theory that could explain observed phenomena, and Einstein's theory was doing that more reasonably than Newton's theory. Nobody, including Einstein, claimed that the theory of relativity explained *everything*. At the time, it was the best theory because it came closest to providing explanations to many phenomena, and could be validated by mathematical analysis.

FINALLY, there was mathematical tradition. For many centuries, mathematics and logic were the cornerstone of formal reasoning. In geometry, for example, one does not define what a point is. Geometry is a mathematical system that starts out with some axioms. An axiom is something that is taken to be true without definition, like a point in space. Once the set of axioms is defined, one can use principles of reasoning to deduce the theorems of geometry. Most high school students understand how this works. But high school students would not know how to prove that two parallel lines do not meet. They find out later on in college that that statement could not be proved and was one of the axioms of Euclidean geometry. An important question with respect to an axiomatic system is:

- Is mathematics powerful enough so that in any axiomatic system with deductive inference you could prove that a statement is either true or false?

If this was indeed the case, then one could use mathematics as a tool to validate propositions in the sciences. In 1931, Kurt Gödel proved a very remarkable theorem. He showed that in an axiomatic system, like arithmetic, if you could produce a proof for *every* true statement that could be made within that system, then there would have to be some inconsistency in your reasoning principles. And if the reasoning principles were determined to be consistent, then the axiomatic system would be incomplete in the sense that there would be true statements that one could write down, but would not be able to prove using mathematics. This theorem came as a shocker to many mathematicians and scientists of that period. It placed a limitation on logic and mathematics, and changed the tradition of mathematics. A popular example of this theorem is to ask whether the following sentence is true or false.

This statement is false.

If someone tells you the sentence is true then it is clearly false, and if someone tells you it is false then it is true.

NORM filled up his glass with his second drink. Back in the '50s, he had thought about the various traditions within physics. The Aristotelian tradition was based more on logic and less on observation. The Newtonian tradition was based on experimental observation as well as mathematical justification. Newton had expanded reasoning by inventing calculus to deal with infinitesimal changes. The Einsteinian tradition was based on the speed of light being a universal constant, which led to the concept of relative time. None of these theories satisfied the true goal of science. There seemed to be something missing. The choice of one theory over another was made on the basis of how closely it was consistent with the observed experimental data. Norm was hopeful that there could be another theory that did not need any relativistic correction factor but still satisfied the experimental observations. He had written down the following questions in his journal:

> • *Even if someone articulated this theory, would it be possible to justify it mathematically?*

> • *Or would the incompleteness theorem impose its limitation, in the sense that even if the theory were true one would not be able to justify it mathematically?*

> • *Could this theory be validated experimentally?*

- *Or would the uncertainty principle impose its limitation, in the sense that one would not be able to make accurate measurements of all the quantities of interest?*

- *Is the world of physical phenomena consistent and complete?*

Eleven

As Anita and Chris attended kindergarten in the academic year 1985-86, they learned quite a few things. They learned to recognize the different colors, the days of the week and the months of the year. They learned to write their own names on the artwork they did in school. Chris still wrote in upper case, Anita could write in lower case. They learned how to cut shapes like triangles, squares and rectangles and paste them with glue. The school had been informed about Anita's fear of libraries, and on media center days the books would be brought to her in a cart so she could check out those that she liked. The children by this time knew all about Halloween, Thanksgiving, and Christmas. In February they had to prepare cards for all their classmates on Valentine's Day. When Norm picked up the children after school, he asked Anita, "Do you have any special valentine in school this year?"

"That's for me to know and you to find out," said Anita in a teasing tone.

Norm smiled at her reply. Children learned so many things when they went to school. When he was a child he could not remember ever having spoken like that to any of his elders. Nowadays, it was common to hear kindergartners speak like this. Either they picked this up from school or from TV.

"Grandpa, is Easter coming soon?" asked Chris.

"Yes, Chris. As soon as winter is over, Easter will be here. Then we can go on our Easter egg hunt."

IN the first weekend in March, Meg invited Norm and family for dinner on Saturday night. Whenever Meg called them over, she tried not to cook any food that Anita disliked, especially meat. So she cooked spaghetti and meatballs. This way Anita could eat plain spaghetti with some tomato sauce if she wanted to.

"Grandpa, what is the story of Easter?" asked Chris.

"Easter falls on a Sunday. On the Friday before Easter, the God Jesus Christ was killed. He was crucified by the order of the Roman governor of Judea. But since he was a God, he came alive again on Sunday. Easter celebrates the Resurrection of Jesus Christ," said Norm.

"What is resuction, Major Kay?"

"Not resuction, Anita. It's re-surr-ec-tion. It means rising from the dead."

"Why do we celebrate his death? Shouldn't we be feeling sad that he died?"

"Yes, we are sad that he died. Celebrate does not mean that you have fun. To celebrate means to do something to show that a day or an event is important."

"Like going on our Easter egg hunt, Grandpa?" said Chris.

"Yes. That's a folk custom from many years ago. We go on our hunt because we want to look for that dark black egg, remember?"

"When is Easter Sunday?" asked Anita.

Norm left the room to get a drink as Anita asked this question.

"I think it's the first Sunday in April," said Becky.

"Well, let's see," said Meg. "Last year, Easter was on April 7th. That was the first Sunday in April."

"My birthday was on Easter a couple of years back," said Alan. "I believe April 3, 1984 was Easter Sunday. That was the first Sunday in April."

Norm came back with his drink and heard Anita questioning her father, "Papa, Major Kay told us that Christmas is the day Jesus Christ was born. And Christmas is on December 25th every year. Why is the day he died not a fixed day? Why does it change every year and why does Easter have to be on a Sunday?"

ALAN did not have an answer to her question. Neither did anyone else. Norm was in a trance. He was thinking about something that happened in physics a long time ago—about experiments done to determine the speed of light. In the 1860s, an English physicist, James Maxwell, had proposed a new wave theory to describe electromagnetic radiation. His theory was extended to the light wave and the prediction was that light traveled at a fixed speed. Since the concept of absolute rest had been abandoned in Newton's theory, it was presumed that the speed of light was fixed relative to a substance called *ether* that was present everywhere. So light waves traveled through ether just as sound waves traveled through air. In 1887 the Michelson-Morley experiment was conducted to measure the speed of light. The earth moves in its orbit around the sun, and if there is an ether, then the speed of light can be measured in the direction of the earth's motion and in a direction at right angles to that motion. It was hoped that the two speeds would be different. The result, however, of the experiment showed that there was no change in the speed of light. Various theories were formulated to explain this so-called negative result of the Michelson-Morley experiment but the one that prevailed was Einstein's theory of relativity. Einstein said that if the presence of ether could not be detected, then you could do away with it and also do away with the concept of absolute time.

ALAN was still not happy with the manner in which they had predicted Easter to be the first Sunday in April.

"Does Good Friday have to be in April?" he asked.

"Yes," said Becky and Meg together.

"Well, then we have a problem. What if the first Sunday in April falls on the 2nd of the month? Then the Friday before that would be March 31st and Good Friday would not be in April."

Meg and Becky thought about this for a while. "You're right," they both said. "Easter is not necessarily the first Sunday in April."

"I think we can fix that problem easily," said Alan. "Easter is the Sunday following the *first* Friday in April. Wouldn't that take care of it? Both Good Friday and Easter Sunday would then be in April."

128

Alan looked towards Norm for an acknowledgment at having solved the Easter prediction problem. Norm shook his head and said, "That was pretty scientific Alan, but not quite correct."

NORM left to get another drink. He thought to himself that physics was also guilty of making the same kind of mistakes that Alan was making in predicting Easter. Earth was just one tiny speck in the entire universe. Physicists were drawing conclusions about fundamental aspects of the universe based on local experiments conducted on earth. If the presence of ether could not be detected on the basis of a single experiment, did that guarantee its absence? How could one be so confident that Einstein's theory of relativity was the correct one to believe with respect to the speed of light and with respect to the absence of ether? Certainly it was the most widely-believed theory at the time, but did that mean there was no other way to explain it? He knew that for every phenomenon, one could postulate several hypotheses. What science was doing was choosing from among these hypotheses, a single one that was consistent with the experimental observations and also mathematically justifiable.

AND here were people who were trying to make predictions about Easter based on a couple of years of data. It was simply not correct, in his mind, to draw conclusions based on what he felt were local observations. He came back with his drink and spoke up, "Easter has its roots in the Jewish festival of Passover, which commemorates Israel's deliverance from the bondage of Egypt. Early Christians observed Easter on the same day as Passover. But Passover and all Jewish festivals are determined on the basis of a lunar calendar, not a solar calendar. Later Christians changed the celebration of Easter to the Sunday following Passover if Passover fell on a weekday.

"This is known as Eastern orthodox Easter. The Western Easter that we observe is currently determined as follows. It is the first Sunday after the full moon on or after March 21st. And it need not be in April. It can be in March also. This year I think Easter is on the last Sunday in March."

Everyone was surprised by his answer. Meg hadn't heard about this before and she was somewhat annoyed that she didn't know a fairly simple fact. Becky challenged her dad.

129

"Let's get a calendar," she said, "and check this out."

Meg got a calendar, and sure enough, Easter was on Sunday, March 30, 1986.

"Going back to Anita's question," continued Norm, "I still don't know why Easter is celebrated with a lunar calendar and Christmas with a solar calendar. It's not consistent."

That year, Norm and Anita and Chris went on their Easter egg hunt as usual. Again, they did not find the dark black egg.

Twelve

Joann and Norm were expecting their first child in April 1955. Norm made sure that he spent a lot of time with Joann. He would come back from work and go on long walks with her. Every Sunday they would attend church and Joann would pray for a healthy baby. On April 25 Joann gave birth to a baby girl at 10:15 A.M. She weighed eight pounds and one half ounce and was 20 inches long. There were no complications in the labor and the baby looked healthy. They named her Rebecca.

Norm's job when he came home in the evenings was to hold Rebecca and burp her after every meal. For the first four months or so, Joann nursed the baby and did not give her any solid food. Norm watched Rebecca as she slowly started growing up, and enjoyed spending time with her. His daughter demanded so much attention and being their first child, both Joann and Norm pampered her a lot. Norm did not have any time for himself to pursue his study of physics and metaphysics. As was typical of many families, they had to make adjustments to accommodate a child.

In June 1958, Norm got transferred to Fort Riley, Kansas. Joann was excited, as this would be closer to her home in Ontario, Iowa. Rebecca was three years old and very active. She no longer slid down the stairs on her stomach but could walk down like everyone else. It was easy making new friends in the army and Joann and Norm settled down comfortably in their home in Kansas. On the Labor Day weekend that year, Joann's parents came down to see their granddaughter for the first time. They had a good time visiting with each other and Joann's parents invited them to come over for Thanksgiving that year.

Rebecca adjusted easily to her surroundings and made new friends. As she started getting older, Norm went back to his books and to his journal of questions. He would spend some of his Saturdays in the library at Kansas State University, which was located in nearby Manhattan.

ON July 31, 1961 Norm knew that something was wrong when he returned home from work. Joann's face carried a painful expression as she told him, "I just got a call telling us that your mother is no more."

"Do you know how she died?"

"A heart attack. We'd better get there soon."

They left the next morning for Illinois and Norm attended to all the details regarding his stepmother's death—the funeral arrangements, the memorial service, the obituary in the newspaper, and the death certificate. He took care of all the paper work that needed to be done. Norm knew the procedure because he had gone through it in connection with his father's death a few years back. In times of grief 'like death, he was aware that funeral parlors took advantage of people since nobody had the heart to shop around. Except for ancient Egyptian priests, thought Norm to himself, nobody seemed to do enough to earn the exorbitant prices charged for burial services. After settling Beverly's matters, Norm returned to Kansas.

For a few months after that, he was a very reserved man. He would not talk much, socialize much, or even read his books much. The death of both his parents gave him the feeling that his connection with the past had been completely cut. Joann understood Norm's way of overcoming grief. She had never once seen tears in his eyes, but knew that he felt the pain inside.

IN the spring of 1962 Norm traded his 350cc motorcycle for a 500cc Royal Enfield Bullet Roadster. Known as the "Woodsman," this bike had an improved lubrication system, larger brakes, and a maximum speed of 70 mph. The first person to ride with him was Rebecca. He took her around the block on her first motorcycle ride.

The Midwestern states of Oklahoma, Kansas, Missouri and Iowa get the most tornadoes in spring. In this part of the country, it is typical for houses to have a basement where one would have to go in the event of a tornado. Weather forecasters did not have early warning systems that could predict when and where a tornado would strike. Scientists did not even know how exactly a tornado formed.

On June 23 Norm was riding home on his motorcycle from Manhattan. He had gone up to the library at the university. Several thunderstorms had rumbled through the area the whole day, and weather forecasters had issued a tornado watch. A tornado watch meant that conditions were right for tornadoes to form—a tornado warning was issued when an actual tornado was sighted.

It was drizzling when Norm left the library. He was confident that he would make it home before it rained heavily. Nobody knows what exactly happened on the way back home, but Norm was involved in an accident. A truck driver who was passing by on the opposite lane told the state trooper that a severe wind gust had picked Norm's motorcycle up in the air and literally thrown him about 400 yards away. He fell down on his right side and was unconscious.

NORM was taken to the emergency room in a hospital in Manhattan. The doctors who examined him tried hard to find a pulse or heartbeat, but could not. They began to administer CPR but that did not help either. The only thing remaining was to give him shock treatment.

In the meantime, Norm could see what was going on in the emergency room. He seemed to be up above and could look down below at his lifeless body. His soul seemed to be wandering around. For some reason, it was not going back into his body.

He wandered around some more and suddenly felt very cold. He found himself at the top of a mountain and saw someone sitting there. Norm could not make out the person's face clearly but noticed his blue body, a snake around his neck, and a trident in his hand. He and the blue-bodied person talked for a while. Then Norm found himself at the bottom of the mountain.

He was lost and did not know where to go. Another spirit carried him and took him back to the hospital in Kansas. Although he couldn't see the spirit's face, Norm felt that this was his birth mother, Kitty. He asked her, "Is that you, mother?"

She replied, "Yes. I never got a chance to hold you after you were born, my son. Now, I can hold you and feel your spirit. I gave you the gift of life when you were born on earth, and I am going to do it again by carrying you back to your body. Those are my instructions."

The shock treatment was not successful and as the doctors were preparing to pronounce him dead, Norm's soul came back into his body. He had been gone for about half an hour. One of the doctors suddenly noticed that Norm was registering a pulse.

"What the . . ." the doctor exclaimed. "Do you see what I see?" he asked the others.

The medical team could not understand how this could have happened.

After Norm recovered and was released, he recalled a few of the things that had taken place. He confided in Joann and she was surprised to hear a science buff like him admit what had happened.

"Are you sure you weren't dreaming, dear? What you are saying is so unscientific."

"No, I'm sure it wasn't a dream. I remember talking to my birth mother, but I couldn't see her face."

His conversation with the blue-bodied figure was fuzzy in his memory. What he remembered was the following.

"Are you the soldier who has lost the way?"

"YES, SIR."

"Don't worry. You will find it soon. My Word has been on earth for centuries. Unfortunately you are not looking for it in the proper place. It is there for you to discover and understand. Only when you do so, will you be ready to enter My abode. That is your mission."

The most significant impact on Norm was that he now believed in the existence of God. Who else could talk with such authority? He was determined to find out this God's identity. He had been given a mission by the blue-bodied figure—to seek out His Word and find the way. Only then would he be able to die in peace.

Norm was beginning to find some tolerance for those who could believe in God based on faith alone—people with a strong internal conviction like Joann, who did not need scientific reasons like he did.

AT the time this accident occurred, Norm held the rank of major in the U.S. Army. The fall from the motorcycle had wounded him badly—there was a huge gash that had to be stitched up. The stitches were so deep that they left a permanent scar on the right side of his face.

After he recuperated, the emergency room doctors interviewed Norm as part of a report they had to forward to the army. Norm was very forthright and honest, almost naive, with his experience, and recounted all that had happened to him in those moments when he was absent from his body. He did not, however, disclose the conversation that had taken place with the blue-bodied God. He just mentioned that he had talked to a God-like person for a while but could not recall what was said. The doctors wrote down everything and forwarded the report to the army.

The army psychiatrist called Norm in for a check-up. This time again, Norm stuck to the facts about what had happened after his accident. The psychiatrist asked him, "Is it at all possible that you dreamt about this while you were in a coma-like state?"

"No sir. These recollections are not like a dream. They seem more real than that."

After dismissing Norm, the psychiatrist prepared his report. He wrote that Norm was having hallucinations and that he should not be put on active duty anymore. He stated that his rank of major should be terminal and he should be given minimal responsibilities from that point onwards. He also prescribed some medication for Norm, and advised him to limit his alcohol consumption to two drinks a day.

NORM came back from his check-up and updated his journal by answering some of the questions he had written down. He looked at the first few questions he had entered in his journal and attempted to write down some answers.

- Q. Does the soul consist of matter?
  A. No. If it did, then it would not be able to move freely as my soul had. If it consisted of matter, then the movement of my soul would have defied the laws of physics.

• *Q Is the soul eternal, and is human existence only a manifestation of the soul?*
   A. There is no basis from my experience to answer this question.

• *Q. What existence tests would one apply to determine if the soul exists after death?*
A. When my soul was wandering around, I could hear and feel things, but my vision was not focused. I could not make out anyone's face clearly. Since I could not see clearly, one could argue that I did not truly exist in my out-of-body state and that it was just a dream. Should the sense of sight be on the existence test? But blind people cannot see and they exist just fine. It is difficult to come up with existence tests for things that do not consist of matter.

• *Q. As humans, do we have a basic need to deny our non-existence? Is the reason we believe in God and soul a selfish reason—to establish for ourselves a permanence in the universe?*
   A. No. There is a God and I saw Him on the mountain. People might be led to believe in God for the wrong religious reasons, but that does not mean He is not there.

• *Q. What exactly happens when one dies?*
   A. Based on the conversation I had with the blue-bodied God, I have to find the way before I die. It seems that everyone has a personal challenge, a personal test, to discover the truth, and then his or her soul enters God's abode. What if I don't find the way? Then the soul would reenter the body as in my case, or perhaps find another body and be reborn again on earth.

Norm had answered all his questions dealing with death and the soul. Although he was not sure that his answers were correct, at least they served the purpose of recording his thoughts at the time.

Thirteen

In the fall of 1986, Chris was learning how to read in first grade. Every day, Anita and Chris were required to read a couple of "baggie" books that they brought home in ziploc bags from school. Anita was more proficient at reading than Chris and she checked out the more advanced books. Chris wanted to do the same. The teacher recognized Chris's problem and let him check out one easy book that was at his reading level and one advanced book. Chris would get frustrated trying to read the advanced book at home because it was not at his level. In due course of time, after Norm read many books to him, Chris was able to read the advanced books. He was still, however, not comfortable with reading. Time and practice would take care of that.

Anita and Chris were both growing up so fast. Now they could ride their bikes without training wheels and wanted to learn roller blading. The previous summer they had taken a two-week swimming class offered at the local pool. For Easter, which fell on Sunday, April 19, 1987, Anita and Chris decided to play a trick on Norm. They took a hard-boiled egg, painted it black, and hid it in Anita's back yard. When Norm joined them for their annual Easter egg hunt, they found lots of eggs that he had hidden. Soon, they went to Anita's back yard, and stumbled onto the dark black egg. Norm smiled as he found the egg and said, "That was nice of you, kids. But I'm afraid that it is not the dark black egg from the Easter Bunny's

137

basket. Some day I will have to tell you more about that dark black egg."

DURING the summer Norm, Chris, and Anita joined a Tae Kwon Do class. Norm had practiced martial arts many years ago when he returned from Korea. He still remembered the two rules that his first instructor had told him. Rule number one: it was for defense only. Rule number two: understand rule number one. All of them started out as white belts. Every day they were reminded of the five basic principles— courtesy, integrity, self-control, perseverance, and indomitable spirit. Their instructor, Master Pak, would count in Korean and it all came back to Norm, hanna, dur, set, net, which were the first four numbers. The lesson lasted for an hour, after which everyone bowed to each other as a demonstration of courtesy and respect.

"I think we should put a stop to having Norm baby-sit Anita," Alan told Meg. "Why don't we get a teenage girl to take care of her after school?"

"Whatever for? It's working out all right," replied Meg.

"It seems to be all right because he doesn't complain. Don't you think we ought to respect his age?"

"Alan, it's only for a couple of hours after school. And besides, Anita enjoys spending time with Chris and Norm."

"I'm afraid of that. I don't think it's good for her. Norm's views on things are wacky and dangerous and they may rub off onto her."

"Rubbish," said Meg confidently. "I think Norm's views are much broader than your narrow scientific outlook on life."

"Honey, that's not why I was trying to do it. You know that I care about Anita."

"Care about her? That is utter nonsense. Have you forgotten what you did to her in Pullman? I don't think you care about anyone. If you cared about people you would spend time with them. It's the most important thing you can give to somebody else.

"I thought you cared about science, but Norm tells us that even that's not true. All you care about are your damn research papers and your tenure."

138

"Will you stop listening to that old fart? I tell you he's brain damaged. I've seen his face twitching many times and he has a spaced-out look that's pretty scary."

"You're just making excuses. I think it's hard for you to accept criticism. There are many good books on personal growth that you ought to read."

"What? All those self-help books? I don't have time for all that."

"I think I've proved my point. Anita is very happy with Chris and we're not going to change that. And that's final," said Meg, emphatically.

"Well, excuse me. I'm the head of this household and I should be making all the important decisions. I bring in more money than you do." He would regret making that last statement.

"Is that all you care about?" Meg was now angry. "Does money give you power? We're both in this together and I should have as much power as you do. Who do you think has taken care of the house all these years? I have a job, too, you know. I've never once seen you volunteer to do household chores like cooking and laundry."

"I cook waffles on Sunday morning."

"Yes, Mr. Big Shot. And who makes the last-minute dash to get the syrup? You've never even gone to the grocery store. Bringing in more money? That's a terrible thing to say to someone you love."

"I have to go now, Meg. I'm late for work," said Alan, leaving in a hurry.

IN the fall Anita and Chris entered second grade. One evening when they came back from school, Anita was angry. Norm asked her what was bothering her.

"I didn't pass the running test again," she said.

"What test is that?" asked Norm.

"In P.E., we all have to run a mile in less than 12 minutes. My P.E. teacher says I didn't pass it."

"Did you pass the mile test, Chris?" asked Norm.

"Yes, Grandpa. I ran the mile and finished third. Anita thinks she also finished the mile on time."

"Major Kay, why does the P.E. teacher think he is correct and I am wrong?"

"Well, he's the one who measured the time, isn't it?"

"Yes, but he could have made a mistake. How could he see both his watch and me at the same time?"

It caught Norm completely by surprise. In some sense, Anita was absolutely right. The P.E. teacher could not simultaneously look at his watch and the finish line. So, either the time would not be accurate or the runner's position would not be accurate. If the P.E. teacher was looking at his watch all the time, he would have to sense the finish by physically standing in the runner's lane and sensing the body contact when the runner crossed the finish line. But then, with his body there, it could no longer be called a *line*. If the P.E. teacher was looking at the finish line, then the time measurement would not be very accurate, unless he had a stopwatch, in which case his eyes could be focused on the finish line and he could mechanically stop the watch by pushing a button.

"Does your P.E. teacher use a stopwatch to measure time?" asked Norm.

"No, Grandpa. He uses a watch that he wears on his hand," said Chris.

"Well, he's been a P.E. teacher for many years, Anita. You have to believe what he says and try harder next time. Okay?"

"But he might have been wrong every single time, Major Kay."

"Yes, he might have been. The accurate measurement of time is not at all easy. Don't worry about it. I'm sure you will run faster next week."

THE problem of the finish line is analogous to the problem faced by cognitive scientists when they try to explain human consciousness. If we treat the conscious mind as an observer, we have to associate with it a point of view. The idea of a crucial finish line in the brain, marking a place where the order of arrival of events is the same as the order of presentation in experience, is called Cartesian materialism. But if this point of view is located at a single point in the brain where "it all comes together" then there are logical difficulties in explaining events that occur in very short time intervals. Light, for example, travels much faster than sound but the brain takes longer to process visual stimuli than auditory stimuli. Is the finish line for light different than the one for sound? Where is the screen in the Cartesian theater of the brain where it all comes together, and who is the audience?

THE following week Anita ran the mile in six minutes. She beat everyone in her class handily. The P.E. teacher was surprised and remarked, "I've never seen anyone in your age group do that before. How did you do it?"

"Maybe your watch needs a correction factor, Mr. Time Keeper."

Chris was angry when he found out that Anita had beaten him in the mile run.

"I don't like her any more, Grandpa. She's too weird."

"Don't worry Chris. You will run faster than her soon."

Chris, however, would not be easily consoled. He decided to unleash on Anita the worst punishment that a child could ever face.

"This year I'm not inviting her to my birthday, Grandpa."

"Okay Chris. Do as you please."

FOR Christmas that year, Norm decided to give Anita a Sesame Street present. She and Chris enjoyed watching the show on TV. He had more time to go shopping now since both the children were in school from 8:30 until 3:15. He found a new videocassette that had just come out that year called "Don't Eat The Pictures" and gave it to Anita for Christmas.

While Meg and Becky braved the crowd and went shopping on the day after Christmas, the children stayed behind with Norm and watched the movie Norm had given Anita.

The story was about an Egyptian boy who was under a spell in New York's Metropolitan Museum of Art. His parents were stars in the sky and he had to answer a question to be released from the spell. The boy answered the question with the help of his Sesame Street friends, and became a star after having been trapped in the museum for nearly 4,000 years.

Anita and Chris were fascinated by the story of the little boy, Prince Sahu, who became a star in the sky. Major Kay told them that the prevalent belief in ancient Egypt was that you became a star when you died and your soul went up to the stars. When the pharaohs were mummified in their tombs and kept in the pyramids, one of the chambers had a shaft that was open to the sky. This shaft provided a passage for the pharaoh's soul to depart the body and join the stars in the sky.

To appease their curiosity about Egypt they looked up an encyclopedia and found the famous pyramids in Giza.

"Look," said Norm, "they are not in a straight line."

"They look straight to me, Grandpa."

"For them to be on the same line, we ought to be able to draw a straight line through all three pyramids. You can't do that. You can draw a straight line between two of them, but not the third. Try it."

Their interest in stars had been aroused by the movie, and on a clear night they gazed at the constellation of Orion. Norm pointed to the Orion Nebula and three stars that were supposed to be Orion's belt. These three stars were not in a straight line either.

"The ancient Egyptians saw the night skies just like we are seeing it," said Norm. "They considered Orion to be a very special constellation and may have used his belt to position the three pyramids. Let me show you something else."

Norm pointed the binoculars to the east-northeast and exclaimed, "There it is. Look at that little cloud."

"Where, Major Kay? I don't see any clouds at all."

"No, not a real cloud. It's a hazy patch of light that looks like a cloud."

"Yes, I see it. What is that?" asked Anita.

"That's another galaxy like ours. It's called M31 or Messier 31, named after Charles Messier and located in the constellation of Andromeda. It was first discovered by the Persian astronomer Al-Sufi who called it the little cloud."

"It does look like a little cloud, Grandpa. Is it close to us? Can we go there in a rocket ship?"

"If we could Chris, we could get answers to many of our questions. I'm afraid we can't go there yet. It is millions of miles away, over two million light years away."

"What's a light year, Major Kay?"

"It's the distance that light can travel in a year, nearly six million million miles."

"Did Al-Sufi have binoculars?" asked Chris.

"No, he didn't. Al-Sufi and other Sufi poets like Omar Khayyam and Jalal-ud-din Rumi saw a lot more without binoculars than we see today. For them, believing was seeing, not the other way around. One of my army friends, Bill Kaplan, believed that Omar Khayyam's *Rubaiyat* contained deep hidden truths about the universe."

ONE Saturday, when Norm was taking care of the children, they watched the movie about Prince Sahu again. This time, after the movie was over, Anita had a few questions.

"Major Kay, how many days are there in a year?"

"Usually 365 days. Roughly once every 4 years, there are 366 days. Like this year. 1988 is a leap year and the extra day is on February 29th."

"How many days have passed since I was born?" she continued.

"Have you learned multiplication in school?" asked Norm.

"Yes. I know how to multiply numbers," replied Anita.

"On your 8th birthday this year you will be 8 years old. Since every year has 365 days, we have to find out what 365 times 8 is."

"Let me do it, Major Kay. Three hundred and sixty five times 8 is two thousand nine hundred and twenty."

"You have to add in the extra days for leap years. The year 1984 was a leap year, and so is 1988. Anita, on your 8th birthday, you would have lived for two thousand nine hundred and twenty two days. Wow!"

"Grandpa, did you know that Prince Sahu was 4,000 years old?" asked Chris.

"Really?"

"Well, he was four thousand three hundred and six and a half years old," said Anita.

"Can anybody live that long, Grandpa?"

"Not as a person, I think. Just in the movies."

"Major Kay, can we find out how many days Prince Sahu has lived in the museum?"

"I know, I know," said Chris. "He has lived for one million, six hundred thousand and forty two days."

"How did you know that?" asked Norm, a bit taken aback.

"That's what the demon said, Grandpa. Every night the demon asks Prince Sahu to answer a question. The demon said that he had asked the question one million six hundred thousand and forty two times."

143

"How do we know that it's the right answer?" asked Anita.
"We can easily verify that," said Norm. "I'm sure it's the right answer, especially if it's a Sesame Street movie. They don't make mistakes about such things."

Norm got out pencil and paper. He didn't want to use the calculator in front of the kids. Eventually they would find out about it but not from him. He did the multiplication by hand. First he computed 365 times 4,306, which came out to be 1,571,690. Then he added half a year that was roughly 183 days, which increased it to 1,571,873. Oh, and he had forgotten the leap years in between. Roughly one in every 4 years is a leap year. So he added a quarter of 4,306 which was roughly 1,077. That brought the total to 1,572,950. Nowhere near what Chris had said, which was 1,600,042.

"Are you sure of what you said, Chris?" asked Norm. "About the demon asking him the question one million six hundred thousand and forty two times?"

"Yes, Grandpa. I'm sure. I remembered it."

"Let's watch the movie again and find out. Tell me where this part comes," said Norm.

"It's near the end, Major Kay. Before Sahu meets Osiris, the Lord of the underworld."

"Okay. I'll fast forward the tape up to that point."

Norm saw the fragment of the movie for himself. Chris was right. He wondered whether he had made a mistake in his calculation. He excused himself from the room and went to find a calculator. The answer he got from the calculator was identical to the one he got from doing it by hand, and it was different from the one in the movie.

HAD he made a mistake somewhere? Leap years were computed differently in the Julian calendar, which was in use before the Gregorian one was widely adopted in 1752. The correction one made at the time was to add 11 days to the Gregorian calendar. The change had pushed George Washington's birthday from February 11th, the day he was actually born, to February 22nd, the day it is celebrated. These differences could not account for 27,092 days, which was the difference between his answer and that in the movie.

He came back to the family room and told the children that Prince Sahu had not lived for one million six hundred thousand and

144

forty two days, but for one million five hundred and seventy two thousand and nine hundred and fifty days.

"But which one is the right answer?" asked Anita.

"I think our answer is the right one and the answer in the movie is wrong."

"Can you always tell a wrong answer from a right one, Major Kay?"

"What do you mean by that?"

"I mean in 'rithmetic that we learn in school. Can you always tell that some answer is either wrong or right?"

Norm thought for a while about how to answer her question. It was not an easy question for him to answer. On the one hand, he could say that all the problems she would do in school would have a right answer and that her teacher could tell whether an answer was wrong. On the other hand, if her question was really about the power of arithmetic and whether you could prove for any statement that it was right or wrong, she would run headlong into Gödel's incompleteness theorem, which stated that mathematical systems like arithmetic were incomplete in the sense that there would be true statements that one would not be able to prove. Nor could one prove the opposite of the statement. So there would be statements that one would not always be able to tell were either right or wrong.

"Anita, for 'rithmetic problems that you do in school, your teachers can tell you whether an answer is right or wrong. When you learn more math you will also be able to do the same. Okay?"

He hoped his answer would satisfy her. It would take a lot more mathematical maturity than a second grader's to understand Gödel's theorem.

"Major Kay, if you had been seeing the movie like us, would you have known that it was the wrong answer?"

"No Anita. I wouldn't have known at all. I am not smart enough to question the authority of a Sesame Street show. I used to question authority when I was younger, but I had to stop doing it when I retired from the army. My advice to you is to always question all authority, but don't tell your parents I said that. I'll bet that many people don't know it's the wrong answer. Sometimes, in 'rithmetic and science, asking the right question is more important than finding an answer."

145

Fourteen

After his accident in 1962, Norm was eager to discover the identity of the blue God that he had seen. He did not recall any such figure from the Old or New Testaments. He decided to talk to a professor in the department of Religious Studies at Kansas State University. From the description that Norm gave the professor, he at once told him that it was one of the Hindu Gods, named Lord Shiva. The Hindus had a trinity of main Gods—Lord Brahma, Lord Shiva, and Lord Vishnu. Lord Shiva's abode was a snow-capped mountain called Mount Kailas in the Himalayas. In His full form, Lord Shiva is considered the source of all opposites: creator and destroyer, half man and half woman, total rest and remorseless action. Norm asked the professor to suggest a book that he could read on Hinduism. The professor told him that a new book had just been written and he had heard that it was a good book but had not read it himself. The book was *Hinduism* by R. C. Zaehner, a professor of Eastern Religions and Ethics at the University of Oxford.

This was Norm's starting point in the study of Hinduism. It was an ancient religion, about 4,000 years old, maybe older than that. Unlike Christianity and Judaism which were monotheistic religions believing in One God, Hinduism seemed to have several Gods. The Gods themselves were not as important as a fundamental concept called '*dharma*.' *Dharma* was supposed to be a very subtle concept and difficult to understand. One interpretation was that it meant Hindu law as written in the sacred texts of the Hindu religion.

Another interpretation was that it was the religion on which these laws were based. A third interpretation was that it was far more fundamental and referred to a natural law that governed the universe. As he read this Norm was excited. Here at last was a religion that might give him some clues about the goal of science. Science was also in pursuit of this natural law, a grand unified theory that would explain the universe and human existence. If there was a connection between *dharma* and a theory of the universe, Norm was determined to find it.

As Norm read Professor Zaehner's book, he realized that Hinduism had a lot of sacred literature. There did not appear to be any sort of canon to produce a condensed version of the sacred texts as in the case of the Old and New Testaments. So to study it in its entirety, one would have to read all the literature. Fortunately for him, Zaehner had focused on summarizing the essence of Hinduism and for the time being he was content with that.

THERE were quite a few concepts that were foreign to Norm's thinking and background. The main tenets seemed to be *dharma, moksha, karma,* and *brahman.* The roots of all these words were in Sanskrit, which was the sacred language of the Hindus. *Moksha* was a liberated or blessed state that freed an individual from the bondage of existence—it transcended space and time and cause and effect. The meaning of the word *karma* in Sanskrit is 'action' and the law of *karma* states that any action whatsoever is the effect of a cause and is, in its turn, the cause of an effect. All existence was subject to and conditioned by an endless causal past, the 'eternal *dharma*' or *sanatana dharma* of the universe. The word *brahman* had two meanings: one was the eternal substratum of the universe, not only the state of *moksha* but also the source of all existence; the other meaning was the Brahman caste.

Unlike the religions of Judaism, Christianity, and Islam, Hindus believed that their religion was free from dogmas. That, however, is not the case. Brahmanic orthodoxy and Vedic righteousness are exactly what spawned the birth of heterodox sects like Buddhism and Jainism. Hindu scholars disagreed on various portions of the principal tenets; for instance, some believed an individual could attain *moksha* on her own while others believed that you needed the assistance of a superior power to attain this state.

147

There were some principles that all the scholars agreed upon. They were:

- Time was cyclic rather than linear.
- The individual soul was governed by the same law of cause and effect that governed the universe. What affected the microcosm also affected the macrocosm.
- Unless you attained *moksha* you would be reincarnated into another existence, but release from this existence was ultimately possible for all beings.

While it was clear that Hinduism was not monotheistic, it was not clear whether it was pantheistic (the doctrine that God is everything and everything is God) or polytheistic (worship of more than one God). It depended on which sacred text you were reading. The closest that Professor Zaehner and other scholars had come to describing Hinduism was a pantheistic monism—they did have an Absolute One but it was identified with the individual soul. The sacred writings can be divided into what one might call the classical texts and the great epics. The classical texts are the Vedas and the Upanishads. The Vedas represent the eternal Word of God heard by the sages of antiquity, and the Upanishads represent what was remembered and transmitted from generation to generation. Sometimes, the Vedas appear dualistic but this is misleading. There is a strong belief in one Supreme Being worshipped under different aspects—'He is one, though wise men call Him by many names.' The Upanishads focus on events that are prior to all existence. They do not separate man from creation or its creatures, and ask not only the question 'Who am I?' but also 'Who is the knower?'

THE two great epics are the *Mahabharata* and the *Ramayana*, which have great rhetorical power. In the middle of the *Mahabharata* lies one of the most influential Hindu scriptures, the *Bhagavad Gita* or 'Song of the Lord.' The Gita is not an easy text to study, as it sometimes appears inconsistent with itself and the rest of the *Mahabharata*. It describes a conversation between Arjuna the warrior and Lord Krishna, his charioteer. Arjuna is on the battlefield to fight a fratricidal war—between two branches of a royal family known as the Pandavas and the Kauravas. He is one of the five Pandavas fighting against his hundred brothers, the Kauravas. He cannot bear to kill his own brothers and is consumed by a deep internal conflict. He collapses into a coma, lays down his bow and arrows and surrenders himself to Lord Krishna for guidance. From the standpoint of 'eternal *dharma,*' Arjuna had an obligation to carry out his duty as a warrior; from the standpoint of 'individual *dharma,*' or duty toward oneself, fighting against his own brothers was bothering his heart and his conscience. Norm related well to this conflict. When he was in Korea, he had to shoot the enemy soldiers and it bothered him quite a bit. Even though the enemy soldiers had killed Bill Kaplan, they were still his brothers of humanity—just like him, but with a different cultural background who fought the war from a different viewpoint.

The *Bhagavad Gita* was organized into 18 chapters. Each chapter consisted of several verses, each verse being two lines in Sanskrit. Norm had bought an English translation of the "Srimad Bhagavad Gita" by Swami Vireswarananda of the Ramakrishna Mission. Most of the chapters were a dialogue between Lord Krishna and Arjuna to help Arjuna resolve his conflict. The Lord's answers revived and recharged Arjuna by giving him a vision of the bigger scheme of life and its purpose. After this, Arjuna fought the battle and the Pandavas emerged victorious.

Some chapters that Norm found intriguing were Chapter 7 on The Way of Knowledge and Realization, Chapter 8 on The Way to the Supreme Spirit, and Chapter 13 on Discrimination Between Nature and Soul. Since his near-death experience Norm was particularly interested in any literature on the soul. In Chapter 13, Lord Krishna had described two fundamental principles, Purusha and Prakriti, and had said that whoever understood these principles fully would not be born again. Norm was not the type of individual who would read something and accept it without detailed scrutiny. To him, even though what he read was the recorded Word of God, it had to make sense in the real world, in the world of science. The challenge, of course, was to find an interpretation of the writings in the Gita that would withstand scientific scrutiny.

The other great epic of Hinduism is the *Ramayana.* This epical narrative with its many stories describes how Lord Rama is exiled into the forest for 14 years by his stepmother who wants her son to occupy the throne. Rama's wife Sita is captured by a demon *(rakshasa)* and Lord Rama and his brother Lakshman fight the ten-headed *rakshasa* Ravana and rescue her. Whereas the *Mahabharata*

149

describes the many aspects of Hinduism, the *Ramayana* focuses on how to live life in the world. Lord Rama was an incarnation of the God Vishnu, and his life was a model of the perfect life that one could live.

AN influential and holistic school of thought is the Vedanta that focuses on the concept of Brahman. Its most celebrated exponent was Adi Sankaracharya. While one school in Vedanta tolerates a degree of dualism, Sankara and his school were strictly non-dualistic, preaching the doctrine of advaita (literally, 'not two'). The basis of their teaching is the identity of the self and the Absolute—all entities are identical with each other through their common origin in Brahman, the substratum of all phenomena. Vedantists reject the dualism of mind and matter as unreal: 'All sense-objects, including the body, exist solely as notions, they exist only when thought of. The sole Reality alone exists eternally and the world owes its appearance to the mind alone.'

Hinduism appeared to contain a mixture of classical literature, epical narratives, and numerous rites and rituals, ceremonies and celebrations. The Hindus themselves were not always clear about this mixture. Norm learned that they were not polytheistic but did believe in an Absolute Reality. Why, then, did they not concentrate on one God, one ritual and one practice like other religions? The answer was not clear to Norm from his first reading of Hinduism.

IN May 1963, Norm was transferred from Fort Riley to his new post at Fort Belvoir in Virginia. His rank continued to be Major and he was told that he would not be promoted any further. The official reason given was that he was medically unsuitable to obtain a higher rank. They packed up their belongings and moved to Virginia. Rebecca was now 8 years old and a bit sad to make the move and lose her friends in Kansas. Joann thought it was a good move because Norm had become so withdrawn into himself after the accident and did not socialize at all.

As they drove from Kansas to Virginia, Norm had plenty of time to think about what he had read. The Hindus believed in reincarnation—a doctrine of rebirth for those who did not attain *moksha*. He seemed to recall some writings from the time he studied the Old Testament that had mentioned reincarnation. Perhaps it was Josephus who had mentioned it as a belief among Jews of that period. In some of the discussions that Jesus Christ had with his disciples— discussions that do not appear in the New Testament—the possibility that He believed in reincarnation could not be ruled out. Some of the Greek philosophers such as Plato and Socrates also believed in reincarnation. So it appeared that the concept of reincarnation was not unique to Hinduism. The question that was most puzzling to Norm was whether or not he had died during his accident and was now reborn. That was not how reincarnation was explained—it was an actual rebirth as a totally different being. In a spiritual sense, however, Norm felt strongly that he did have a rebirth—his beliefs about the existence of God and soul were totally different now from what they had been before the accident.

At the mountaintop, Lord Shiva had given Norm his mission: to seek out His Word and understand It. Lord Shiva had assured him that His Word had been on earth for centuries. Norm asked himself whether His Word was in the *Bhagavad Gita*. Perhaps there were some chapters or verses that could be interpreted to construct a model that could be subjected to the laws of physics, or rather, be subjected to the observed evidence about the universe. Norm made a big distinction between the laws of physics and observed evidence. The laws of physics were merely selected hypotheses chosen from among a multitude of hypotheses, and by no means the *only* way to explain the observed evidence. Maybe there was another model that would have different hypotheses, different from Einstein's view and different from Newton's view, and yet be a tenable model. But the *Bhagavad Gita* was Lord Krishna's Word (who was an *avatar* or incarnation of Lord Vishnu) and not Lord Shiva's Word. Were they one and the same God? Norm decided to dig deeper into Hinduism to find out if there were any writings like the Gita that were attributed to Lord Shiva.

Finding answers to the questions he had raised in his journal and fulfilling his mission given to him by Lord Shiva had now become his individual *dharma*— his duty towards himself.

Fifteen

Every summer after school got over and summer vacation began, Chris would spend two weeks with his father in Chicago. His dad, Robert Stewart, worked as an engineer for Motorola and had remarried after his divorce. Robert's wife, Sheryl Thomas, was an attorney for a private law firm. Sheryl was very nice to Chris—in the summer of 1988 she took him to the museum, to the top of Sears Tower, and to the circus. Both Sheryl and Robert went with Chris to the Six Flags amusement park, which had plenty of rides and was a whole day affair. Robert told Chris that in fall, he would have him over for a weekend to see a Chicago Bulls basketball game. Chris, like everyone else in Chicago, was a big fan of the Bulls, especially Michael Jordan. Chris asked his dad to get an extra ticket because he knew that Anita would also love to see a Bulls basketball game.

Anita had turned 8 years old in May and was getting interested in geometry.

"Do parallel lines meet somewhere, Major Kay?"

"No, Anita. Parallel lines don't meet except at infinity."

"Can you prove that?"

"No. It's one of the axioms of geometry. You don't prove axioms. Axioms are statements that are considered true by default."

"Can we have parallel light rays in space?"

"I don't see why not."

"If one of the light rays is close to the sun, won't it get bent by gravity?"

"Hmmm. I don't know. Check it with your dad. Are you ready to go?"

"Yes."

Every day, when the children were in school, Norm did some volunteer work—he read the newspaper and a book chapter or two to blind people. Anita had become his helper. Some of the blind people stayed in apartments and some stayed in a retirement home. They would each read to four blind people every day. As they drove around from place to place, Anita asked Norm, "Can blind people see?"

"No, they can't."

"How do you know that?"

"Anita, their eyes don't function. How can they see?"

"They can't see like we do, but they may be able to see things that we cannot see. Right?"

Norm had to agree. "That's right, Anita. Nobody knows what we can see with our inner eye."

"Major Kay, what do you think about all the time?"

"Oh, lots of stuff. This and that."

"Do you think about the dark black egg that we haven't found yet?"

"I'll tell you what. How about coming over on Saturday, and I will tell you about the dark black egg and some of the other things I think about all the time. Okay?"

"Okay."

ALAN was busy that year preparing his resume for tenure. His tenure document would have to be ready in the fall and it would be discussed and evaluated by his department, by the college, and by the university. He was entering his sixth year and it was mandatory that the university either granted him or denied him tenure. For his portion of the document, Alan had to submit a statement describing his research, a statement describing his teaching, and a list of his publications and grants. In his research, Alan used computers to solve some of the physics problems he was working on. A couple of years ago in 1986, the university, with the help of a federal grant, had established a supercomputing center—The National Center for

Supercomputing Applications, and Alan was part of a group of researchers learning how to use supercomputers. Supercomputers had more computing power than ordinary computers and could carry out computations that would take ordinary computers much more time to do. They were used to solve many scientific and engineering applications as well as for weather forecasting.

When Norm came over one Friday morning to mow Alan's lawn, he asked him, "How's your tenure process coming along?"

"It's coming along fine. I think I end up spending more time preparing my credentials than doing research," replied Alan.

"What do you mean by that? Don't you have a resume on file that you turn in?"

"I wish it were that simple. I have to prepare statements about my research and teaching. And I have to suggest to the committee the names of a few external professors who can review and critique my research work."

"Whatever for? Don't your publications get reviewed before they are published? By this time, after so many years at processing tenure, they ought to have a litmus test for it: x publications, y dollars of funding, and z graduate students."

Alan laughed as he said, "Those administrators don't get paid such high salaries to do simple counting that Anita could do for free. They have to justify their time by claiming to be the watchdogs for quality. But wait, there's more to it.

"For every article that I publish jointly with others, I have to list out the names of all the authors in the order in which they appear in the paper and also include the percentage of my contribution in that publication."

"I don't understand what you mean by that Alan."

"Let's say I work on a paper with two other people. Then I have to list out their names so it is clear who was the first author, the second author and so on, and quantify my contribution, that is, give an actual number like 33%, or 40%, or 50%."

"Aren't the names listed in alphabetical order?" asked Norm.

"A few people list it that way, but many don't. There is a widespread belief that the first author is the primary driving force behind the paper. That's another thing to include in your litmus test: w publications as first author."

"In quantifying your contribution, how do you compute the percentage? Would all the co-authors agree with your figure?" asked Norm.

"The percentage figure that one reports is hard to verify. If the co-authors are within your department one can track them down and ask them. But if they are at other universities, it is difficult to verify the percentage. My publications are either with my graduate students in which case I always list them as first author, or with colleagues in my research group."

"You still haven't told me how you compute the percentage of your contribution?"

"It depends on how much work was involved in putting the paper together. For example, if a paper had six sections and I was responsible for 2 of them, then my contribution would be one third."

"What does being responsible for a section mean? Don't you ever get stuck in a section and need someone else's help in getting unstuck? It happens to me all the time."

"Yes, that can happen. You may have developed an idea and done 80% of the work, but still need a crucial step to prove it. I'll admit that in such cases, the person who provides that important step should receive a lot of the credit, perhaps even 50%. But I doubt you will find many people who are conscientious about such things."

"What if you are the sole author of a paper? What's the percentage in this case?"

"Norm, now you're beginning to sound like a picky administrator. Even they don't need the percentage in such cases. It's obviously 100%."

"Really? Where do your ideas come from, Alan? Are they generated within you, or do they get generated in the cosmos with your brain a mere receiver?"

"When I said 100%, it was a practical answer, not philosophical."

"I wish you all the best in your tenure decision, Alan. I can see that academia is becoming more marketing-oriented and less quality-oriented. I shudder to even think that Albert Einstein would not have received tenure at your university. He was a patent clerk whose hobby was physics when he published his famous paper in 1905. He would not have passed your tenure litmus test.

"I hope we still have the university around in the next millennium, but I don't think I would bet on that. What I would bet

155

on is a university provost telling people that the contribution of the Wright brothers in the construction of a Boeing 747 is 0%."

NORM left to mow another neighbor's lawn. The following day would be Saturday and he remembered that he had asked Anita to come over. He had promised to explain to her what he was thinking about all the time. It was going to be difficult. He thought back to the time when he had first met her, at the age of four, and she had asked the question about First Cause. Which came first, the chicken or the egg? She really wanted to know.

After he got done with his yard work, Norm took Anita to a shopping mall in Champaign. They had lunch in the mall—a slice of pizza—and Anita scraped the cheese off before she ate it. While strolling through the mall, something caught Norm's attention in the bookstore. It was a new book titled *A Brief History of Time* by Professor Stephen Hawking. As he leafed through the book he saw that it was going to be useful for his talk with Anita. He bought the book and told Anita that he would be ready to tell her many things the next day.

That night as he sipped his scotch, Norm started reading Stephen Hawking's book. He had read some of Hawking's papers before but this was the first time he had seen a book that explained scientific concepts in language that was easy to grasp by a non-scientist. In an early chapter in the book, Stephen Hawking had directly addressed one of the problems that physics was facing in the search for a grand unified theory, namely, that the general theory of relativity which described the universe on a macroscopic scale was not consistent with quantum mechanics which described the universe on a microscopic scale. So the search was on for a new theory, a quantum theory of gravity, that would reconcile the inconsistencies.

THE next day Anita came over to Norm's place after breakfast. Norm sat outside with her on the patio.

"Anita, do you remember asking me about the egg the first chicken came from?"

"Yes, Major Kay. You said this egg was a dark black egg in the Easter Bunny's basket. Isn't that the egg we have been looking for every year?"

"Yes and no. A few months back when we looked up at the night sky and saw the constellation of Orion, did you ask yourself whether the stars have been there all the time or where they came from?"

"Chris and I know the answer to that one. The stars are all ancient Egyptians."

"Ancient Egyptians?"

"Yes. That's what we learned from Prince Sahu."

"Oh, from that movie?"

"Yes."

"Seriously Anita, when we look towards the sky and see the moon, the planets, and the stars, we have to ask ourselves how and why they got there in the first place. Whether something caused constellations like Andromeda and galaxies like M31 to be there.

"When I pull the string on the lawn mower, the lawn mower comes on. The cause is the pulling of the string, and the effect is the starting of the lawn mower. The question that philosophers have been asking for centuries is 'What was the first cause whose effect was the birth of the universe?' It is just like the question you asked about chicken and the egg."

"Who are philosophers? Have they found the answer?"

"Philosophers are people who use reasoning to search for truth. Before I tell you whether they have found the answer, let me talk about First Cause a little more. Not only did philosophers ask this question but so did scientists. The laws of science can explain many events that we see as being caused by some earlier events. For example, science can explain how rainfall occurs. For rain to occur, there must have been some water that first went up in the sky, and then fell down as rain. Science tries to explain things that we see around us but is not very clear about how the universe started.

"Nearly two thousand years ago there was a Greek philosopher named Aristotle. He believed that we were at the center of the universe and that the sun, the moon and the stars moved around the earth. Since the telescope had not been invented nobody could check what he said, and Aristotle was famous enough that all the people believed his reasoning especially because it gave them a lot of importance to be told that they were at the center of the entire universe.

"Science has constantly been changing the beliefs of many philosophies and philosophers by conducting experiments and gathering information about the universe. Around the year 1600, the Italian astronomer Galileo observed the night sky with a telescope and disproved Aristotle's theory."

"What's a theory?" asked Anita.

"Good question. When a scientist tries to explain things, she does so by building a model of what goes on. This model is not real but exists only in the scientist's mind. It has a set of rules and the scientist uses these rules to predict what would happen next. That's what is meant by a theory. A good theory makes correct predictions most of the time.

"Philosophers still do not have an answer for First Cause. And scientists believe that the universe started with a big bang—a big explosion—it is called the Big Bang theory. That is the closest that scientists come to answering First Cause. But they have a major problem with their answer. Their theory says that the laws of science do not apply at the beginning because of something called a singularity. A singularity is when mathematics and science break down in their explanations. It does not say anything about the universe, it only says that we cannot explain it at the beginning."

"Father Anthony told us that God made the universe. Did God make that first egg?"

"Science and philosophy have not found the answer to First Cause. Therefore, religion tells us that it has the answer. Its answer is that First Cause is the Supreme Being we all call God. Grandma Joann believed that God made everything."

"Do you believe that, Major Kay?"

"Yes, I do believe in God, but not in the way Father Anthony says we should. The religion that is taught to people in the churches and temples of the world is not always accurate. Remember you asked a question about why Easter was not celebrated on the same day every year but Christmas was. Lord Jesus Christ was born on Christmas eve and Easter observes his resurrection after he was crucified. If Christmas is observed on December 25th using the solar calendar, then Easter should also be observed using the same calendar. Easter, however, always falls on a Sunday and is determined from a lunar calendar. There are quite a few inconsistencies like this and the Bible does not contain all the sayings of Jesus Christ. So I don't believe in God because religion asks us to believe in Him. I have my own reasons for believing in God."

"Why do you believe in God?"

"I'll tell you some other time. The answer to First Cause is like a scavenger hunt. There are many clues to help us—clues from religion, clues from science, and clues from philosophy. Each group, however, is looking only at its own clues and nobody has been able to get all the clues and find the treasure. Many times these groups are so caught up in their own ideas that they don't look outside themselves for answers. Take the example of the Big Bang theory. Since science cannot explain what happened at the very beginning because of a singularity, it is possible that they have the wrong theory. Maybe there is another way to explain what happened at the very beginning, but nobody has found that theory yet. That is what I keep thinking about all the time. A theory of the universe that will answer some of my questions.

"Last night I was reading Stephen Hawking's book. He is the second scientist I know, after Einstein, who has openly addressed the concept of a Creator of the universe. I hope he gets the Nobel Prize soon. He wrote about an expanding universe, by which he meant that all the galaxies we see in the sky are moving away from us and so the universe is expanding in all directions. But if there is some other kind of matter, some form of dark matter that we have not detected, then it is possible that the universe might collapse back again. That is another thing I think about, the existence of dark matter. It might explain some of the inconsistencies in various scientific theories. Many years ago I had read the Gospel of the apostle Thomas, whose writings are not part of the New Testament. I remember reading that the real kingdom of God is light present inside dark matter. So when you asked me which egg the first chicken came from, I told you it was a dark black egg. Dark matter is one of the keys that can unlock the mysteries of the universe for us.

"When Chris comes back from Chicago I am going to read, everyday, a few pages to both of you from Stephen Hawking's book. It will be difficult for you to understand everything, but if you keep asking questions as we go along, I will try to help you understand what science has accomplished so far and what the goal of science is. I think it is an excellent way to learn about science. Okay."

Norm's lecture sounded like a homily, a broadside, and Anita detected a strange look in his eyes, the look of a madman who was disgorging something from his memory.

Sixteen

They arrived in Fort Belvoir in June 1963. Situated in lush woodland amid rolling hills along the west bank of the Potomac River, about 20 miles southwest of Washington D.C., it was a pleasant change of scene from the plains of the Midwest and one of the most beautiful army bases that Joann and Norm had seen. The Potomac River separates the state of Virginia from Maryland. The capital of Virginia is Richmond and its largest city is Norfolk down in the southeast corner of the state by Chesapeake Bay. Both cities are major industrial areas in the state, Richmond known for its tobacco products and Norfolk for shipbuilding. The proximity of Fort Belvoir to Mount Vernon, where George Washington grew up, to Alexandria, which had many 18th-century buildings, and to Washington D.C. made it easy for Norm's family to make weekend trips to the museums and other historic sites.

It took a few months to settle down, unpack the boxes and find a school for Rebecca. Norm adjusted well to his new posting. Even though he knew that his rank of major was terminal, he didn't care. The intellectual and scientific pursuit of religious philosophy had consumed his entire being. Joann tried her best to distract him but it was of no avail.

"I think you'd better stop all your reading," Joann pleaded. "I need your help in raising our daughter."

"You're on our own, dear. I've simply got to get to the bottom of this. It's important to me that I focus on my mission. Have you forgotten my accident and what happened to me?"

"That was a year ago and the doctors didn't seem to think it was real."

"Damn the doctors and damn you. Leave me alone from now on," he yelled. After a few minutes he calmed down and added, "You're doing a good job with Rebecca. I don't think you need me to mess it up."

DURING the winter of that year, Norm continued his study of Hinduism. He was very intrigued by the *Bhagavad Gita* the first time he had read it, and decided to read it again slowly. This time he jotted down some of the verses in his journal. Swami Vireswarananda's translation did not contain any superfluous commentary and this helped Norm to figure out his own interpretation of each verse.

It (self) is not born and it does not die at any time. And it does not again come into existence by being born. It (self) is birthless, constant, eternal, and ancient; it is not slain when the body is slain. — Bhagavad Gita 2: 20.

Is the self the same as the soul? This verse states that my soul is eternal, and therefore my existence as a human is a manifestation of my soul, or a transient phenomenon superimposed over the eternal reality of my soul.

This (self) is indeed incapable of being cut, of being burnt, of being moistened, and of being dried; it is eternal, all-pervading, stable, immovable, and primordial.— Bhagavad Gita 2: 24.

This verse says that my self or soul does not consist of matter and hence does not pass any test that matter can be subjected to like being cut or being burnt.

The dull-witted, whose minds are full of desires, who regard heaven as their highest goal, who are enamored of the panegyric statements in the Vedas and assert that there is

nothing else (higher than this), speak familiar flowery words about numerous kinds of rites (prescribed by the Vedas) . . . as the means to enjoyment and power. Those who are attached to enjoyment and power, and whose minds are carried away by these (flowery words) do not attain single-minded determination leading to concentration on the Lord.
— Bhagavad Gita 2: 42–44.

Dull-witted indeed? If this passage does not constitute a slap on the wrist of the high priests of Hinduism, then what does? The point being made is that any kind of desire, including the desire to control people by preaching the Word of God through rites and rituals is not a path to truth. The practice of such rites and rituals are not only prevalent in Hinduism but in other religions also.

THE *Bhagavad Gita* was a tiny portion of the great epic, the *Mahabharata,* yet it was not easy to understand. In his book, Swami Vireswarananda had divided the Gita into three parts: Chapters 1 through 6 dealt with the different ways one could attain *moksha,* Chapters 7 through 11 dealt with the nature of God, and Chapters 12 through 18 described the gospel of the love of God for man. Norm's interest in the Gita was to search for verses that could somehow be used in formulating a scientific model of the universe.

Presided over by Me, Prakriti brings forth the world of moving and unmoving things; for this reason, O son of Kunti (Arjuna), the world revolves. — Bhagavad Gita 9: 10.

This makes perfect scientific sense as it describes the revolution of the earth around the sun. Is Prakriti analogous to the fundamental particle?

Earth, water, fire, air, ether, mind, intellect and egoism— thus is My Prakriti divided into eight categories. This is My lower Prakriti; different from this O mighty-armed one, know that higher Prakriti of Mine in the form of the individual soul by which this world is sustained. Know that all beings have these two for their origin; I am the origin of the entire universe as also its destroyer. — Bhagavad Gita 7: 4–6.

This is the first reference to a duality associated with Prakriti, consistent with the matter-wave duality of physics. I find the reference to ether somewhat surprising.

THE Michelson-Morley experiment had not been able to conclude the presence of ether, and hence Einstein had rejected it. Norm was sure that there was no experiment that guaranteed the absence of ether, and while it was a plausible concept, one would have to explain a lot of other observations if one admitted the existence of ether. For the time being, Norm decided to keep an open mind about the presence or absence of ether.

In Chapter 11, Lord Krishna revealed his celestial form to Arjuna. In Hinduism, the ultimate goal for a person was to attain the state of *brahman,* the state that characterized *moksha* and the source of existence; yet, when Arjuna saw the celestial state of the Lord, he thought that this celestial state was more desirable than *brahman.* When Norm had seen Lord Shiva on the mountaintop, he did not recall that vision as being celestial. Lord Shiva's body appeared blue in color but Norm could not see his face. The chariot in which Arjuna rode was a metaphor for a self-controlled person who could understand and derive the benefit from spiritual instruction. This was exactly how Norm himself felt as he read the Gita—he was trying his best to understand it and derive some intuition to construct a model of the universe. He had noted down bits and pieces that could be useful, but there was nothing that he could immediately use from any of his readings of Hinduism. There was nothing that obviously stood out from a scientific standpoint. He also found out that there was nothing similar to the *Bhagavad Gita* that contained the Word of Lord Shiva.

NORM'S study had taken him four years of nights spent in solitude, sitting on the carpet and using his dad's kidney-shaped coffee table for updating his journal. At the end of it he was somewhat disappointed, as there were no easy answers to his questions. The study had generated more questions and he was getting more and more entangled in its web.

When he came back from work, he would start pacing up and down in the kitchen, smoking to high heaven.

"Will you please get out of the way?" begged Joann.

"Sure. Do you want me to move my body out of the way or my soul?"

"What's the difference? Just go away and let me get dinner ready. I have enough problems dealing with Rebecca."

"Your soul, my soul, everyone's soul is the same. That's why I can't move my soul out of the way."

"Oh, shut up Norm. I've had enough of your metaphysics. Leave me out of it. There are many problems to worry about in the real world. I haven't seen you reading the newspaper in the last four years."

"I read the sports section everyday, especially the baseball scores."

"I don't think you get it. I'm worried about your grip on reality."

"Don't worry. I'm all right, A-OK."

Joann had stopped entertaining visitors at their home, as it had become embarrassing to deal with Norm's antics. He had started talking to himself and it was difficult to follow what he was saying. If one listened carefully, it sounded like quatrains from *The Rubaiyat* of Omar Khayyam.

Up from Earth's Centre through the Seventh Gate
I rose, and on the Throne of Saturn sate,
And many Knots unravel'd by the Road;
But not the Knot of Human Death and Fate.

The Moving Finger writes; and, having writ,
Moves on: nor all thy Piety nor Wit
Shall lure it back to cancel half a Line,
Nor all thy Tears wash out a Word of it.

On October 7, 1967, Joann came back early in the afternoon from grocery shopping. She was surprised to find Norm at home.

"Everything under control?" she asked him.

"Yes. I have a severe headache."

She turned on the radio and Norm went ballistic.

"Turn it off," he screamed. "It's too jarring."

"Just a minute dear. The news comes on soon."

Norm couldn't stand it any longer. He picked up the radio and threw it to the ground, smashing it into a hundred pieces.

"Next time, TURN IT OFF when I ask you to."

"I think you're the one who has gone off. You need help, Norm. Why don't we go see the doctor?"

"Leave me alone. I'm going to get something to eat."

"Be careful on the street."

When Norm left the house, Joann started cleaning up the debris from the radio, which contained several glass pieces. He came back in a little while with a take-out from McDonald's, and started eating the bag instead of the food.

"What's the matter with YOU, Norm? Why don't you act normal?" said Joann, having now reached the limits of her patience.

"I *am* normal. The paper bag tastes better than the food."

This was the straw that broke Joann's back. She knew now that Norm needed psychiatric treatment. She went over to her neighbor's house and called Edgar Root and Hemant Lal, two of Norm's bridge buddies, and explained the situation to them.

WHEN Rebecca came home from school later that day, she saw her father being physically held down and given an injection. Then he was carried into a car and taken to the psychiatric ward of the army hospital.

The next day Joann went to the hospital after Rebecca had gone to school. "How is he?" she asked the doctor in a nervous tone.

"So far we've diagnosed him with acute hallucinations and paranoia."

"Is he going to be all right?"

"Yes. His condition can be treated easily with shock therapy and medication."

After a week of shock treatment, Norm was allowed visitors. Joann was the first to see him. He looked very weak and subdued.

"My God, Norm. What have they done to you?" she asked him.

"I don't know. I still have headaches but they're somewhat dull now."

A couple of weeks later, Norm got used to the medication and started regaining some of his strength. He had four visitors—Joann, Rebecca, Edgar Root, and Hemant Lal.

"How about a game of bridge?" suggested Hemant.

"We need a fourth. Joann doesn't play."

"Let's play gin rummy then," said Edgar, dealing out the cards.

"When are you going home?" asked Hemant.

"I don't know. I have to pass the exit interview first."

Every Friday, the more normal inmates were interviewed to see if they were ready to leave the psychiatric ward. The doctor held up his forefinger and thumb together in the shape of a circle and asked them "Tell me what this reminds you of?"

"Thursday," replied Norm.

"A white dwarf in M31," said another inmate.

"The revolving substratum of the universe," said a third.

When they learned that none of them had passed the test, Norm muttered to himself, "At least my answer was the most logical of them all." The next time Hemant Lal visited him, he heard about the doctor's question.

"What's your reason for saying Thursday, Norm?"

"That's how I was taught the days of the week. The pinky and thumb is Monday, the next one is Tuesday, the middle finger and thumb is Wednesday, and the forefinger and thumb is Thursday."

Hemant laughed and said, "Norm, that's not the normal answer the doctor wants to hear. He wants you to tell him that it's a circle. Trust me."

"But the doctor's question was 'What does it remind you of?', not 'What shape does it resemble?' If he had asked the right question, I'm sure many of us would have given him the normal answer."

At the next interview, Norm gave the normal answer and got out of the hospital. The psychiatrist told Joann that he would have to take some medication everyday of his life. The first thing Norm asked for when he came home was chicken soup. Joann's chicken soup, garnished with Minute rice that was crunchy at first and became softer halfway through, was good for his soul. It tasted so much better than the lousy hospital food he had eaten for two months.

JOANN requested him to stop reading and lead a more relaxed life. Norm listened to her advice and completely stopped his inquiry into metaphysics. He packed up all his books into three boxes and stored them in the basement. He had spent 20 years in the army and decided it was time to retire. Joann, too, thought it was a good idea.

The release from the army was an unceremonious Section 8 discharge—the medical instability from 1962 and the recent mental breakdown were part of his permanent record. Fortunately, he would get retirement benefits and they moved to Orlando, Florida, like so many army personnel who retired there to get a tax break.

Getting a job in the private sector would be hard with his health record, so Norm decided to open up his own business. Like his father, he was good at fixing things, and started a lawn-care operation, taking care of people's yards and their swimming pools. Joann was by his side and between the two of them they managed to get it operating smoothly.

Seventeen

When Chris returned from Chicago in the summer of 1988, Norm got him and Anita into the habit of listening and questioning as he read everyday to them for an hour from Stephen Hawking's book, *A Brief History of Time*. Progress was slow as the children did not understand the basic concepts and constantly interrupted him. They learned about the solar system, about the rotation of the earth on its axis, about the revolution of the earth around the sun, and about gravity. Gravity was a hard concept to explain, but Norm had a couple of magnets with him and told them that gravitational attraction was similar to the attraction between unlike poles of a magnet. There were days when they would barely read a paragraph from Professor Hawking's book—Norm would spend almost the entire hour answering the questions that were generated, or at least trying to answer the questions as best he could so the children would understand a particular concept.

"Major Kay, does the moon revolve around the earth?" asked Anita.

"Yes, the moon revolves around the earth just like the earth revolves around the sun. The moon is like a satellite of the earth, and the earth is like a satellite of the sun."

"Grandpa, will the moon hit the earth some day?"

"Hopefully not Chris. The earth's gravity will prevent that from happening. Have I ever showed you an eclipse in the sky?"

"No, Grandpa. What's an eclipse?"

"There are two kinds of eclipses. When the earth, in its movement around the sun, comes directly between the sun and the moon, the shadow of the earth falls on the moon. At this time, we cannot see the moon because the earth hides it from the sun's light. That's called a lunar eclipse.

"When the moon, in its movement around the earth, comes directly between the sun and the earth, we cannot see the sun because the moon blocks our view of it. That's called a solar eclipse.

"Ancient priests who knew how to predict eclipses, would use their knowledge to control people by telling them that eclipses occurred when God was angry with the moon or the sun and would make them disappear for a while."

"Do priests still do that, Grandpa?"

"Yes," replied Norm, as his beady eyes bobbed up and down. "Today's priests and scientists still terrorize us into believing things that may not actually be true. Let's read some more."

NORM read to them about Aristotle's beliefs that the earth was at the center of the universe, and that all the planets and stars and the sun revolved around the earth. As they read more and more, Norm visited the library and checked out books on science that could explain concepts at their level. He believed that it was a better way for them to spend the summer than watch TV most of the time.

Later on in the summer, the Olympic games held in Seoul, South Korea, took priority over science. The venue brought a flood of nostalgic memories to Norm—the last time he was there was the 1950s during the Korean War. The games were covered on TV and Norm watched them intently along with Chris and Anita. With Korea in the limelight, they went for Tae Kwon Do thrice a week. They had progressed from white to yellow to orange over the last two years, and just passed the test to become green belts.

IN the fall that year, the children entered third grade. Chris had sharpened his reading skills and was able to read books at his level quite easily. He wanted to be more independent and conveyed that to Norm.

"Grandpa, from now on I'm going to walk to school by myself."

169

"Are you sure, Chris?"

"Yes, Grandpa. And one more thing. Don't hold my hand anymore when you come to pick me up. I hate it when you do that. People might think I'm still a baby."

That time, Norm got told by his grandson what was expected of him in school.

The children's activities started piling up and there was no time for science everyday. They read once a week on Saturday afternoons, but not on the pleasant fall days that were meant for enjoying the outdoors and raking leaves.

During the rest of that year, Norm became their science tutor. He taught them some of the basic definitions they would need before appreciating what Hawking had said in his book. Both the children had ruled notebooks and they wrote down whatever he told them.

"Major Kay, why does matter have mass?" asked Anita.

"Because when you lift matter up, it is heavy, isn't it? That's why it has mass."

"What you're telling me is a property of matter. I asked you why it has mass?"

"What else can it have?"

"I don't know. Maybe it has energy."

Even though he could not answer her question, Norm was happy because his science tutoring was paying off. Unlike her father, Anita was zeroing in on the fundamental questions of science. The question about why matter had mass was the central unanswered question in particle physics.

"What's momentum, Grandpa?"

"For a moving body, it's the mass multiplied by the velocity. If you and I run a race at the same speed, who has more momentum?"

"Of course you do, Grandpa. You're much heavier than me."

"Yes. A force can be explained as something that causes a change in a body's momentum."

"Is there a difference between mass and weight, Major Kay?"

"Sometimes. Have you seen weight-loss commercials on TV?"

"Yes, we see them all the time," they both replied.

"There's a new one that's being patented. It works by people joining NASA, becoming astronauts, and visiting the moon. The weight of a body is its mass multiplied by the acceleration due to

170

gravity. Since the moon's gravity is one-sixth that of the earth, these people will have an instantaneous weight loss on the moon, even though their mass remains the same."

The laughter that rang out from him as he said this sounded like that of a madman. His face started twitching and Chris and Anita were somewhat taken aback but joined in the merriment.

"Major Kay, who makes up all these definitions in science?"

"That depends on whose theory you are studying. Every theory makes a few assumptions called postulates and defines its own terms. The definition of force I gave you was Newton's definition. Before his time, people used Aristotle's definition of force, which is different from Newton's definition. We shall see later on that Einstein's theory is different from Newton's theory."

THE winter passed by quickly and in the spring it was hard to motivate the children to pursue science. The snow had thawed and there were so many outdoor activities to cure their cabin fever. Norm sensed that Chris was not at all interested in science and would rather play basketball and computer games.

A few days after Easter, Alan heard that he had received tenure at the university. He was somewhat relieved to hear the news—he had been anxiously waiting for a decision since last October.

During the summer of 1989 Chris joined a basketball camp. That was his ticket out of Norm's boring science lessons. There were more important things in life—basketball and computer games. Norm had to let him go. If the horse wasn't thirsty, there was no point in forcing it to drink the water.

Anita, however, continued to study science with Norm. They read Stephen Hawking's book and watched the television show "Cosmos" by Carl Sagan. Sagan's excitement about the cosmos rubbed off onto Anita. She was already fascinated by the night sky and knew the positions of several constellations. She learned that a galaxy had about 100 billion stars and that there were about 10 billion galaxies in the visible universe. By studying the behavior of visible matter, Sagan had said, astronomers had concluded that the bulk of the universe was invisible. The only way we could infer its presence was because of the gravitational effects they produced on visible matter.

Norm and Anita studied the laws of conservation of energy, of momentum, and of mass.

"How does the law of conservation of mass work, Major Kay?"

"Easy. When you don't eat well and your body loses mass, I make up for it by eating more and gaining more mass. That's why I am getting heavier as the years go by," replied Norm, patting his stomach.

"Seriously, Major Kay?"

"Okay, okay. In classical physics, the law of conservation of mass states that the total mass in a closed system is constant. But Einstein changed that by saying that mass is just another form of energy. So in relativity physics the laws of conservation of energy and mass are combined into a single law of conservation of mass-energy."

They moved on to Newton's laws of motion. There were three laws and the basis of these laws were the experimental measurements made by the astronomer Galileo.

Newton's First Law: A body continues in a state of rest or uniform motion unless acted upon by a force.

Newton's Second Law: The rate of change of momentum of a body in a given direction is proportional to the force applied to it in that direction.

Newton's Third Law: For every action there is an equal and opposite reaction.

"Major Kay, can you give me an example of uniform motion?" asked Anita.

"Yes. A car traveling on the interstate at a constant speed of 55 miles per hour is an object in uniform motion."

"Hmmm. According to Newton's law of gravitation, the force of gravity would always be acting on the car, wouldn't it? How can you say the car is traveling in uniform motion if there is an attractive force between the car and other cars on the interstate?"

Norm was trapped. He had tried to give an easy example of uniform motion and had hoped that Anita would be happy with his explanation. It now appeared that he was going to have to find some way to tell her that there was no uniform motion in the entire universe, nor was there an absolute standard of rest according to Newton's theory.

"Anita, you are right. There is no uniform motion in the universe as described by Newton's first law. That is because there are some fundamental forces in nature and scientists are trying to discover what these forces are. Some scientists who are in search of a grand unified theory believe that there is just one basic force that governs nature. Other scientists believe that there are four fundamental forces in nature. Gravity is one of the four forces and every particle in the universe feels the force of gravity. The car, the road it is traveling on, and every atom feels this force of gravity. Since the car is being acted on by a force, it is not in uniform motion according to Newton's theory. And even though the speed of the car is constant at 55 miles per hour, it is constant *relative* to the surface of the road. If the road itself was moving, then we could not say what the absolute speed of the car was—it would depend on how fast the road was moving. Relative to the road, the speed of the car would be fixed. The road does move, you know, because the earth rotates around its own axis and also orbits around the sun."

"What are the four fundamental forces?"

"The prevalent belief that there are four fundamental forces in nature is based largely on experimental evidence. It is possible, however, that with a different model of the universe, there may be more forces or fewer forces. Only time will tell whether or not scientists have fully understood what the fundamental forces of nature are."

NORM was continually amazed at Anita's pluck and courage in asking questions about science. When Becky was in college, he had wished very much for her to major in physics. After Becky, he thought that Chris would take an interest in science. Chris was still growing up though, and could change with time. Anita was like the daughter or granddaughter that Norm never had but had great admiration for. She reminded him of himself when he was younger. At that time, women were not encouraged to learn math and science and would mostly concentrate on other subjects in college. The concept of women in the work force was not a popular concept. Over the years education had changed, and everybody was encouraged to learn whatever they liked. Women were not being discouraged from learning math or science. That was fortunate for Anita because she had such a keen interest in science and Norm hoped that her interest would continue in future. If she was too smart, however, she would face obstacles in the male-dominated scientific camp.

"How is Einstein's theory different from Newton's theory?" asked Anita.

"Einstein's theory examines the effect of forces on objects that travel at very high speeds, like the speed of light. The speed of light is roughly 186,000 miles per second. Einstein proposed his theory of relativity in which the speed of light is constant. Pretend that a pulse of light is sent from a lighthouse to a ship at sea. Also pretend that many people are observing this event, some at land, some at sea, and some in the air. In Newton's theory, all observers have to agree on the time taken by the pulse of light. They would not necessarily agree on the distance traveled by the light pulse. So if they measured the speed of light, which is distance traveled divided by time taken, each observer would measure a different speed for the light pulse.

"In Einstein's theory, the speed of light is fixed. That is, everybody agrees on how fast light travels. They still would not agree on the distance traveled by the light pulse, so now they would have to make an adjustment to the time taken by the light pulse to obtain the same speed for light. In essence, Einstein was saying that the people at land observing this event, those at sea, and those in the air, would have their own measure of time even if they were using identical clocks."

"How can that happen? The clock in my house shows the same time as the clock in your house."

"Are you sure? There may be a few differences but certainly they can be adjusted to show the same time. What Einstein was saying in his theory applies to objects that move very fast—at or near the speed of light."

"You just said from Newton's law that nothing could move at a fixed speed—it has to be fixed relative to something."

"Good point, Anita. I need to explain that more clearly. You know what a wave is, don't you? Like waves in an ocean or ripples formed in a lake when you throw a rock into it."

"Yes, I've seen waves in the water."

"Light is also like a wave, but we can't see the waves because they are very close together. Such waves have been used to

174

describe magnetic forces—like the force between magnets that you and Chris have played with, and also electrical forces. In fact, the electro-magnetic force is a fundamental force of nature.

"James Maxwell predicted that light waves should travel at a fixed speed. The fixed speed was measured relative to a substance called *ether* that was present everywhere in the universe. Light waves would move through ether just as sound waves moved through air."

"What is ether, Major Kay? Can we see it?"

"That was a question many scientists asked. An experiment to detect ether was carried out by two scientists named Michelson and Morley. They believed that the speed of light ought to change as the earth moved through the ether in its orbit around the sun. If ether had an effect on the speed of light at a given time, then six months later as the earth would be moving in the opposite direction around the sun, the speed of light should be different. So they measured the speed by bouncing a pulse of light off a mirror. They did this in the direction the earth was moving and in a direction at right angles to it. The purpose of the experiment was to measure the time difference between the two round trips and find out the relative velocity between the earth and ether, assuming that the ether was at rest.

"And guess what happened. The experiment was performed many times, at various times of the year, and in many locations. In every single case, there was no time difference observed. The time taken by the light to travel from the source to the mirror and back was the same in both cases. So the experiment had a negative result in the sense that the presence of ether could not be detected.

"Therefore, Einstein, in his theory, said that the whole idea of ether was unnecessary and postulated that the speed of light was a constant in vacuum."

"If the experiment could not detect ether, Major Kay, does it mean it is not there?"

"That's a difficult question to answer, Anita. If we cannot measure something by scientific experiments, then we look for a different theory to explain the observations. In a sense, Einstein's theory offered a different way to explain the observations—a theory where ether was not needed. So it is not right to conclude that there is no ether. Just that it is not necessary in Einstein's theory, provided we give up on the idea of absolute time. This means that all clocks do not have to agree on the same time."

"I'm a little confused by this experiment. Newton's law says that nothing can be at rest or in uniform motion. Why is it assumed that ether is at rest? Is it possible that ether is also moving?"

"Hmmm. That's a very interesting question. I will have to think about it. I'm not sure what would happen to the result of the Michelson-Morley experiment if ether was moving."

It was clear to Norm that Anita had grasped the scientific way of thinking. Children are so unbiased in their approach that sometimes they can ask questions that experienced scientists don't bother asking but can't answer either. The question about an ether that was moving was an intriguing one.

Eighteen

In March 1968, Norm broke ground for his lawn care business in Orlando. Unlike the northern portion of the country, Florida was warm throughout and there was work to be done all year round. This kept him so busy that he had little energy to pursue physics and metaphysics. He felt a deep sense of failure from two sources: the first was his army career that terminated in a Section 8 discharge, and the second was his failure to find the Word of Lord Siva and fulfill his mission. With Joann by his side to support him in whatever he did, he had no regrets. Financially, they were doing all right after his retirement from the army. Personally for Norm, lawn mowing was a sort of therapy—he could spend a lot of time thinking by himself about several things, and on many occasions his customers had noticed that he was in some sort of trance as he mowed their yards. Little did they suspect that his thoughts were focused on concepts in physics and metaphysics—for all external appearances Norm was just an ordinary lawn-care person. Nobody knew where he had been or where he was trying to go and they probably didn't care as long as their yards were well maintained.

For his birthday on March 18th, Joann fell sorry for Norm and bought him a book. It was *The Teachings of Don Juan : A Yaqui way of Knowledge* by Carlos Castaneda. Norm started reading it with great interest. Carlos was describing his adventures with a Yaqui Indian warrior named Don Juan. Far from being a ladies' man, Castaneda's Don Juan was a true seer of knowledge. As was the custom with Yaqui Indians, Don Juan consumed peyote before he went on vision quests. Castaneda described him as a 'man of knowledge,'—a phrase that Norm had come across in the *Bhagavad Gita*. There was one passage in the book that Norm enjoyed so much that he wrote it in his journal.

> *Any path is only a path, and there is no affront to oneself or to others, in dropping it if that is what your heart tells you . . Look at every path closely and deliberately. Try it as many times as you think necessary. Then ask yourself, and yourself alone, one question . . . Does this path have a heart? If it does, the path is good; if it doesn't it is of no use.*

Castaneda was a doctoral student in anthropology at UCLA and claimed that the book was a real occurrence based on his experiences with a Yaqui Indian tribe. Don Juan had told Carlitos, as he affectionately addressed him, that there were two concepts in the exclusive realm of men of knowledge—tonal (toh-na'hl) and nagual (nah-wa'hl).

> *The tonal is everything we are, Carlitos. Anything we have a word for is the tonal. The tonal is everything we know. It begins at birth and ends at death.*

> *The nagual is that part of us which we do not deal with at all. It is the part of us for which there is no description— no words, no names, no feelings, no knowledge.*

The idea of a state of consciousness, the nagual, distinct from ordinary reality is similar to the dualism between the mind and the brain. Is the conscious mind a part of the brain or something beyond it? The Yaqui Indians believed that the world of enlightenment was not to be confused with any conceptual pattern of thought, a belief embraced by Hindus and Buddhists as well as by Robert Pirsig. It almost dragged Norm back into his inquiry—something he had promised Joann that he would abandon. His cooler head prevailed and after reading the book he packed it away in one of his boxes.

Norm would later find out about the controversy over Castaneda's writings. It arose when Carlos claimed that his work was scientific anthropology, yet nobody but him could ever meet Don

Juan in person. Richard DeMille, in particular, had written that Castaneda's writings were more an eclectic mishmash of Eastern doctrines than rigorous scientific work. Nevertheless, the dualism expressed by the concepts of tonal and nagual had resonated well with readers.

AFTER her initial dislike of Orlando, Rebecca made new friends in school and became more comfortable. She would soon be a teenager in April and incur the wrath of the universe.

"What are we going to do with her?" asked Norm, a little nervous about his daughter who had grown up so quickly.

"What do you mean by that?" replied Joann. "She's going to live with us just as she's been doing all along."

"You know what I mean. About how long she can stay out and all that."

"Are you worried that she's going to start dating, Norm?"

"I didn't say that. I guess I am. Have you told her the story of the birds and the bees?"

"Yes, yes, Norm," Joann replied, laughing. "That was in our time. Rebecca knows about all this stuff already."

"That's what I was afraid of."

"Take it easy Norm. Nothing's happened at all. There's no need to get so worried."

After a month or so in school, Rebecca told her parents to call her Becky. That was the name she liked and that was what they called her in school. Joann and Norm did not have any problem with that. They had always been supportive of decisions that their daughter made, and were not the sort of parents who would impose anything on her, not even religion. Norm told her that as she grew up she would be free to pursue whatever religion she liked.

Over the next few years Norm and Joann underwent the trials and tribulations of dealing with a teenager. In her sophomore year in high school, Becky passed the driving test and was eligible for a driver's license. She started driving with Norm by her side.

"How did it go, dear?" asked Joann after one of their test-drives.

"Great, Mom. I think I can go by myself now."

"No, you can't," shouted Norm. "You have to be 16 years to drive by yourself. Okay? Try to understand that."

Becky sulked into her room as Joann chided Norm, "Did you have to scream at her like that? Take it easy."

"Take IT EASY! It's easy for you to say that. I'm the one whose hair and knuckles are turning white. She can't even make a smooth lane change. Take it easy! Next time you go with her. Let's see if you come back alive."

"Okay, okay. Settle down, Norm."

Like any regular teenager, Becky attended parties with her friends and hung out with them. Norm insisted that Becky come home by 10 o'clock at night, which ruled out late night movies. For her first prom night Becky pleaded with her mom to negotiate a midnight curfew, and Norm agreed.

Upon graduating from high school, Becky decided to go to college. Her parents told her that they would not be able to afford private colleges and encouraged her to attend one of the state universities in Florida. Becky enrolled in the University of Florida at Gainesville. Unlike Norm, Becky's interests were in history and literature, not science.

WHEN Becky left for college, their house became empty. Joann and Norm would look forward to the times when she would visit them. Gainesville was only 110 miles from Orlando, and Becky would come home on long weekends. Norm didn't like the idea of Becky owning a car and so she would either take a bus or find a ride with someone from the university. Sometimes, Norm himself drove up to bring her home. With a little whining, he allowed her to drive the car on the way back. Now that Becky was gone from the house, Joann found plenty of time with nothing to do. She told Norm that she wanted to open a shop that sold handicrafts. Norm checked into their financial situation and told her it would be all right. Joann's shop was called the Craft Patch. Her idea was to stock a variety of decorations and crafts so that her shop would be a one-stop place for people who wanted different things. There were decorations for the usual celebrations of Halloween, Thanksgiving, Christmas, and Easter. There were decorations for weddings and parties, decorations for ribbons, beads, wreaths, and dolls, instruction books on knitting, crochet, sewing, and woodcrafts and many different types of eyes that could be used for self-made dolls. Norm occasionally asked her when she would start carrying magic carpets.

180

Within two years of its opening, the Craft Patch became a very popular place. Joann couldn't take care of it by herself and hired a person to assist her. During the summer of 1975, when Becky came home from her junior year, she told her parents that she had a steady boy friend and that they were planning to get married the following year after graduation. His name was Robert Stewart and he would be getting his masters degree in electrical engineering at the same time that Becky would graduate with a baccalaureate degree in history. The wedding date was set for July 18, 1976. Joann's shop took care of all the wedding arrangements.

Norm had ambivalent feelings on the wedding day—he was happy for Becky but sad that she was leaving home. After marriage, Becky moved with her husband to the Chicagoland area. Bob had found a job with Motorola in Schaumburg, which was a northwest suburb of Chicago. Becky's marriage created a vacuum in the lives of her parents. In her college days she lived quite close by to them in Gainesville, now it would be hard for her to visit them often. Every other week Joann and Norm would call Becky and she would do the same. They spoke to each other once a week during the first year, and then it became less frequent, like once a month.

In March 1979, there was some good news and bad news from Becky. The good news was that she was expecting a baby in November. The bad news was that she and her husband were not getting along together. Her parents just encouraged her and told her to do the best she could. Norm advised her to pick up some skills that would help her find a job if necessary. At 10:05 P.M. on November 17, 1979, Becky gave birth to a baby boy, who weighed eight and a half pounds. She named him Christopher after her grandfather whom she hadn't seen.

IN September of the next year, Joann gave Norm some shocking news. She had felt a small lump in her right breast for quite a few months and had just visited her doctor. The doctor conducted an examination and told her that it might be breast cancer. She would have to undergo a number of tests in the next few weeks. While Norm had heard about cancer, it was not an easy matter to deal with when it happened to some one very close to him. Although he had some knowledge about science, outside of physics and metaphysics Norm was a big zero. He didn't know anything about medicine at all.

He decided that the only way he could help Joann and himself was to be with her during the check-ups and get all the information the doctors gave him on her condition. He put his manager in charge of the lawn-care business and did the same with Joann's Craft Patch.

The first test that her doctor carried out was a mammogram. Mammography is an X-ray process that tells the doctor the location and size of the lump and provides other useful information. Since there was always the possibility that a lump was benign and not malignant, the doctor had to also do a biopsy. A biopsy is a procedure for removing a small amount of tissue from a living organism and examining the pattern of cell disruption under a microscope. It is usually done with a surgical incision. Norm's self-determined role was to get as much information as possible about the tests, take some notes of his own, and discuss these with Joann in the evenings after dinner.

The results of the biopsy confirmed that Joann's lump was malignant. But there was some good news. The cancer had not spread too far into the rest of her body, and the doctor had hopes of curing her. He gave Joann two options. One was a lumpectomy in combination with radiation therapy and chemotherapy. The lumpectomy would focus on removing the malignant lump. If, however, there were other small lumps that were present in the breast but did not show up in the mammogram, then the lumpectomy could not guarantee that the cancer had been totally destroyed. The other option was a mastectomy. This would remove the entire breast and sometimes the surrounding tissues and muscles. Since the cancer had not spread beyond the breast, a mastectomy would assure that the cancer was totally destroyed. The doctor told her to think about it for a while and tell him within a week which option she wanted to go with.

It was around Christmas when the decision had to be made. Becky visited them for a few days with Chris, and Joann and Norm were so proud of their grandson. Chris was 13 months old and could walk by himself but needed supervision on stairs. Going up was easy but coming down was not. Norm would walk Chris in his stroller every day. Becky had a long talk with her mother and suggested that she talk to some of her friends who had undergone either a lumpectomy or mastectomy before making her decision. She also told her dad that in case he needed help, he could always give her a call and she would be there right away to help him.

Lumpectomy or mastectomy? It was a difficult decision. Norm did not pressure Joann at all in making her choice. His job was to support her and give her all the information about both options. Ultimately she would have to choose between them. With either option there would be some X-ray treatments, perhaps more in the case of a lumpectomy. Joann talked to some of her friends and eventually decided to have a lumpectomy. They conveyed their decision to the doctor.

The doctor told Joann that before doing the actual lumpectomy he would prescribe some medication and radiation therapy. Joann would have to undergo radiation three times every week for a couple of months. Norm accompanied her on all the radiation treatments. The radiation therapy left Joann very exhausted. It was in the middle of March when the doctor suspected that the radiation therapy was not having the intended effect on Joann. He performed another mammogram and biopsy and told them that the cancer had spread further. A lumpectomy was no longer an option.

The mastectomy was scheduled for May 14, 1981. The operation went off very well and Joann's right breast was removed. She stayed in the hospital for a week after that and then came home. Becky arrived from Chicago to spend a few days with her. Besides her mother's operation, Becky's other worry was that Chris, at the age of one and a half, had not yet learned to speak.

Joann still had to undertake some X-ray treatments in the next few months. The radiation therapy, the medication, and the mastectomy had weakened Joann so much that she would constantly feel exhausted. Norm had never seen her so tired before and asked the doctor whether it was a normal condition. The doctor told him that it would take some time for her to recover fully and be her usual self again. He advised Norm to be patient.

In the months that followed, Joann was like a complete invalid. She used to become so breathless that Norm insisted that the doctor give her a thorough examination. The doctor checked her up and found nothing to be alarmed about. Norm took charge of looking after the house, the cooking, and the cleaning. Meanwhile Becky and Bob Stewart were having marital problems, and in November of 1981 they decided to get separated. Chris was almost two years old and had still not spoken a word. Joann was very sad when she heard the news about the separation. Norm consoled her by saying that it was not right for Becky and Bob to live together if they had fallen out of love. Perhaps, in the long run, this was best for Becky and Chris. They offered to help Becky out financially but she said she would manage just fine. The divorce and the settlement would take some time and the details were in the hands of their attorneys. Joann insisted that Norm send Becky some packages of food now and then like oranges and cuts of meat.

THE following year Joann was still as tired and breathless as before. She would sit up in her bed and talk to Norm about her hometown.

"How I wish I was back on my farm in Ontario, Iowa. I miss it badly."

"Yes, dear. Those are usually the best years of one's life, carefree and innocent."

"I still remember spending precious moments with my dad. He would never talk much but when he did, it used to inspire me from within. So much of my inner strength comes from him.

" 'Have you seen the corn grow?' he would ask me. When I shook my head he would say, 'When you do, you will learn the art of seeing.'

" 'Have you heard the corn grow?' he would ask me. Again I would shake my head and he would say, 'When you do, you will learn the art of believing.' "

On Friday, April 9, 1982, Joann had breakfast and then went in to shower. It was raining heavily outside and Norm was at home reading the newspaper. He heard the bathroom door open and soon after that he heard a thud. Joann cried out his name and Norm rushed to her side. She had collapsed just outside the bathroom door.

"O Lord, O Lord," she implored, "please take care of my husband."

Norm held her head up in his arms and wanted to put her up in a chair before calling an ambulance. As he held her up, she started foaming at the mouth and a couple of minutes later she stopped breathing. The end was swift and peaceful and like Bill Kaplan in Korea, she had died in his arms. Norm rushed over to call 911.

The paramedics tried their best to revive her but in vain. The autopsy indicated that she had died of pulmonary embolism, a blockage of an artery in the lungs. The pathologist said that the possible cause was a detached blood clot, perhaps from some of the tumor tissue. In looking for cancer cells, her regular doctor had not bothered to check her arteries at all. Had he done so, he might have found the blood clot. Norm didn't care much about the autopsy report. He knew that Joann's time to depart had come, and nothing could have stopped it.

WITH Joann's death, Norm became more withdrawn. He sold his lawn-care business and went into retirement. He still kept Joann's shop open in honor of her memory. A full-time manager was put in charge of running the Craft Patch. She was as capable as Joann with quite a bit of business savvy. Norm lived one day at a time. He had no motivation to do anything. He wished he had been a different person in his life, a regular person who would work from 8 to 5 and spend the rest of his time with his loved ones. Every day he would take a long walk for roughly 6 miles. On those walks he would think often about Joann's faith in God. About how she used to pray every single day of her life—a simple prayer of thanks, not one of needs or desires. If at all she wanted something in life, it was for Norm to give up smoking and to be normal—to be a person who would believe in God like she did, and enjoy the simple pleasures of life. Do good unto others and give a helping hand to those not so fortunate as yourself—that was her motto in life. She didn't need any scientific reason for her belief in God, nor did she ever question the authority of religion. To her, religion was not something she did in church only on Sundays, it was something she practiced every single day of her life—to be kind to all her fellow human beings.

Hemant Lal was in Orlando for a bridge tournament in early June and visited Norm for a couple of days.

"It's during times like this, my friend, that one turns to religion and God," he said to Norm.

"I'm beginning to believe that," Norm replied.

"I think the *Bhagavad Gita* will help you understand what has happened. Do you still have your copy?"

"Yes. Let me find it." Norm searched one of his boxes, and found the copy to show Hemant.

"Very interesting, Norm. I will tell you a story about the person who translated your book, Swami Vireswarananda.

"He was born as Panduranga Prabhu and lived a normal life until the age of 24 when he was studying law in Trivandrum. Then he experienced a strange awakening within himself, described best as a spiritual phone call. He left his law studies and took a train to northern India to join the Ramakrishna Mission, an order of monks who follow the Gospel of Sri Ramakrishna. Panduranga's uncle tried to get him back a couple of times, but so strong was the spiritual calling that he did not succeed in changing the young lad's mind."

"Who was Sri Ramakrishna?"

"Sri Ramakrishna was a Bengali Brahmin who experienced ecstatic mystic visions as a child. He became a priest at the temple of Kali near Calcutta and believed that all religions were directed towards the same God along different paths. People who knew him believed that he was an incarnation of Lord Vishnu."

"Did Swami Vireswarananda meet him?"

"No. Sri Ramakrishna passed away in 1886 at the age of 50."

"Thank you Hemant. I will read the *Gita* again. Every time I read it, I learn something new."

After Hemant Lal left, Norm wondered whether Joann had attained *moksha* as explained in Hinduism. Was the path to liberation of the soul a path of knowledge, or were there other paths to liberation? Then one day he read a verse from the *Bhagavad Gita:*

> *He who at the time of death remembers Me alone and passes out, leaving the body, attains My being—there is no doubt about this. — Bhagavad Gita 8:5.*

IF the Lord Himself had said this, Norm had no doubt in his mind that Joann had indeed attained *moksha*. She had always thought of Him her entire life. There were many paths to attain the truth and Joann's path was different from his path.

On his 58th birthday the following year, Norm decided to give up smoking completely. It was a habit he had acquired since his college days and it had stuck with him throughout his army career. Giving it up was a small gesture on his part in honor of his dearly departed wife of nearly 30 years.

When people close to him passed away, Norm remembered them by doing something special on the day they died. The two special people who were close to him were Joann and Bill Kaplan. He had promised Bill that he would keep his memory alive and that he would not be forgotten. Bill had introduced Norm to the Sufi poet Omar Khayyam and his quatrains known as *The Rubaiyat*. During the big bug-out on November 27, 1950, Bill had been badly injured along with a 5,000-strong Turkish brigade. The Chinese ambush proved deadly and only a handful managed to escape. Bill died later that day in a MASH unit. Norm was at his side when he took his last breath. Every year on November 27th, Norm always found time to read *The Rubaiyat,* a piece of poetry Bill had really liked. He did a similar thing to remember Joann—every year on April 9th, he read pages from the New Testament, a book that was very sacred to Joann's heart.

In 1984, Norm was happy to hear that Becky needed his help with Chris. He made plans at once to leave for Urbana. The feeling of being needed by someone was a very comforting feeling.

Nineteen

In the fall of 1989, Anita and Chris entered fourth grade in school. The schoolteachers had recognized Anita's interest in science and she was placed in an accelerated learning program.

In late September, Alan got a phone call from Seattle.

"Hey bud, what's happening?" asked Kali.

"Nothing much. I'm still here at Urbana. You'd be surprised at the amount of work I have to do after tenure. Man, those student days were cool."

"You should have bought stock in my company when I asked you to in 1986. We're doing really well now. I might be a millionaire soon."

"No kidding."

"No, I'm serious. Every year the company gives me stock options and when the stock splits my shares get doubled."

"Good for you. Looks like you're one step closer to attaining your *dharma* in life, uh?"

"I don't know. The downside is that I have to put in many 18-hour days to get products finished on time. Since last year, I've developed arthritis in my wrists."

"Too bad. Don't work so hard, man. How's Lila?"

"That's what I wanted to talk to you about. I'm thinking of leaving her. She's very crazy about money. Every time I bring up the matter of retiring from Microsoft, she gets mad. She wants me to stay here and earn more money. I don't know what to do. I'm worried about my health."

"I thought your purpose in life was to make money. Has something changed?"

"Yes. I thought that was my purpose when I started working. But now I think my health is more important. I wish I could ask Nitya to guide me."

"You can always go back to her."

"No, I can't. Nitya's joined a priory. Maybe I ought to visit India and talk to her."

"You're not the only one with problems, Kali. Meg and I are not happy either. We're both so busy with our own jobs that we don't spend time together any more. And even if we get the time, we don't know what to do because we've grown apart. Meg's been acting strangely of late, reading all kinds of self-help books on spiritual mush. There seem to be new gurus popping up every minute nowadays. They enlighten her and our checkbook as well."

"Sorry to hear that, Alan. I've got to go now. Talk to you later, man."

THE following month Alan attended an annual physics conference held in Vail, Colorado. The previous year, when it was held in Orlando, Alan had been introduced to Pat Duran of Boston College. She was also working in the area of fundamental particles. They had spent an evening in Church Street Station and the ambiance and beer and Pat's infectious laughter and olive complexion spawned a chemistry between them that nurtured and bloomed for a whole year through e-mail. The affair was consummated during the conference in October 1989.

In early December Alan was invited to give a colloquium in the physics department at Boston College. When he returned Meg noticed the smug grimace on his face.

"Do you know that we've been getting strange phone calls lately? Last month when I picked up the phone, on at least half a dozen occasions as soon as I said hello the other person hung up. Do you know anything about it?" Meg asked him.

"No dear. It's probably a student prank."

189

Meg had been suspicious of him for some time and shared her feelings with Becky. "Have you noticed any change in my husband's behavior recently?" she asked her.

"Well, he's shaved his beard and is dressing a lot more decently nowadays."

"He's also traveling quite a bit and spending less time at home. He keeps going often to Washington D.C., to review proposals he tells me."

"I hope it's not proposals from women."

"My God, Becky. I think you're right. Do you think he's having an affair?"

"I was just kidding when I said that Meg. He's probably reviewing proposals for the National Science Foundation."

"No, no, what you said makes perfect sense. His whole behavior is different now. I've been getting strange phone calls that hang up on me. Add it all up, Becky. It's clear as day."

"Relax, Meg. You don't have any real evidence about this you know."

"Evidence-shevidence. I'm going to find out right now."

"How?"

"I'm going to ask the bastard to his face," said Meg, who slammed the door and rushed home.

"ANITA," she said, "I want you to go up to your room, NOW. I need to be alone with your father." Anita left quietly.

"Alan," she continued, "stop what you're doing and listen to me."

Alan turned toward her and said, "What's up?"

"Are you having an affair? Admit it. I know it's true."

"Nonsense, honey. You know I'm married to my work."

"You're supposed to be married to ME." He could sense that this was going to be a serious conversation. He hadn't seen her so angry before.

"I've got proof you know," she continued. "Don't think I'm a fool. The phone calls, the clean-shaven face, the trips to the East Coast, they all add up. Tell me, is it true?"

"If it's true, it's true. If it's not, it's not. So what?"

"Look, I don't care how circular you are in your damn research papers. Just give me a straight answer."

190

Alan squirmed for a while and decided to get it over with.

"Okay, DAMMIT. It's true. What are you going to do about it? It's all your fault."

Meg started sobbing.

"I knew it, I knew it," she said. "Why? What is it that you don't get in this house?"

"I don't know. She's a physicist like me specializing in the area of particle physics. We've been working closely on an interesting problem—high-energy collisions between gravitons and gluons."

"Oh yeah. What kind of high-energy collisions?"

"Come on, Meg. You know what I meant."

"No, I DO NOT. Why don't you tell me?"

"Well, at the conference in October our discussions got intense, and after the bar closed we continued it in my hotel room. That's when our bodies consumed each other. It could have happened to anybody."

"How can you justify what you did? What about your morals? Don't you know that you're a married man?"

"Yes, in the eyes of the world we're married. But you've been neglecting me of late. All you do is read spiritual books my parents dump on you. I picked up one of them and this is what it said, 'Far from condemning sexual desire, Taoism feels that sexuality mirrors the cosmic flow of energy between yin and yang. Ch'i is increased by sexual stimulus which nourishes life.'

"And Pat told me that I wasn't making love to her but to the Absolute made manifest in her. We were uniting male and female principles operating throughout the universe."

"Pat? Does that THING have a name? Bitch."

"Meg, you of all people should understand that it was a spiritual exercise. Isn't spirituality what you've been searching for lately?"

"Don't you dare make a mockery of my spirituality. You can't trivialize solemn religious literature with your weak moral standards. You men have no backbone at all. I don't want to talk about this any more."

Meg and Becky had lunch the next day. "It's true," said Meg. "I asked him last night and he admitted it, the creep."

"That's too bad."

191

"In all my life I've never heard such utter nonsense. He's justifying what he did by blaming me. He claims it was a spiritual exercise and he made love to a manifestation of the Absolute. I just can't get over it."

"I think both of you need to be separated for a while. It'll be good for you."

IN January 1990 soon after the new year, Meg decided to get separated from Alan. The rift between them had been present for a long time, and what precipitated the separation was Alan's affair and the fact that Meg had received an offer from Nieman Marcus in Chicago and did not want to pass up the opportunity. They both agreed that whatever their differences were, Anita should not have to suffer too much. Since finding the right school district in Chicago would be a problem, they decided that it was best for Anita to continue in Urbana and visit Meg whenever she got a chance.

When Anita was told the news, she started to cry. Her first question was whether she was responsible for the divorce. Her parents told her that they were just getting separated for the time being, not getting divorced. She rushed over to Norm's house and gave Chris the news.

"Chris, my parents are separating just like yours. My mom is moving to Chicago."

"Anita dear, when did you find this out?" asked Norm.

"Just now, Major Kay."

"Are you going to move to Chicago?" asked Chris.

"I don't know," replied Anita.

Later on, Norm went over to visit Meg and Alan and confirmed what Anita had told him. He was happy with their decision to leave Anita in Urbana, as he felt that it would be in her best interest.

"Does Anita need to attend counseling?" he asked.

"I think she might," replied Meg.

"Are both of you going into counseling?"

"No, not me," shouted Alan. "She's the one who needs it," he carried on, pointing to Meg.

"See what I mean," said Meg, shrugging her shoulders and looking towards Norm.

"Alan, counseling works only with both people present. It takes two hands to clap," said Norm.

"Whatever. I'll pass up on it for now."

"If I were you I would discuss my problems with a counselor. Sometimes talking loudly about your feelings is a good way of understanding them."

Meg left Urbana in the last week of January. Her job in Chicago started on February 1st. Chicago, situated on the shores of Lake Michigan, is called the windy city. Meg soon found out why. When she walked outside without earmuffs, her ears were frozen stiff in less than 200 yards, especially in February.

During spring break that year, both Chris and Anita went to Chicago together. Chris spent time with his dad and Anita spent time with her mom. Chris's dad took the children to a Bulls basketball game. The Bulls were playing pretty well with Michael Jordan but had not won a championship yet. Anita loved to watch basketball but she was not as interested in playing the game as Chris was. They had a wonderful time in Chicago and Meg told Anita that she would be in Urbana for her birthday in May.

WITH all the changes in her life, Anita's science education had slowed down quite a bit. Norm did not push her at all and waited for her to take the initiative. On Friday, April 13, 1990, Anita told Norm that she wanted to understand the theory of the expanding universe.

"You remember Newton's law of gravity don't you? Gravity is an attractive force between any two particles in the universe.

"A question that is interesting is whether the stars, because of gravity, will eventually attract each other and collapse together at some point."

"Is that going to happen soon, Major Kay?"

"I don't know, Anita. Scientists have not observed many stars falling in this manner. What they believe is that if the universe is infinite and gravity is always an attractive force as Newton defined it, then the universe cannot be static, that is, it cannot be stationary— it must be dynamic, either expanding or contracting."

"But if the universe is either expanding or contracting, has it always been like this or did it start at some point in the past?"

"Good question, Anita. One of the implications of a non-static universe is that it must have had an infinite density in the past.

It is presumed that a few billion years ago, a huge explosion called the Big Bang occurred, and this is thought to be the beginning of the universe."

"Was this before the dinosaurs?"

"Yes. Much before the dinosaurs. Much before any life form that we know could have even existed. This might have happened ten or twenty billion years ago."

"Do scientists know whether the universe is expanding or contracting?"

"The belief in the 20th century is that it is expanding. With the invention of powerful telescopes, we now know that there are many galaxies in the universe. Our galaxy is called the Milky Way. There are other galaxies like M31 in Andromeda. The existence of these galaxies was shown by Edwin Hubble and he measured the distance between us and them."

"How did he measure distance using a telescope?"

"He could tell how far a star was by finding out how bright it was and by studying the spectrum of its light.

"Hubble observed that the frequency of the light waves from a star in another galaxy always appeared smaller and smaller and the conclusion drawn was that the star was moving away from us. The further away a star was from us, the more rapidly it was moving away. Hubble's observation led scientists to conclude that the universe was expanding, not contracting."

"I don't get it," said Anita.

"Let's pretend that you stand outside on the sidewalk and a motorcycle approaches you. When it is far away its engine sound is soft, corresponding to a low frequency of sound waves. As the motorcycle approaches you, its sound becomes louder with a corresponding increase in the frequency of the sound waves. And as the motorcycle passes by you and moves away, the sound becomes softer. So if I were to blindfold you and place you on the sidewalk, you could tell whether the motorcycle was coming towards you or whether it was going away from you just by listening to its sound. Right?"

"Yes, Major Kay, now I understand why the universe is expanding. The frequency of light waves from stars is becoming less and less and that's why they are moving away from us."

"Exactly."

Norm and Anita took a small break. Norm went to fix a drink and Anita got a snack to eat. When she finished her granola bar, she told Norm that she was still confused. Norm repeated his motorcycle analogy.

"Now do you understand it?" he asked.

"No."

"I don't see why not. It's pretty simple."

"Here's the part that is confusing me. You said from Newton's laws that there was no uniform motion and no absolute rest. So what you say about the motorcycle is all right if the observer is standing still. But what if the observer is not standing still? What if the observer is also moving?"

"If the observer is moving, then so too is the motorcycle, and in a relative sense these two motions will cancel each other out."

"What if the observer is moving faster than the motorcycle? Let's pretend that the observer is blindfolded as before, but this time she is placed in a car. And the car moves in the same direction as the motorcycle, but at a faster speed. If the observer does not know that she is moving, then by listening to the sound of the motorcycle's engine alone, she would think that the motorcycle is moving away from her in an opposite direction, when actually it is moving towards her in the same direction. Wouldn't that be a contraction and not an expansion?"

It was Norm's turn to be surprised. The monkey was on his back now.

"Will you please repeat that, Anita?"

Anita explained her concern one more time. Norm had to agree because what she said made perfect sense.

"Yes Anita, if the car is moving in the same direction as the motorcycle and the observer does not know that the car is moving, then by listening to the sound of the motorcycle alone, she would come to the wrong conclusion that the motorcycle is moving in the opposite direction. It could be moving in the opposite direction but it could also be moving in the same direction. The reality is that the distance between her and the motorcycle increases with time. The experiment would not be able to distinguish any more than that."

"Major Kay, is it not possible that the earth and the stars and all the galaxies are moving towards some center of the universe and at different speeds? We just read that in the days of Aristotle people thought that the earth was stationary. Now we know that the earth is moving around the sun, but we still can't be sure that it is not moving in any other way. If the earth is like the car and a distant star is like the motorcycle, then by measuring the frequency of the light wave, all we can say is that the distance between the two is increasing. We cannot conclude that the universe is expanding. It could also be contracting, couldn't it?"

"Where would it be contracting to?"

"In the same space that it is assumed to be expanding into."

Norm was amazed by her explanation. The discovery of the expanding universe had been hailed by many as one of the great intellectual revolutions of the 20th century. Here was little Anita, barely 10 years old, challenging that great discovery. He was somewhat puzzled by the nature of her questions. A few months back she had raised the question about an ether that was moving and the effect it would have had on the Michelson-Morley experiment. Now she had raised a question about a contracting universe. It was clear to him that he was soon going to reach the boundary of his own ignorance. He recalled asking the question about the existence of ether himself a few years back when he was studying Hinduism, but the concept of a moving ether did not occur to him.

WHEN Anita went back home that night, Norm thought about what she had said. He searched for some of his physics books and found one that explained redshift, which described the fact that the characteristic lines in the speçtrum produced from the light of a galaxy appeared at longer (or redder) wavelengths. How did this observation lead to the conclusion of an expanding universe, he wondered? As he read some more, he found a definition of redshift:

"A redshift is the increase in wavelength that a ray of light undergoes when its source is receding from the observer."

No, that couldn't be a definition, he told himself. How could redshift be defined in terms of a recession velocity? The only conclusion that could be drawn from the observed evidence was that the distance between source and observer was increasing with time. Then a light bulb came on in his head. In physics, velocity was *defined* as the rate of change of distance with time. Therefore, to explain redshift it was natural to associate a recession velocity with the emitting source. What other nice, elegant way would there be to characterize it other than to use one of the definitions within the system? At a fundamental level, however, the two concepts of distance increasing with time and recession velocity are quite different.

IF the notion of an expanding universe depended on recession velocity, it was on pretty thin ice as far was he was concerned. The velocity interpretation of redshift was based on a radial line-of-sight component of the velocity, disregarding any other complex velocity field that might be present for matter in the universe. Was the concept of the expanding universe based on an interpretation of the evidence instead of the actual evidence? Could there be an alternative explanation for redshift? It certainly appeared that way to him as he wrote Anita's questions in his journal.

• *Is it possible that the substratum ether is not stationary, but accelerating?*

• *Is it possible that the universe is contracting right now, not expanding?*

Twenty

In the summer of 1990 Norm offered to take Chris and Anita to Orlando. He had to take care of some business matters that dealt with Joann's Craft Patch, and the children would have an opportunity to visit some of the area attractions. Both Anita and Chris had a blast. They visited the Magic Kingdom and Epcot Center in Disney World, and also spent a day at Sea World.

The Disney World theme parks each take a full day to visit, but with the summer time crowds it takes a little more than a day for each park.

Norm bought 3-day world passes for each of them so that they could spend enough time visiting the Magic Kingdom and Epcot Center. Personally, Norm just enjoyed the Carousel of Progress and the train that went around the Magic Kingdom. Anita and Chris were old enough and tall enough to go on all the rides by themselves, so Norm escaped from having to go on the dreaded Space Mountain. On one of the days, Norm kept track of the time they spent in Disney World. Out of a 10-hour day, from 9:00 A.M. to 7:00 P.M., which amounted to 600 minutes, the total number of minutes actually spent on rides was 94 and a half. The rest of the time was spent sweating in lines, or walking from one ride to another with an hour and a half for an expensive lunch in between. But the children didn't mind the lines at all and as long as they were happy, Norm was happy.

198

DURING the fall of that year, the children entered fifth grade. Anita had become very interested in mathematics and philosophy. She started studying the theory of cones by herself, from an old book, *On the Conics of Apollonius,* which Norm had given her. Early Greek religion and philosophy captured her attention after she read two famous sayings of Heraclitus:

All things come out of the one, and the one out of all things.

You cannot step twice in the same river for fresh waters are ever flowing in upon you.

Her study of Greek philosophy led her to Pythagoras, whose well-known theorem about the hypotenuse of a right-angled triangle we all remember from high school geometry. Pythagoras lived in the sixth century B.C. and was a mathematician and a mystic, combining theology and science. He founded a religious order that abstained from eating flesh because it was cruel and from beans because they excited the passions. He believed in reincarnation and thought that the only way to escape the 'wheel of life' was to become a philosopher who pursued science.

After Pythagoras came Plato who developed the dualistic view of the world, separating the mind from the body, reason from emotion. In *Phaedrus,* Plato compared the psyche to a charioteer controlling two horses, one representing the appetite and the other emotion. Plato taught the traditional Greek religion, which believed that if man mastered the world, God would punish him for his arrogance. *Hubris,* pride before a fall, would be followed by *nemesis,* revenge. Greek thought from Plato onwards rejected the idea of hubris and forgot about nemesis. Thereafter it became common for man to believe that he could dominate Nature and exploit her resources.

One school of thought that did not conform to this view was Neoplatonism. Its principal founder was Plotinus of Alexandria. Like the Hindus and Buddhists he believed that all was one and one was all. The human soul was of divine origin but imprisoned in material clothing that made it tainted, gross and dark. It was the individual's duty to cleanse the soul of its bodily form so that it might return to God. The Neoplatonists encouraged dualism by separating mind and body, spirit and matter, and practiced extreme asceticism, fasting, and chastity to purge the soul from its impurities.

Plotinus's ideas about the soul being immortal left a deep impression on Anita. She started to believe that God's light was present in everything that existed. Sometimes one could see it and sometimes one could not. She was beginning to understand Norm's pursuit of an explanation of the divine mystery of light and darkness.

WHEN winter set in that year, Anita went back to her study of physics.

"What's the smallest particle you can think of Anita?" asked Norm.

"A grain of sand. No, no, a grain of salt. A grain of salt is smaller than a grain of sand."

"Uh-huh-huh. Those are things that you can see with your eyes. Scientists have asked the question whether there are particles smaller than that, those which we can't see with the naked eye.

"The Greek philosopher Aristotle believed that matter was continuous, that is one could always divide a piece of matter into smaller and smaller bits. Other people believed that matter was made up of smaller bits called atoms that could not be divided further. The word *atom* means indivisible in Greek.

"The debate continued for centuries without any experimental evidence until Einstein published a paper in 1905 that gave evidence in favor of the existence of atoms."

"Is the atom the smallest particle there is?"

"Not quite. After Einstein's work, further experiments showed that the atoms were not indivisible after all. They consisted of smaller particles—electrons, protons, and neutrons."

"Can scientists see these particles, Major Kay, but we can't?"

"No. Certainly not. Scientists conduct experiments and based on the results of the experiments they deduce the existence of these particles. Some particles like the electron have a negative electric charge, and this helps in detecting them in some experiments."

"What's a negative electric charge?"

"Electric charges are the carriers of electricity through a medium. The basic unit of charge is the charge on the electron. These charges exist because of an electromagnetic force—a fundamental force like gravity but much stronger than it."

"Are the electron, proton, and neutron the fundamental particles?"

"No. A few years ago, maybe 10 or 15 years ago, more experiments were conducted, and these experiments indicated that there are still smaller particles called quarks. There are several different types of quarks and all these particles spin around their axis, just like the earth's rotation.

"Why don't you stand up and face me? Now turn around so that your back faces me. Make another half turn and face me again. You are back to your starting position. With one full turn you are in the same state that you started.

"Now, let's take the Queen of Spades from this deck of cards. Look at it with the picture facing you. Give the card a half turn."

" Okay, Major Kay, with half a turn, the card looks exactly as it was before."

"Good. That's what is meant by the spin of these fundamental particles. It's how much you have to turn them by to get back to their starting position. Some particles need to be moved half a turn and others need to be moved a full turn.

"But there's one strange thing that happens with some particles. You have to turn these particles two full turns before they come back to their starting state."

"How is that possible?"

"That's what scientists have observed, though it's not easy to explain why it happens. Maybe it's because of the uncertainty principle."

"What's that?"

"I'll try to explain it, although I'm not an expert on the subject. To predict the position and speed of a moving body at a later time, we need to know its current position and momentum. For a small particle such as the electron, the only way we can measure its position is by shining light on it. The light waves bounce off the electron and we can thus locate its position. The accuracy of the measurement is determined by the frequency of the light."

"Can't we increase the frequency to get more accuracy?"

"In principle, yes, but there is a slight problem. A scientist called Max Planck found out that even though light was composed of waves, it sometimes behaved like a bunch of particles that moved in packets, each packet called a quantum.

"To generate light waves of higher frequency, the quantum of light requires higher energy. This higher energy of the quantum, however, disturbs the velocity of the electron and the measurement of its momentum is not accurate.

"So the uncertainty principle of quantum mechanics states that we cannot measure the position *and* momentum of a particle very accurately. We can measure either position or momentum, but not both."

"Why can't we first measure the position, and then the momentum?"

"That can be done, although the values will not be useful in predicting the future state of the particle. If we measure the position first and the momentum later, the electron would have moved during the time taken by the measuring process, and the measurement of momentum will not correspond with its position.

"Quantum mechanics treats light as both a wave and a particle. This duality is used as follows: if it is easier to explain something by taking the particle view of light, then it lets you do so; if it is easier to explain something by using the wave view, then it lets you do so. Quantum mechanics makes a clear distinction between actual reality and the mathematics used to describe this reality."

"Is the particle-wave duality similar to Plato's dualistic view of the world that separates mind and body?"

"I don't know, Anita. Many philosophies and religions embrace the concept of dualism. The problem with dualism, however, is that it clashes with the Supreme Being principle. The monotheistic view of world religions stresses the importance of one absolute being and the dualism of matter and soul or mind and body is unacceptable. The same holds true when we try to understand human consciousness. If we accept dualism, then we can't explain it very well.

"The philosopher William James believed that reality and experience were much richer than what we could express by our concepts. We deceive ourselves, he said, when we believe that reality is exhausted by our conceptual patterns of thought.

"I think James's vision of the world was more consistent with quantum mechanics than Einstein's, who did not like unpredictability and once said, 'God does not play dice.' "

"So was James more scientific than Einstein?"

"That's not a good way to characterize it. There is a rift between science and religion, between the mystics and the scientists. Mystics believe that the fundamental nature of reality is outside language. Scientists believe that assertions about reality must be validated by observational evidence. Einstein, like Pythagoras, wanted to be in both camps. You see, science does not answer all the interesting questions, and neither does philosophy."

"What is meant by validation of observed evidence?"

"As in all scientific work, an experiment is repeated by many scientists. If all of them get the same result, then it's true."

"That can't be right, Major Kay. If all of them get the same result, what we can conclude is that there is no observational error. How can we conclude that the scientists are correct?"

"You're absolutely right, Anita. What we can conclude from observational consensus is that scientists have the best explanation for a given event at a given time. In other words, their best explanation can change as more information is obtained or as new assertions are proved."

"I've been reading some Greek philosophy and find it very interesting. Are there other philosophies that are dualistic?"

"I think some branches of Hinduism take a dualistic approach to reality. I'll go through my stack of books and find something for you to read."

Twenty-one

In January 1991, the United States entered into the conflict brewing in the Persian Gulf. In August of the previous year, Iraq had invaded and occupied Kuwait, a small country with plenty of crude oil. The invasion united the entire world community into opposing Iraq's aggression, and many countries formed a broad-based coalition to confront Iraq both diplomatically and militarily. The Security Council of the United Nations passed a number of resolutions condemning the invasion and gave Iraq a deadline of January 15, 1991 to withdraw from Kuwait. When Iraq did not comply with the resolutions there was no option but to engage in a military conflict. The United States deployed more than half a million troops and 2,000 aircraft to Saudi Arabia and Kuwait. Several other countries that were part of the coalition also sent troops to assist in the war. General Norman Schwarzkopf was the commanding officer of the non-Arab troops and General Khalid Sultan was the commanding officer of the Arab troops. Together they devised and implemented a strategy of intensive air attacks ending with a ground battle. When President George Bush was asked for a reason to get involved in Iraq, the official line from Washington was that it was to oppose aggression. But everyone knew that the real reason was to preserve the security of global oil supplies.

Norm was glued to the TV, intently following the war on CNN reported by Susan Rook and Bernard Shaw with Peter Arnett from Baghdad. He had no time to read science with Anita. He recalled the involvement of his country in World War II, in Korea where he himself had fought for a couple of years, and in Vietnam— a war in which the United States did not emerge victorious. This time, the country looked stronger with the coalition backing the decision to go to war.

CHRIS and Anita asked Norm to tell them stories about the army and about war. Norm told them that it was not easy being a soldier. Sometimes it was easy because there were rules for everyone to follow and as long as you followed the rules, there was no problem. In situations such as wars, however, it was possible to have conflicts between your own personal beliefs about killing people and the orders given to you by your superiors.

"Killing somebody is not easy, at least for me," Norm told them.

"Can war be completely avoided, Major Kay?" asked Anita.

"That would be everyone's hope, although sometimes it is not possible. Let's pretend that you and Chris are selling lemonade for 10 cents a glass outside the house. A big bully of a kid comes and drinks two glasses of lemonade, but does not pay for them. You might let him get away with it a few times, but if he repeats his behavior all the time, then something ought to be done about it. The boy needs to get punished. Fighting wars is somewhat like enforcing punishment for bad behavior. We try our best to tell people who do not respect the rights of others to clean up their act. If the advice is ignored and the bad behavior persists, there is no option left except to enforce the punishment. That's what happened in the Persian Gulf war.

"When I was your age and misbehaved, which I did many times, I would get a good spanking. In your case, the punishment is either a time-out or grounding. I wish it were that simple when dealing with disturbances in the world. Unfortunately, it's not."

AFTER the war, it was difficult for Norm to focus on physics, and he suggested to Anita that they continue their reading of science in the summer. Easter fell on March 31st that year and the weather started getting warmer in early April. On the Saturday after Easter, Anita had gone over to Norm's house.

"Major Kay," she asked him, "are my parents ever going to stay together?"

"That's entirely up to them," replied Norm.

"Can't they make up like Chris and I do?"

"It's not as easy when you grow up, Anita. Somehow, making up becomes harder as you get older. As human beings, we have four distinct aspects of our lives that we have to understand—a physical aspect, an emotional aspect, an analytic aspect, and a spiritual aspect.

"If you get married, it would be ideal to find someone who connects with you on each of these aspects. But that happens only to very few people. Take grandma Joann and me, for example. In the analytic aspect, we did not connect at all. In the spiritual aspect, she had such a strong faith in God and always believed in Him. I am different. My spirituality has been turned topsy-turvy by things that have happened to me."

"What kinds of topsy-turvy things happened to you?"

"When I was young, I questioned the need for humans to believe in God. It seemed as though belief in God was related to the uncertainty that all of us faced in our lives. God and religion were concepts bigger than we were, and people naturally believed in a Supreme Being. I wasn't happy doing what everyone else was doing. It occurred to me that death was the greatest uncertainty of all, and religion's message was that your soul or spirit did not die when you died and hence you had a permanence in the universe. Many people like to believe this because it removes their uncertainty and adds meaning to their lives."

"Father Anthony told us that God removes the dark clouds in our minds and brings sunshine to our lives. Is that what Grandma Joann believed?"

"Grandma Joann and me disagreed a lot on religious aspects, yet we stayed together because we understood and respected each other's viewpoints. When you love somebody, you have to respect their positions on each of the four aspects without passing judgment. Sometimes I wish I could have spent less time reading and more time with her.

"I guess your parents have to sit down and talk from the heart. It is still possible that they have strong resentments against each other, in which case it is better to stay apart."

"What changed your spiritual aspect, Major Kay? Do you believe in God now?"

"Yes, now I do believe in God. Something strange happened to me in 1962. I was riding my motorcycle in Kansas when a strong gust of wind picked me and the motorcycle up and hurled us about 400 yards. I fell down on the road and became unconscious. I was rushed to the hospital and after a few minutes, I could see the doctors working on my body but they had not yet found a pulse on me. It's as if my spirit was outside my body and I was watching them from up above. They thought I was dead because my heart had stopped beating.

"My spirit wandered and I found myself at the top of a cold mountain. A blue-bodied God spoke to me. He said to me that my mission was to seek out the Word of God. Only then would I be ready to enter his abode. Since the accident I found out that he is a Hindu God, called Lord Shiva. After my meeting with this God, my spirit came back and I was alive once more."

"Did this God have a snake around his body?"

"Yes. He had a snake around his neck. How did you know that?"

"I imagined it. Just a guess, Major Kay, just a guess."

"After this experience my spiritual aspect was awakened and I started believing in God. I have still not satisfied Lord Shiva's mission and hope to do it someday soon."

ON April 2nd, a series of small explosions had taken place on the volcanic islands of the Philippine archipelago. Volcanoes are vents in the earth from which molten rock and gas erupt. The molten rock forms a hill around the vent, and can sometimes flow out in liquid form. Its ultimate source is thought to be the decay of radioactive isotopes within the earth's crust combined with residual heat from the time when earth must have first formed. Scientists still do not have accurate methods to predict volcanic eruptions, although it is widely believed that small explosions are precursors of bigger ones.

The Philippines is an independent island nation in the Pacific consisting of about 7,000 volcanic islands off the coast of southeast Asia. The archipelago extends from Luzon in the north to Mindanao in the south. The Pacific floor under the islands is unstable, leading to frequent earthquakes and volcanic activity. The small explosions had taken place in the vicinity of Mount Pinatubo in central Luzon and officials promptly evacuated about 5,000 people in the vicinity of the mountain.

The following month Meg visited Urbana for Anita's birthday. Upon Norm's suggestion, Alan and Meg decided to jointly visit a marriage counselor. Norm had told them to speak frankly from the heart—it could not hurt but only help. They did so, and made some progress. The counselor advised them that they should continue to meet at least once a month.

School was over the week after Memorial Day and the children were excited to go to Chicago. Chris's dad had got tickets for them to watch the Bulls play in their first NBA championship. That year the Bulls led by Michael Jordan won the entire event—it was the first championship victory for the franchise. Chris was so excited, like every Bulls fan in Illinois and the whole country— Gatorade became his favorite drink and he set his goal in life to be like Mike.

DURING the second week of June, the first of a series of eruptions took place on Mount Pinatubo. A huge column of volcanic ash rose up in the sky to a distance of about 12 miles and slowly started moving in a southwesterly direction. The number of people evacuated increased to 60,000. The eruptions continued with increasing frequency through June 15th. It was one of the worst volcanic eruptions of the century and had it not been for the precursor explosions in April, the loss of life might have been much more.

On the same day that Mount Pinatubo had its first major eruption, Anita and Chris were at Norm's place. Around mid-morning Anita had to visit the bathroom. While she was in there, she let out a loud scream for help. Norm was terrified and asked her what was the matter. She shouted out through the bathroom door that there was blood in the toilet and it had probably come from her. Norm asked her if she had any cuts in her body or if it was hurting anywhere. Anita said that there was a slight pain in her stomach but nowhere else.

He did not know anything about medicine but did know that when you discharged blood it had to be a serious matter. He quickly called the doctor's office and told the nurse on duty what had happened, and whether Anita should be rushed over to the emergency room right away or not. He was in an utter state of panic but pretended to act calm in front of Chris. The nurse asked him to give the phone to Anita. She asked Anita how old she was, and asked to speak to her mom. When Anita explained that her mom and dad were separated and that her mom lived in Chicago, the nurse asked whether there was any other older woman that she knew. Anita told her that Chris's mom, Becky, was a person she could talk to. The nurse then got Becky's phone number from Norm.

At lunchtime, Becky came home from work. She sent Norm and Chris outside and told them that she wanted to be alone with Anita. Becky gave Anita a sanitary pad and showed her how to use it. She explained to her that what she was undergoing was part of the female reproductive cycle, and that it would occur for a few days every month.

"What are they called, Becky?" asked Anita.

"They are called periods, but my mom told me they were my chums—friends who would visit me regularly once a month without fail. The nurse told me that you might have a fever and if you do, you should take Tylenol—one tablet every six hours. Okay?"

"Okay, Becky. I'll do that."

Becky left after lunch and when Norm came in he asked Anita,

"Everything okay?"

"Yes, Major Kay. Everything is okay. My chum decided to visit me today, and I'm fine now."

Over the next couple of days Anita developed a fever and stayed in bed most of the time. Norm gave her some hot vegetable soup for lunch on both days.

PERHAPS it was the counseling sessions that Alan and Meg had jointly attended, or perhaps it was the fact that Anita had now matured and had no one at home to take care of her—whatever the reason, the effect of it was that Meg decided to come back to Urbana. She wanted to be there for her daughter as she was approaching her adolescent years. It would be difficult for Alan to deal with the problems of a teenage girl. Meg was not sure whether it was she who needed Anita more or whether it was Anita who needed her more. Living by herself in Chicago had made Meg somewhat lonely and she felt good about coming back.

209

"Thank you, Norm," Meg told him, "for taking care of Anita. I don't know what I would do without you."

"My pleasure entirely. She's such a delightful girl to be around, always asking interesting questions."

"I'm a little worried about what happened to her during the recent volcanic eruption."

"Don't worry. Everything was all right. Becky came home from lunch and took care of her."

"I'm not worried about that. I think there's a deeper connection between her and volcanic eruptions. Do you know how she was born?"

"No. Please tell me."

"Just before she was born, my water bag burst at the exact same time that Mt. St. Helens erupted. I don't think it was a coincidence, but Alan does not believe me. Pullman had become pitch black by 2:30 in the afternoon and it was in such darkness that she came out into the world. There are times when I think she is someone special who has been sent down to earth to deliver a message."

As soon as Meg said that, Norm went into a trance. He thought about all the inquisitive questions that Anita had been asking. These questions would simply not occur to a normal ten-year-old like his grandson. If there was any truth to what Meg believed, perhaps Anita *was* someone special who had been sent to help him fulfill his mission. He decided to pay closer attention to her questions in future.

Twenty-two

A week after her chum had visited her, Anita told Norm that she had something important to discuss with him.

"Major Kay, do you remember your motorcycle accident in 1962? And what happened to you after that?"

"Yes. I remember it distinctly. My insistence on the fact that it was not a dream caused me lots of problems in the army."

"A similar thing happened to me last week. I don't want to tell anyone else about it. They might think that I'm loony or something. It's as if a model of the universe was shown to me in a dream, but I can still remember all the details, which I usually cannot with my regular dreams. My regular dreams just come and go away but this one is still so clear in my head."

"Go ahead Anita. I'm listening."

"Imagine a tornado like the one that picks up Dorothy and takes her to the Land of Oz, but much more humongous than that. There is a low pressure in the center of the tornado just like the eye of a hurricane. This humongous tornado is the entire universe. There is a substratum ether present everywhere in the tornado except in the low pressure center, which I call the Void."

"Why is the substratum not present in the Void?"

"That's my postulate, Major Kay. The substratum is the most fundamental form of matter and it exists everywhere except in the Void.

"Because of the Void, a pressure is exerted on the ether above it and ether starts moving into the Void, just as a tornado tends to suck objects into it. Due to the inward pull of the Void, three forces manifest in the universe—a gravitational force that pulls objects inwards, an anti-gravitational force that pulls objects outwards, and a revolving force that spins objects around."

"The inward force is called the centripetal force and the outward force is called the centrifugal force," interjected Norm.

"Due to the three forces, revolving masses of ether form matter at many places. The stars, the sun, the planets, and atoms are all formed in this manner. The substratum of the universe and all matter including the stars, the planets and the atom have a void around their center and are spherical objects like the earth.

"The pressure of the void from within and the ether from outside retains the ether as a packet of waves. Light is also a manifestation of ether.

"The earth looks stationary to us and in the days of Aristotle it was believed that the sun went around the earth—a wrong belief that lasted for more than a thousand years. Similarly the substratum ether, with all objects on earth, accelerates, and this acceleration is not evident to us."

Just then Anita got a phone call from her mom reminding her that they had to go shopping. She excused herself and told Norm that she would return later.

NORM wrote down what she had said in his journal. He could easily understand the tornado analogy and the postulate. He knew the result of the Michelson-Morley experiment, which could not detect the presence of ether, but the experiment never guaranteed its absence. Before Einstein came up with his theory of relativity, two scientists, Lorentz and Fitzgerald, who had admitted the existence of ether in their theories had tried to explain the negative result of the Michelson-Morley experiment by suggesting a contraction to distance and proposing a factor called the Lorentz-Fitzgerald contraction factor. They stated that this contraction was a property of matter.

When Einstein proposed his theory of relativity and postulated that the speed of light was constant in vacuum, he took the position that the existence of ether was not necessary provided the notion of absolute time was abandoned. He, too, had to explain the negative result of the Michelson-Morley experiment. He did that by suggesting a contraction to time, proposing a factor called relativistic correction.

In experiments done with the atom in the early 1900s, a correction factor had to be given to the gravitational field of the atom to conform to experimental findings.

In each of these cases, the correction factor was

$$\frac{1}{\sqrt{1 - v^2 / c^2}},$$

where v represented the relative speed between two systems and c represented the speed of light.

However, it had always been assumed that ether was at rest and not in motion. Anita had just told him that in her theory the substratum ether was accelerating. If it was accelerating by exactly the amount specified by the correction factor, it would provide a neat solution to the Michelson-Morley result and get rid of relativistic correction. The speed of light would still be a constant, but in this case it would be a constant relative to the acceleration of the substratum.

"No, this can't be," he told himself. "There must be a mistake somewhere. There are so many pieces of evidence to support Einstein's notion of relative time."

Norm recalled from physics that light lost energy when traveling upwards against the gravitational field of the earth. This had been tested in 1962 by mounting a pair of clocks at the top and bottom of a water tower. The theory of relativity predicted that time would appear to run slower near the surface of the earth than far away. This was verified by the test—the clock at the bottom of the tower ran slower than the clock at the top of the tower.

Anita's theory would explain this differently. The light wave when moving against the gravitational field would decelerate and hence lose energy. To someone high up who does not take into consideration the acceleration of the substratum ether and light, everything down below would appear to take longer to happen.

What other observed evidence could be explained by her theory? That was one question that Norm asked himself. But he also asked another important question. What observed evidence could *not* be explained by her theory? Norm was aware that in the scientific method, one could generate any number of hypotheses to explain natural phenomena. For a theory to be accepted, it would have to explain all the observed evidence. For a theory to be wrong, it would have to fail in only a single instance. The problem was to find a single instance of observed evidence that this theory would fail to explain.

HE made an appointment to see Alan in his office to check Anita's hypothesis of an accelerating substratum. Ever since Norm's direct attack on the power of science over the masses, Alan kept a safe distance from him.

"So this is where you hang out, Alan. It's a pretty big office."

"It's not big enough to store all my papers. Excuse the mess on my desk. The workstation takes up so much space."

"What's the real university up to these days? Teaching anything useful?"

"We take great pride in teaching all branches of learning. Our president stresses that in every strategic plan we write."

"Yaaas. I read his trash in the newspaper. But do you also teach the roots?"

"Well, I suppose we do. What do you want to talk about? Can I get you a cup of Java?"

"No thanks. I'm here to discuss something that Anita told me."

"I don't know why she's so interested in science. I hope she gets back to doing normal girlie things."

"You've always discouraged her, Alan. Maybe you should listen to some of her theories."

"Okay."

"You know the Michelson-Morley experiment, don't you?"

"Yes. I remember studying it in graduate school."

"So, you're aware of the correction factors proposed to explain its negative result—the Lorentz-Fitzgerald distance correction factor and the Einstein time correction factor."

"Of course. Everybody who's studied SR knows relativistic correction. It's a fundamental concept in the Special theory of Relativity."

"But the need for these correction factors arose because ether was assumed to be at rest. Anita is questioning this assumption. According to her the substratum ether is accelerating."

214

"What?"

"An accelerating substratum."

"Where is it accelerating to? And what force is making it move?"

"I don't know, Alan. What I want to know is whether an accelerating substratum can explain Einstein's time correction factor."

"Norm, you can't walk in here with such an outrageous notion and no equation to back it up. We need formulas, diagrams, and numbers to explain things. We're interested in quantitative understanding, not qualitative knowledge. Mere ideas are useless to science. Anybody can come up with ideas."

"But do you think it's a good idea?"

"It's going to be mighty hard to disprove the theory of an intellectual giant like Einstein. Maybe there are philosophers who will entertain such questions, but for me it's not useful without a mathematical model. Without the math, there is no true understanding."

NORM knew that he would not get help from Alan, but he was the only scientist he could talk to. Alan was trapped into a mode of publishing papers, not stepping back to see the big picture. The true scientist seeks both a qualitative as well as a quantitative understanding of reality. Norm recalled something that Abdus Salam, a Nobel laureate, had written:

> . . . the particle physicist, after years of experience, learned that there are very few systems he can quantize exactly — very few cases where he can solve the equations of quantum field theory. His experience has taught him that a frontal attack on any problem in quantum field theory is pointless. He has learned to proceed heuristically, conjecturing solutions, extending the domain of the solutions he knows by methods which may appear atrociously vile to those brought up in the strict mathematical disciplines . . .

Norm wondered whether Alan had ever read any of these writings by the top experts in his own field. He was a little disappointed at the lack of enthusiasm shown by Alan, and when he

215

met Anita he told her, "Anita, you have to do a little better with your idea of an accelerating substratum. You need to find some observed evidence to support your claim."

"That's easy, Major Kay. The evidence lies in the redshift of light from distant galaxies."

"The redshift? That won't be useful to you at all. The redshift is an indication that the universe is expanding. In your tornado model, the acceleration of the substratum would produce a contracting universe. You can't use that as evidence to support your theory. It would disprove it."

"No, it would not. In my model the universe is contracting, not expanding."

"You mean there is a possibility it will contract in the future, because its expansion was proved by Edwin Hubble."

"Uh-huh-huh. I mean that it is contracting right now. The expanding universe is just an illusion."

"I've got to hear the explanation for this."

"When the big bang explosion took place billions of years ago, the substratum expanded. It continued to expand until it reached a stable state. The outer boundary of the universe is like the outer boundary of the tornado. The centripetal force from the Void sucked the substratum in and it fluctuated for a while till it settled down. Right now, the universe is contracting, and the acceleration is moving us towards the Void."

"Anita, that still doesn't explain why the galaxies are all redshifted. The acceleration should produce a blueshift if there is a contraction."

"I'm coming to that part. Let's pretend there is a star in a galaxy near the periphery of the tornado and let's pretend we are in the middle of the tornado. When we observe the spectrum of light from the star, it's true that the frequencies are smaller, shifted to the red end of the scale. The further away the galaxy is, the greater is the shift towards the red. The conclusion, however, that the universe is expanding is an illusion.

"The far-away star is accelerating towards the Void due to the effect of the gravitational field. We are also accelerating towards the Void. Since we are closer to the Void, the effect of the force on us is more than that on the distant star. Hence, we are moved a greater distance towards the Void than the star, and the distance between the star and us increases. The further away the star, the greater the distance between us and the star, giving us the illusion that the universe is expanding."

"What about a star that is closer to the Void than we are?"

"Same thing, Major Kay. That star will be moved a greater distance towards the Void than us, and again the distance between the star and us increases. So the accelerating substratum, which produces a contracting universe, is consistent with the observed evidence.

"Are you convinced of this?"

"No. I'm not fully convinced, but I can't seem to find any mistake in your reasoning. I'll have to think some more about what you just said. I'm sure it's got to be wrong."

ANITA left to go play with Chris. Becky had bought him a personal computer and he showed Anita how to play computer games. As they played Hangman and Brickles Anita had a lot of trouble adjusting to the computer's mouse.

Norm thought about the contracting universe that Anita had just explained. The existing evidence indicated that the universe was going to expand forever but scientists had not excluded the possibility of some other form of dark matter, not yet detected, that could raise the density of the universe up to the critical value needed to halt the expansion. So the possibility of contraction existed, but that possibility was in the future and not supported by the measured spectra of light from distant galaxies. The burning question was whether Anita's explanation of the observed evidence was incorrect.

When Alan came back that evening, Norm told him, "Alan, your daughter just proved to me that the universe is not expanding, but contracting."

"How on earth did she convince you?" asked Alan, a little incredulous.

Norm repeated Anita's explanation giving Alan the analogy of the motorcycle and the car that Anita had told him the previous year. At first Alan could not find any error in the explanation, but was sure that there had to be a mistake somewhere. The notion of the expanding universe had been widely accepted by many scientists. It was not something that could be challenged by an 11-year-old girl.

"Norm, now her theory has got my attention. I'm going to think about it some more," said Alan.

Twenty-three

The next day Alan called on Norm when he returned from work. Norm was sipping his first scotch and offered him a beer. He wasn't going to waste his 12-year-old Black Label on somebody who couldn't appreciate it.

"Norm, I've found a flaw in Anita's claim of a contracting universe. I'm going to bounce it off you and you can then tell her. She's been acting strange with me lately."

"Okay. Let me get my journal."

"Here's how she explained the contraction of the universe. She visualized looking at a star in a distant galaxy right at the periphery of the tornado. Let's assume that we are in the middle of the tornado, and we draw a straight line from the Void to the sphere that represents the tornado. This line crosses us also. So the star we are talking about is directly above us, like a zenith star, as shown in this figure." Alan showed him the diagram he had drawn in Figure 1.

"The zenith star, P, at the periphery accelerates towards the Void and so do we at E. Due to the acceleration of the substratum and the inward contraction of the universe, the point *new E* indicates the new position of earth and the point *new P* indicates the new position of the distant star. Since earth is pulled more towards the center of the Void, the distance between the new positions of E and P is greater than the original distance EP. Hence, the distance between the star and us has increased, but we can't tell from the Doppler effect whether the star is moving away from us or towards us. In a contracting universe the star would be moving in the same direction that we are moving, namely towards the Void, but slower than we are. In an expanding universe the star would be moving away from us.

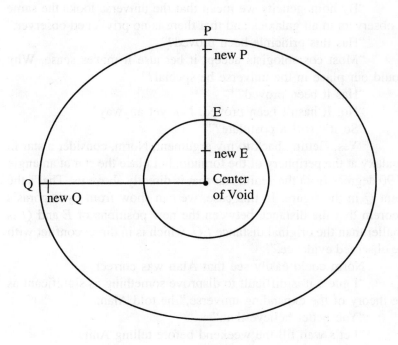

Figure 1.

"If another galaxy happens to be on the same line but closer to the Void than we are, then a star in such a galaxy moves a greater distance towards the Void than we do, again increasing the distance between us and the star. But we could still be in a contracting universe. So far, there is no problem with Anita's theory.

"Any theory about the large-scale structure of the universe has to be consistent with the Cosmological Principle of isotropy and homogeneity."

"What's that?"

"By isotropy, we mean that the universe should appear the same in whatever direction we look."

"That can't be true when we look at the night sky and the different constellations."

"I know. What isotropy looks at is the density of observed matter in each direction and that should be the same."

"What's homogeneity?"

"By homogeneity we mean that the universe looks the same to observers in all galaxies and that there is no privileged observer."

"Has this principle been proved?"

"Most cosmologists accept it because it makes sense. Why would our place in the universe be special?"

"Has it been proved?"

"No. It hasn't been proved. Not yet anyway."

"So it's still a postulate?"

"Yes. Getting back to my argument, Norm, consider a star in a galaxy at the periphery of the tornado, but place the star at an angle of 90 degrees from the zenith star that is directly above us. That's the point Q in the figure. In this case, we can show from Pythagoras's theorem that the distance between the new positions of E and Q is smaller than the original distance EQ, which is in direct conflict with the observed evidence."

Norm could easily see that Alan was correct.

"I guess it is difficult to disprove something as significant as the theory of the expanding universe," he told Alan.

"You better believe that."

"Let's wait till the weekend before telling Anita."

"Sounds good."

THE three of them got together after lunch on Saturday. Norm started the discussion.

"Anita, we may have found a problem with your explanation of the contracting universe. It is not consistent with the observed evidence."

"I thought I convinced you, Major Kay. Let me see where you are stuck."

Norm showed her the diagram in Figure 1 and Alan explained to her that at the point Q, the new distance would be smaller than the original distance, which was not consistent with the observed evidence. The point Q, he said, would have to produce a blueshift according to your theory.

220

Anita studied the diagram for a few minutes.

"I'm afraid that both of you are making a simple mistake and have not understood a few things," she said. "This figure contains a two-dimensional representation of what I described. That's all. It does not imply that you are capturing reality."

"What the heck do you mean by that?" asked Alan, somewhat annoyed.

"Calm down Alan. Let her explain what she means," said Norm.

"This is what I mean, Dad. The tornado that represents the universe is extremely huge. Our solar system is a tiny, tiny speck within this tornado. Surely both of you have heard about the theory of cones in mathematics. Consider an ant trapped within an ice-cream cone. As far as the ant is concerned, the inside walls of the cone limit its vision. The ant simply cannot see things outside the cone. It would have to be mighty arrogant to claim that it knew how big the world was outside the ice-cream cone, even if it had a very powerful ant-telescope.

"Our galaxy is within a cone of the tornado. We cannot expect to see stars like the one marked Q because such stars are outside our scope of vision. Let me correct the diagram for you."

She reached over and drew a couple of lines in Alan's diagram. The diagram now looked like the one shown in Figure 2.

"When we observe things from earth, we can only see objects within the cone that I have drawn. In fact, we cannot even be sure that we see much of the cone. Nearer the wall of the cone there is a lot of dark matter that is not visible to us. So, the observed evidence about the decreasing frequency of light waves from stars is limited to a small sphere around us and this sphere lies inside the cone. Within this sphere it is possible to explain the observed evidence by a contracting universe."

Alan was up in arms when she finished her explanation. "Anita, you are positing an unknown effect for objects that we haven't observed which would support your model. This is bad science. There is, simply put, no observed evidence for this."

"Is that so, Dad? What is the evidence for the expanding universe? Hubble did not observe galaxies rushing away from us. All we are sure of is that the lines in their spectra are shifted towards the red. The conclusion that it is expanding is a leap of faith based on the postulates of homogeneity and isotropy. Not admitting that leap of faith openly—*that* is bad science!"

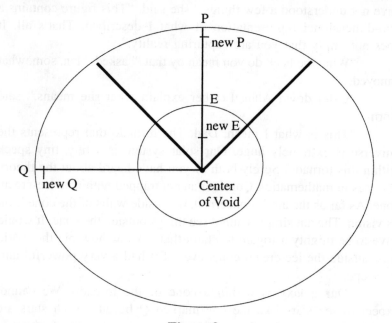

Figure 2.

"The cosmological principle of homogeneity and isotropy has been established by the microwave background radiation," retorted Alan.

"Dad, electromagnetic radiation may not be isotropic. That's an assumption. And the microwave background radiation just puts a time stamp on the origin of radiation. You can't conclude that every pair of galaxies is rushing apart, and then state that since they are rushing apart that they must have once been closer together. You miss out on alternative explanations for the observed evidence. I want to show you something."

SHE went inside and brought her violin.

"Dad, let's pretend that you live on the *A* string. Your home is two on *A* and that's all you can hear. A musician plays the note three on *E*. You can't hear this note because its frequency is higher and it's outside your range. Now the distance between this musician and you starts increasing with time. Eventually you will begin to hear her music because the frequency will decrease until it reaches the frequency of two on A. If, however, the velocity of propagation of her music is slower than what you think it should be based on your experiments on the A string, successive wave crests of her music will take longer to reach you and her notes will appear to you to have a lower frequency, maybe one on A. You will say that these notes are redshifted and you will draw many conclusions about this musician.

"Another musician plays the note three on D. You can't hear this note either because its frequency is lower and it's outside your range. Now the distance between this musician and you starts decreasing with time. Eventually you will begin to hear her music because the frequency will increase until it reaches the frequency of two on A. If, however, the velocity of propagation of her music is slower than what you think it should be, successive wave crests of her music will take longer to reach you and her notes will appear to you to have a lower frequency, maybe one on A. You will say that these notes are redshifted and again you will draw many conclusions about this musician.

"The phenomenon that occurs with redshift is somewhat like this. If you assume the cosmological principle, you arrive at one set of conclusions. If you don't, then you leave open the possibility of arriving at another set of conclusions.

"You, my dear Dad, will live forever on the A string, never be able to play Twinkle Twinkle Little Star, let alone wonder what the star is trying to tell you."

THERE was a poignant silence when Anita finished. Alan, however, wasn't about to give up. In a few moments he carried on, "What about two stars on the same ring and stars very close to the Void? Shouldn't you expect to see a blueshift in at least one case?"

"Yes. Galaxies like M31 in the Local Group are blueshifted. That's because these galaxies are in the same ring as us. Something that is explained away as occurring due to local gravitational effects. These galaxies are two million light years away from us to talk about them being affected by *local* gravitational effects."

"The expanding universe is the *only* self-consistent explanation of the redshift. It's what all the experts believe and they have to be right," said Alan.

"Dad, why is the relationship between redshift and distance a linear relationship and not a square one like gravity?"

"That's easy. It follows immediately from Hubble's law."

"Come on Alan," interjected Norm. "Is there a distribution system that ships Hubble's paper to the galaxies and they study it and follow his law?"

"No. That's not what I meant," said Alan angrily. "The experimental observations suggest a linear relationship between redshift and distance. I don't know why it is linear. Do you?"

"Yes Dad. The acceleration in the substratum produces uniform rectilinear motion. That's why the relationship is linear."

NORM was bewildered by Anita's explanation. He decided to approach what she had said as objectively as possible. The interpretation of the redshift had implied an expanding universe. The view of physicists was that the wavelength of a ray of light increased in proportion to the separation of galaxies as the universe expanded. That is, wave crests of light were being pulled farther and farther apart as the universe expanded. Conclusions drawn from these observations all rested on the assumption that the speed of light was a universal constant.

If, however, as Anita had so cleverly pointed out through her interpretation of Twinkle Twinkle Little Star, the speed of light was not a universal constant, that electromagnetic radiation could be anisotropic, then incorrect conclusions would be drawn between the position of these far-away objects and us.

Twinkle Twinkle Little Star
How I wonder what you are

would have a different meaning with Anita's interpretation. Was it possible that there was an acceleration in the substratum and that the expanding universe was an illusion?

Twenty-four

In the fall of 1991 Anita entered sixth grade. Norm recognized that she would not be challenged in school and encouraged her to enroll in classes at the university. Her teacher discussed the matter with a university committee, and they agreed to let her take two classes—one in math, and one in physics. Norm tutored her a little in the beginning and chauffeured her back and forth from the university campus.

Chris had become interested in computers and asked Alan what he should do to learn programming. Alan decided to call Kali to get advice.

"How's the millionaire doing? Bought any sports franchises yet?"

"Get lost, man. That's for billionaires like Gates and Allen. I'm basically small fry."

"Yeah. Yeah. If you're small fry, then what are we people? Termites?"

"I'm thinking of quitting next year, Alan."

"You've been saying that for the last three years. Are you still with Lila?"

"Yes and no. We stay together, but we don't have a marriage. We sleep in separate rooms."

"You're crazy. I thought Indian wives were easy to control."

"Not her, man, not her. You live and you learn. When I was in the hospital last year, she didn't even come to see me until the last day when I was released."

"Gosh. I didn't know that. Anything serious?"

"No. I'm all right now."

"What happened to you?"

"Don't ask. I'm embarrassed about it."

"You can tell me. We go way back."

"Oh, all right. Promise me you won't laugh."

"Promise."

"With all the Twinkies and junk food I was eating, I got an ulcer."

"That's nothing to be shameful about. Many people get it."

"But this was in the rectum. A rectal ulcer."

"Jeepers! That's weird."

"Boy, was it painful."

"You better quit while you're ahead, pal. Forget Lila's advice and focus on your health. Maybe I should ask my parents to drill some sense into you. There's got to be a limit to how much money one needs. And even with all the money, you're still not happy.

"By the way, the reason I'm calling is because one of Anita's friends wants to learn computer programming. What software should I get for him?"

"Get Visual Basic. That's what I work on day in and day out. It's a great product and very easy to use. I'll send you a version with a manual that you can give to him."

"Thanks, Kali. You take care now."

ANITA and Alan settled down into their fall semesters and were quite busy. Norm had plenty of time to himself and decided to work alone on her theory. It struck him that she was on the right track—a track he had wanted to be on all his life. He had raised many questions about the fundamentals but had come up empty on the answers. Perhaps her theory would take him a step closer to fulfilling the mission given to him by Lord Shiva.

The very notion of a contracting universe motivated him to describe the theory in a formal manner. Formal in the mathematical sense, not in the tuxedo sense. He updated his journal with his understanding of Anita's theory of the universe.

226

• *The universe is like a tornado with a Void at its center.*

• *The substratum ether is the most fundamental form of matter and exists everywhere except in the Void.*

• *Matter and light are a manifestation of the same ether.*

• *There is an acceleration taking place in the substratum.*

• *This acceleration accounts for the time contraction factor, and also explains why the universe is contracting, not expanding. However, it is still consistent with the observed evidence of redshift.*

During Anita's discussion of the contracting universe, Norm recalled a reference made to the cosmological principle and its assumptions of homogeneity and isotropy. Alan had mentioned the isotropy observed in the cosmic background radiation and Norm wanted to learn more about it.

THE general scientific position on the Big Bang is that the universe was infinitely hot in the beginning and cooled down as it expanded. As it cooled down its temperature continued to drop. There would have been plenty of radiation emitted from the early hot state, and an interesting question that nobody had asked was whether or not this radiation could still be measured. The answer was found in the belly of a horn antenna in northern New Jersey.

The microwave background radiation is like music to the trained ears of astronomers. Not the rock and roll of the 20th century, nor the fugues of Bach, nor the classical music of Ravi Shankar. This music is the sound of silence, with tiny fluctuations representing pauses between successive instants of silence.

Discovered accidentally by Penzias and Wilson, it is the decisive factor in the belief that our universe is the relic of a primeval fireball known as the Big Bang. In the spring of 1964, Arno Penzias and Robert Wilson of the Bell Telephone Laboratories set out to measure radio waves emitted from our galaxy. They started their observations with radio waves of short wavelengths known as microwave radiation. Radio waves are much like the static or *noise* one hears when tuning a short-wave radio set.

To their surprise, they found that their detector was picking up more noise than it ought to have. This noise was the same independent of the direction the detector was pointing, it was the same during the day and night, and it was the same throughout the year as the earth orbited the sun. The only possible conclusion was that this noise was from beyond the galaxy and since it was the same in every direction, the universe ought to be the same in whichever direction we look, at least from a large-scale viewpoint. The explanation for the noise was that this was the light from the early glow of the universe— light that reached us after millions of years and was so greatly reduced in its frequency that it appeared as microwave radiation. However, the noise did vary by less than one part in ten thousand but this variation was not significant compared to the noise level and it was attributed to the sensitivity, or the lack thereof, of the detector.

The startling discovery by Penzias and Wilson supported the mathematical models of the Big Bang put forward by Einstein, de Sitter, Friedmann and Lemaitre in the 1920s. The steady-state cosmology of Bondi, Gold, and Hoyle, which predicted that the universe has always been the same as it is now, fell by the wayside.

The hot big bang model was in agreement with the observed evidence but scientists had raised some important open questions that this model did not have answers to. Norm wrote down the following questions, intending to ask Anita for an explanation.

• *How does your theory explain the microwave background radiation?*

• *Why was the universe so hot at the moment of the big bang?*

• *The microwave radiation measured by Penzias and Wilson is the same in every direction, but why is it the same? Why does the universe appear so uniform on a large scale?*

• *What are the forces that hold the universe together?*

As Norm was painstakingly researching and recording all that he had learned over the last couple of years, Anita and Chris were busy with other things. About the beginning of November, just before his birthday, Chris had an accident while playing basketball and fractured his right elbow. His hand had to be put in a cast for six weeks. Norm took a break from his pursuit of physics to take care of Chris. Since Chris could not write, Norm had to copy down what was done everyday in class from Anita's notes. The cast was removed after Christmas, and the following year Norm got back to Anita's theory.

ONE Saturday in February 1992, Norm told Anita that he needed answers to a few more questions. Since February that year had one extra day, he argued that it should be possible to spare a day for him from her busy calendar. Anita agreed. Alan came in as they were starting and joined the discussion.

"Anita, I need to ask you about the forces that hold the universe together. Your model has to satisfy the laws of conservation of energy and momentum," said Norm.

"Gee, how thoughtless of me. I forgot to tell you that in addition to the acceleration, the substratum revolves in uniform motion. The entire tornado is spinning around with a single unit of momentum."

"Can this be observed, Alan?" asked Norm.

"A truly absolute uniform motion cannot be detected by any experiment. Ergo, it must not be present, because even if it is, it is not important to our understanding of reality," replied Alan.

Alan's smug answers usually got under Norm's skin and he started twitching as he said, "The only place in the universe I can detect absolute motion is in the bathroom. Other than that, absolute uniform motion, if it is present, has to be deduced from other considerations. Isn't that right, Alan?"

"That's correct. You don't have to be so sarcastic. Yes, we may be able to deduce absolute uniform motion."

"And quite easily," said Anita.

"Just a minute," interrupted Norm. "If it is true uniform motion you are talking about then it would have to be present at the time of the Big Bang, wouldn't it?"

"Yes, Major Kay. This uniform motion is always present in the universe. But I believe the concepts of Big Bang and Big Crunch have different meanings in my model."

"Poppycock. Sheer poppycock," screamed Alan. "This is not science, Anita. You can't tell us that something exists when we can't measure it. How do we know it's there?"

"Dad, sometimes the answers to big questions are found in small things. To explain the macrocosm, we have to look at the microcosm. The existence of this motion can be deduced from the spin one-half of the electron."

"This is going from bad to worse, Anita," said Alan.

"Give her a chance," interjected Norm. "Carry on please."

"When was the last time you both rode on a carousel?"

"I don't know. It's been ages," said Norm.

"Time to buckle up. We're going on a ride.

"Imagine a carousel that has a giraffe and a horse on opposite ends. Also, imagine a carousel directly on top of this carousel. The carousel on the top has a circular base but no animals to ride on. The base is as big as that of the bottom carousel. I'm standing on the top carousel directly above the giraffe.

"My job is to run around the top carousel. Your job is to observe me running and you have a camera that takes snapshots at fixed time intervals as I run around. For all other purposes, you are blindfolded and you don't know whether either carousel is moving or stationary. You don't even know how fast I am running.

"I run around the top carousel and complete one revolution in one minute. You take a picture of me, and if I am directly above the giraffe then you would conclude that I have come back to my starting state. Correct?"

"Correct," they both replied.

"Now, suppose that the bottom carousel is moving at the rate of 1 revolution in 1 minute and I am running at the rate of two revolutions in one minute. At the end of half a minute, if you take a snapshot, you will see me but this time I will be directly above the horse and not the giraffe. If you take a snapshot after another half minute, then I will be directly above the giraffe."

"But you would have completed two revolutions before you got back to your starting state," said Norm.

"At least two, maybe a multiple of two—that depends on how fast I am running, Major Kay. If we are not aware of the 1 unit of uniform motion of the bottom carousel, then we get inherent errors in measurement. We see fundamental particles that have a spin of one-half—particles that have to be turned twice before they get back to their starting position! The bottom carousel represents the uniform motion of the substratum, my running on the top carousel represents the acceleration of ether relative to thē substratum."

BOTH Norm and Alan were completely taken aback.

"What is that single unit of momentum?" asked Alan.

"That's something you ought to be able to work out, Dad. I call it one Golliwog. One Golliwog of momentum."

"I'm still confused by this uniform motion, Anita," said Norm. "You are aware, of course, of the law of conservation of energy and the law of conservation of momentum, aren't you? How do you account for this one Golliwog of momentum?"

"Trust me, Major Kay. It's there. You will have to come up with the equations and fill in the gaps. Do you know why there is a square factor in Einstein's famous equation, $E = mc^2$?"

"No. Other than the fact that it has been experimentally validated, I don't know why it is squared and not cubed," replied Norm.

"One velocity component is from the revolving substratum, the other one is from the acceleration relative to the substratum. That's why it is squared."

"It's just a little too mystical for me," remarked Alan. "Science does not rely on analogies because they're usually flawed. You need mathematical formulas to support what you're saying. You can't explain Einstein's equation that easily. It's got to be more complex than that because thousands of papers have been written on it."

"There is a mathematical equation, Dad. It's the Einstein-de Sitter model of elliptic curvature for space-time. This model produces an oscillating universe but it is not known how the universe can go through more than one cycle. I think scientists are not aware of the revolving substratum."

"Where did you learn all this?"

"I learned about the Einstein-de Sitter model in my physics class. It's being taught by Professor Michell."

"I don't think you should believe all that he says. He's considered quite a dangerous radical."

231

"Alan, she's just giving us the intuition. We can't expect her to give us equations also. That's something we have to figure out," said Norm, defending Anita's viewpoint.

"Okay, okay. We'll see where this goes. I don't know from where you're getting all these strange ideas, Anita," remarked Alan.

"Not from the same place you do, Dad, not from my brain but from my consciousness."

"She's beginning to talk like you, Norm. What have you been teaching her?"

"Nothing, Alan. I'm not half as smart as she is."

IN mid-March Alan's application for a sabbatical the following academic year was approved. He would spend the 1992-93 academic year at Cairo University. Both Meg and Anita were excited to visit Egypt. Anita, who had been fascinated by the Sesame Street movie she had seen a few years back, told all her friends that she would be visiting the Great Pyramids at Giza and would look for lost mummies trapped by ancient curses.

On April 19th that year, a month or so before her twelfth birthday, Anita's breasts came. Every teenage girl waits anxiously for this to happen, and some get worried when their friends get them and theirs are late in coming. Mothers have to assure their daughters that eventually they would come—it is just a question of time. From the day she got them, Anita became very shy and conscious of her body. Wearing a bra was something she had to get used to. Gone was the resilient lively behavior that had been present in her earlier years. She was approaching womanhood.

Twenty-five

In the spring and summer of 1992 the excitement of going to Egypt was foremost in everyone's mind. The only event that distracted them was the Chicago Bulls repeating as NBA champions. Alan was a little worried about taking Meg and Anita with him because many countries in the Middle East disliked foreigners, especially Americans. Norm assured him that the support that the United States had received from the coalition during the Persian Gulf war was terrific. Egypt, he said, would be a lot safer to visit than other countries. Whatever worries Alan had were quelled by Anita's and Meg's excitement.

Before they left, Anita met Norm and told him, "Major Kay, you have been asking many questions about my theory. I know that you and dad do not believe it to be true."

"That's not right, Anita. We just want to make certain that it is consistent with the observed evidence. A true scientist has to believe things only after thorough investigation. You do understand that don't you?"

"I suppose so. But what is going to help you understand my theory is Sankhya."

"Sankhya? What's that?"

"It's a Sanskrit word."

"Yes, I remember now. It means knowledge. I'm willing to admit that I need knowledge to understand your theory. I've long since reached the boundary of my ignorance."

233

"No, no. That's not what I meant. I meant the philosophy by that name, a Hindu philosophy."

"A philosophy called Sankhya? There is no such philosophy. The cornerstone of Hindu philosophy is the Vedanta System, and it has been so for centuries."

"Major Kay, this philosophy existed long before Vedanta. Please look it up in Zaehner's book on Hinduism."

"Okay Anita, I will check it out. And one more thing, when you return from Egypt please call me Norm."

"All right, I will."

In September Norm drove them to O'Hare airport. Anita promised to send him and Chris a postcard every month.

"Can we get you anything from Egypt, Norm?" asked Meg.

"A few years ago I would have loved to smoke Egyptian cigarettes. Now that I have quit smoking, I don't need anything particular. Maybe a memento from the Great Pyramids."

WHEN Norm got back to Urbana he looked up Zaehner's book and found a reference to the philosophy that Anita had mentioned, but it was spelt Samkhya not Sankhya. This philosophy did not recognize a personal God, but saw the universe as a result of two forces, Purusha and Prakriti.

Holy kullolee! He recalled that he had come across the same terms in the *Bhagavad Gita* many years back. Lord Krishna had described two fundamental principles, Purusha and Prakriti, and had said that whoever understood these principles fully would not be born again. This must be it, he thought to himself. This must be what I have not been able to find all these years.

ANITA's first letter from Egypt arrived in a few days.
> *Sept. 20*
> *Dear Major Kay and Chris,*
> *We reached Cairo safely on September 12th. I was tired from changing so many planes and slept for the first three days. They call the airport here Cairo aerodrome. The city is very crowded with about 11 or 12 million people. The university is in the suburb of Al-Jizah, southwest of Cairo*

and close to the famous pyramids. Al-Jizah is the actual name for what we call Giza. As we drove from the airport past the Corniche, the main street of Cairo, I could see many high-rise buildings like in Chicago. The streets here are called boulevards. We crossed the famous Nile river which runs north-south through Cairo and on into the Mediterranean Sea.

I love the bread here in Egypt and the flavored rice with eggplant. There are so many things to see and we plan to visit all of them—the Great Pyramids and the Sphinx, the statue of Ramses II in front of the railroad station, the mosque of Mohammed Ali inside a 12th century citadel built by Saladin, and the famous Egyptian museums. Chris, if I find Prince Sahu in Queen Hatshepsut's temple I will let you know.

The city is congested and polluted and noisy and we don't go there often. But the people are very friendly and nice. The students dress like we do in Urbana except girls wear a scarf to cover their head. Some girls have a veil in front of their face but only a few of them do this.

I will write more about our adventures in my next letter.

Love,
Anita

THE Sankhya system classifies existence into 25 principles or *tattvas*. Twenty-four of these are evolutes of Prakriti and the twenty-fifth principle, Purusha, is neither productive nor produced. There is no twenty-sixth principle of a Supreme Being.

Norm read this last part again to make sure he understood the philosophy. Yes, there was no Supreme Being principle. Sankhya believed in the plurality of souls but did not seek the source of the individual souls in a common universal soul. It was not a pantheistic monism where *moksha* was the merging of the individual soul into an Absolute *Brahman; moksha* in Sankhya was the release of the individual soul from the bonds of Prakriti.

He wrote down the basic principles in his journal.

- *Purusha: neither productive nor produced*

- *Prakriti: the only productive principle*

- *Buddhi: a combination of intellect and will*

- *Ahankara: ego-principle; similar to Immanuel Kant's "apperception"*

- *Manas: mind*

- *Sense organs: there are 10 of them, five sensory and five motor*

- *Subtle elements: sound, touch, sight, taste, and smell*

- *Gross elements: akasa or space, air, fire, water, and earth*

Besides these principles, there was a creative force and this consisted of three gunas: *sattva, rajas,* and *tamas,* which were translated as goodness, energy, and dullness respectively. Theism, as it was understood in modern times, was a view of reality that postulated a Supreme Being principle as the creator and sustainer of the universe. The Sankhya philosophy with its 25 principles did not give place to such an Absolute God.

ON October 12, 1992, there was an earthquake reported in Egypt. The epicenter was 20 miles southwest of Cairo and the suburb of Giza was badly hit. The quake measured 5.8 on the Richter scale and killed about 370 people. Many apartment buildings, or flats as they were called in Egypt, came crashing to the ground. People were trampled to death as they stampeded in panic and in one high school in the Cairo area, nearly 100 children died. The tremors of the earthquake were felt as far away as Alexandria to the northwest and Jerusalem to the northeast.

Norm waited anxiously for some communication from Meg. The phone lines did not work in the aftermath of the earthquake and it was impossible to get through to them. A couple of days later he received a cable from her saying that all of them were fine and had suffered only minor injuries. Anita's second letter came a few days later.

> Oct. 7
> Dear Major Kay and Chris,
>   The weather here is great, I'll bet much warmer than back home. Yesterday, mom and I went shopping in Old Cairo. The streets are narrow and winding, filled with bazaars where you can get anything. I almost bought a Sony walkman but mom thought the price was too high. One little urchin boy was so charming—he ran around me the entire time saying 'Hullo! Where is your country?' We saw many crumbled mosques with older women sitting in a circle and gossiping.
>   People bargain all the time at the bazaars. I keep telling mom to do that but she doesn't listen. We have to be very careful when shopping here. We are told that merchants increase prices when they see foreigners like us. When you buy something, they don't give you a sack and they don't give you any receipt. All sales are final once you pay them the money. You can't return anything. I'm going to bring some trinkets for everyone in our class, Chris, and I'll bring something special for you.
>   We still haven't seen the Great Pyramids. I'll write about them soon.
> Love,
> Anita

THE little he read about the Sankhya philosophy whetted his appetite tremendously. Zaehner's book contained only a summary, and Norm wanted to track down the original source. He searched the public library but couldn't find a copy of it. He asked a professor of religious studies in the department of philosophy who told him that it was not in the university's library either. The professor told Norm that his best chance to locate it would be the Ramakrishna Mission in Chicago.

Already, Norm had established a connection between Anita's theory and the principles of Sankhya. Prakriti was ether or the fundamental particle, the three gunas were the three forces in the theory, and the Void had to be Purusha. There was some confusion in his mind about the association of Purusha and Void. In the Sankhya system, Purusha was the individual soul; in the theory, it was a place that did not contain ether and could easily be associated with an Absolute Principle.

DURING the Thanksgiving break that year, Chris's father had arranged for him to take a short course in computer programming at Northwestern University. Norm told Chris that he would drive him to Chicago as he wanted to spend a few days there himself. He found the Ramakrishna Mission and fortunately for him, they did have a copy of the Sankhya philosophy. The copy, however, was quite old and tattered and they would not let anyone check it out. Norm was more than welcome to sit there and read it if he wished.

The author of the text was listed as Vachaspati Misra and it had been translated into English in 1896. Norm started reading it at once. Just like the *Bhagavad Gita*, the Sankhya philosophy consisted of several verses called Karikas. Prakriti was the one rootless Root of the universe, endowed with the three gunas and evolving through these, every kind of existence except of course the Purusha or Spirit. The first two Karikas explained in a nutshell the nature of the philosophy: it was practical and directed to meet the practical end of removing pain; it was rational and relied upon reasoning and discriminative knowledge; and it's purpose was to release one's soul from the bondage of Prakriti.

"Can I copy some parts of this, please?" Norm asked a monk.

"All right," said the monk, observing Norm's serious countenance from the corner of his eye. "We don't have a copying machine, but you can write down the parts you are interested in."

"That will take lots of time."

"We're open every day of the week. If you don't finish today you can come back tomorrow."

"I've actually come all the way from Urbana."

"Oh. How long do you plan to stay in Chicago?"

"Four days. My grandson's taking a computer class at Northwestern."

"Do you have a place to stay?"

"No, I was going to check into a hotel later on."

"You're more than welcome to stay here. Gratis."

"Oh, thank you, thank you so much. That will give me enough time to write down everything."

"You're welcome. I'll show you to your room. If you want you can sit there and work."

Norm started writing down all the Karikas, one by one. A few of them are reproduced below.

- Karika 2: The revealed is like the obvious, since it is connected with impurity, decay and excess. A method contrary to both is preferable, consisting in discriminative knowledge of the Manifested, the Unmanifested, and the Knowing (Spirit).

- Karika 3: Nature or primordial matter, the root of all, is not produced; the Great Principle (Mahat or Buddhi) and the rest seven being both producer and produced; sixteen are produced and the Spirit is neither producer nor produced.

- Karika 8: The non-apprehension of this (Nature) is due to its subtlety, not to its non-existence; since it is apprehended through its effects. These effects are the Great Principle and the remaining effects (some of) which are similar and (some) dissimilar to Nature.

- Karika 10: The Manifested has a cause; it is neither eternal nor pervading (universal); it is active (mobile or modifiable), multiform, dependent, predicative (or characteristic), conjunct, and subordinate. The Unmanifested is the reverse.

- Karika 11: The Manifested has three constituent Attributes *(gunas)*, it is indiscriminating, objective, generic (or common), non-intelligent (or insentient) and productive. So also is Nature. The Spirit is the reverse, and yet also (in some respects) similar.

- Karika 16: The Unmanifested is the cause; it operates through the three Attributes by blending and by modification, as water, on account of the difference arising from the receptacle of the Attributes, as they are variously distributed.

239

- Karika 21: For the Spirit's contemplation of Prakriti, and its final emancipation, the union of both take place, like that of the halt and the blind; and from this union proceeds creation.

- Karika 41: As a painting stands not without a ground, nor a shadow without a stake, so neither does the Buddhi subsist supportless, without a specific body.

- Karika 42: Formed for the sake of the Spirit's purpose, the Astral body plays its part like a dramatic actor, on account of connection with means and consequences, and by union with the predominant power of Nature.

- Karika 57: As the insentient milk flows out for the growth of the calf, so does Nature operate towards the emancipation of the Spirit.

- Karika 58: As people engage in action to satisfy desires, so does the Unmanifested Principle (Nature) act for the emancipation of the Spirit.

As he copied down the Karikas, the full connection with Anita's theory became clearer to him. Karika after Karika, it all fit nicely with her model. It took four days to study and copy the entire book, but it was worth it—at least to him. Karika 2 embodied the main thrust of the philosophy—that final liberation of the soul (or *moksha* according to Sankhya) was not attainable by religious rites and rituals but by discriminative knowledge. It was a bold and constructive philosophy that demanded a very imaginative interpretation. With Anita's theory, the interpretation became easy for Norm.

WHEN he was about to leave the Mission on the fifth day, he stopped to say good-bye to his monk friend and thank him for his hospitality.
"Why doesn't modern Hindu philosophy talk about Sankhya?" asked Norm.
"That's because it is considered atheistic," came the reply.
"What do you mean by atheistic?"

"It does not admit a Supreme Being principle. The dualism of matter and soul is the bone of contention between Sankhya and the monistic Vedanta. Unlike the absolute monism in Advaita Vedanta in which only Brahman, the impersonal Absolute, is real and everything else is unreal, Sankhya considers everything to be real, both Spirit and Non-spirit.

"That is why it was rejected by the great exponent of Vedanta, Adi Sankaracharya."

"Wasn't Sankaracharya an avatar of Lord Shiva?"

"Yes. Many consider that to be true. He is the founder of the Advaita philosophy."

"One of my Hindu friends told me that Sri Ramakrishna preached dualism. Is that right?"

"Yes. But what he preached was not exactly dualism. Sri Ramakrishna worshipped the Divine Mother Kali. He saw in her the seed of immortality and felt in her breath the soothing touch of tender love. She was to him the only Reality, yet he spoke often about Lila and Nitya as two aspects of her consciousness. He said a man should reach the Nitya, the Absolute Reality, by following the trail of the Lila, the Relative Reality. It is like reaching the roof by using steps on a staircase. After realizing the Absolute, he should climb down to the Relative and live on that plane, serving God in His image found in every human being. The true seer always sees God. Sometimes he comes down to the Lila from the Nitya, and sometimes he goes up to the Nitya from the Lila. The realization of the *Brahman* enables us to recognize reality as the dwelling of *Satchitananda:* sat—pure being, chit —pure consciousness, and ananda —pure delight."

"Thank you for enlightening me. I really enjoyed my stay here. I've read the translation of the *Bhagavad Gita* written by one of the monks of your order, a Swami Vireswarananda I believe."

"Oh yes, the late Prabhu Maharaj."

"When did he die?"

"He didn't die. He was the president of the order from 1966 until 1985 when he attained samadhi."

"What's that?"

"Spiritual leaders like Prabhu Maharaj don't die. Their consciousness enters another state. People who saw him that day in Calcutta say that his face radiated infinite peace like that of a child sleeping blissfully in the lap of its mother."

NORM and Chris drove back to Urbana to find another letter from Anita.

Nov. 20

Dear Major Kay and Chris,

Guess what? We finally visited the Great Pyramids of Giza. They are simply spectacular. Major Kay, they are not in a straight line just like you told us and look much bigger than in the enclosed postcard. They were built from 2700 B.C. onwards to serve as monuments for the bodies of the pharaohs and their close relatives.

The biggest one is Cheops built for King Khufu. It is 750 feet wide at the base and 480 feet high. The smaller ones are Chephren built for King Khafre and Mycerinus built for King Menkaure. There are long lines to get in for the tourists, but if you are a VIP in a Mercedes car then you can enter through a dark hole in the side of Cheops. Each pyramid is supposed to have a temple complex next to it, but only the one in Chephren is still there. The others have disappeared.

I feel that I have been here before, but it's my first time. The Sphinx stands still a short distance from the pyramids and has a mysterious face, as if guarding many precious secrets. The university is near Saqqara where the epicenter of the earthquake was and the oldest pyramid, the Step Pyramid built for King Zoser, is located here. It has a large mastaba—a rectangular stone structure—at its center and six large terraces one built upon the other.

I wish both of you could be here with us. I can't imagine how they moved the huge blocks to build the pyramids. The night sky here looks so big and so too do the constellations—Orion, Taurus, Pleiades and Ursa Major look majestic in their journey across the heavens. The city lights are so bright that I can't see our little cloud in Andromeda. I'll write more later.

Love,

Anita

242

UPON contemplating some more on his recent trip to Chicago, Norm realized what had happened to Sankhya. It had been buried because it did not admit a Supreme Being principle. A similar thing had happened to the philosophy of Neoplatonism in ancient Alexandria. Somewhat similar to Sankhya in encouraging dualism, it was identified with paganism at the heart of a fanatic Christian uprising in the fourth century A.D. By getting people to rally around the Supreme Being principle, the high priests of Christianity had successfully butchered Neoplatonism.

The Supreme Being principle was the only power that religion had over the masses. Without it they would not be in business, the business of interpreting the Word of God for everyone else.

It was a pattern that was becoming all too familiar to Norm: the circumstances under which the canon had been closed for the Old and New Testaments, the death of Neoplatonism and possibly other dualistic philosophies, and the death of Sankhya at the hands of Adi Sankaracharya who lived around 200 B.C. or 800 A.D., depending on which historian you believed.

Norm was thoroughly confused by all this. The mission given to him by Lord Shiva was to seek out His Word and understand it. Anita's theory was the silver lining in the dark clouds that had girdled him since 1962. Her theory was based on the Sankhya philosophy, but it was this very same philosophy that had been rejected by Sankaracharya—an avatar of Lord Shiva Himself.

How could that be? There had to be a mistake somewhere.

Perhaps Sankara's words had been misinterpreted. Or perhaps the Sankhya philosophy had not been fully understood and in the course of simplifying it, some of its principles might have become diluted. He had read in Chicago that Sankhya was recited by an ancient sage, Kapila, in response to a question asked by his mother about the origin of the universe.

Some mystics had claimed that Sankhya was a derivative of Vedantic thought. Their claim was based on the use of the word Purusha in the Rig-Veda and the Upanishads. But the interpretation of Purusha in the Vedas was totally different from its interpretation in Sankhya. Sankhya's dualistic and anti-ritualistic attitudes were too conspicuous to be concealed.

IN January 1993 Anita and her parents visited the historic city of Alexandria. It was founded by Alexander the Great in 332 B.C. Located on the shores of the Mediterranean, it was Egypt's chief port and second largest city. Cairo was the capital and largest commercial and business center. The bulk of Egypt's foreign trade passed through Alexandria, which was connected by railroads and highways to Cairo and other cities in the country. It had a tremendous history right from the time it was founded, through the establishment of the famous museum and library which made it a cosmopolitan city, up to the time of its near destruction by the Arabs in 642 A.D. The emigration of the large foreign population since the 1950s had made it more of an Egyptian city and less of a cosmopolitan city.

As they toured the historic sites, the guide recounted the history of the famous Library of the Serapeum.

"Do you see the headless Sphinx to my right? That was sculpted during the reign of the pharaoh Horemheb, a thousand years before Alexander the Great. And do you all see the microwave tower close to it?"

A few people in the bus nodded their heads and said, "Yes."

"The famous Alexandrian library had once stood between these two landmarks. It was founded by the emperor Ptolemy I and became the literary and scientific center of the Roman era."

Goosebumps started erupting on Anita's body.

"Unfortunately it was consumed by a fire and a million handwritten papyrus scrolls were engulfed in its flames."

When he said this, Anita went into a chill and started shivering so much that she fainted. The tour guide rushed to her side and sprinkled some water on her face.

"I hope she's all right," he told Meg.

"I think she'll be all right. Can you get her some more water?"

"Sure," said the guide. "I'll stop the bus soon and we can all take a break."

Anita recovered slowly but felt considerably weaker the rest of the day.

BACK in Urbana, Norm was struggling with the rejection of Sankhya by Adi Sankaracharya. He started getting headaches quite often.

Becky, who had a vague memory of how engrossed he used to be in her younger days, was beginning to get worried.

"Dad, why don't you take it easy and put away all these books? I thought mom asked you not to get into this any more," she told him.

"I am on to something very exciting now. I can't put it down. I keep thinking to myself that I've come across the name Kapila somewhere, but I don't remember where."

"Are you taking your medication regularly?"

"Don't worry Becky. You treat me like a small child sometimes. I'm taking good care of myself."

"Okay Dad. Remember to relax once in a while. By the way, Meg's driveway needs to be shoveled."

"Really? I'll do it right away."

The crisp winter air was very refreshing. The January snow was powdery and easy to shovel unlike the March snow, which would usually be wet and heavy. He had shoveled half the sidewalk when it suddenly struck him that he might have seen Kapila's name in the *Bhagavad Gita*. When he reached home, he checked out the holy book and finally found a reference to Kapila in Chapter 10.

'. . . and among perfect souls, I am the saint Kapila.'
—*Bhagavad Gita 10:26.*

In his study of Hinduism Norm had observed, on several occasions, how Indian mystics differed so much in their views. These mystics did not give a damn whether one philosophy was right and the other was wrong. But even the most advanced one had not dared to challenge the word of Lord Krishna in the *Gita,* and Norm took that as solid evidence to believe Sankhya. If Lord Krishna thought that Kapila was a perfect soul, then he wouldn't have to worry any more about what Adi Sankaracharya had said.

The nagging question about associating Purusha with an Absolute Principle still prevailed in his mind.

DURING their stay in Alexandria, Alan decided that they ought to spend a couple of days at the Egyptian Riviera in the suburb of al-Raml. Beaches were scarce in Illinois and nowhere had they seen such a deep blue color as the Mediterranean Sea. It was simply too good to be true. While Alan sunbathed on the beach, Meg and Anita went shopping for their mementos.

In a crowded bazaar off Nebi Daniel Street, one of the centers of commercial trade in the city, they ran across an old man selling ancient scrolls of papyri that he claimed were excavated from the desert sands. They had been warned of such frauds by the tour guides and asked to always exercise their judgment before buying anything from the bazaars. Anita was interested in what the old man had to sell and started rummaging around his collection. The old man had a thick beard and looked very different from the other Egyptian merchants.

He pointed to some scrolls and told Anita, "These are originals from the great Alexandrian library."

"Thank you. I'm just looking around."

"Can I interest you in this piece, miss?" he said, showing her a papyrus fragment. "Also very original. It was found last year when the earthquake shook Cairo. Look, it still has some writing on it. See?"

"Let me see it." Anita examined the papyrus and decided to humor the old man by buying it.

"How much does it cost?"

"For you, miss, it'll be half price. You look just like my daughter."

"I don't have any money. I'll ask my mother and be right back." So saying, Anita took the papyrus and left to find Meg.

When she came back with the money, the old man and his stall were nowhere to be seen. Upon inquiring into his whereabouts, the other merchants told her that they had never seen him before.

"Miss, he's not a part of our bazaar. We don't know where he came from," said one of them.

WITH his grip on reality slowly disappearing from him, Norm had once again started talking to himself. Becky was keeping her fingers crossed, afraid that he would have a mental relapse. Chris had never seen his grandfather behave like this before and didn't know how to react. One day when Becky came home, she found Norm sitting half-naked at the dining table and writing in his journal.

"Eureka, eureka, I found it," he exclaimed to her.

"Found what? That your underwear is too tight?"

"No, I found the answer I was looking for."

"Dad, I want you to put a stop to all your nonsense. It's affecting Chris badly."

"Parp-parp-parp. Poor Chris. Affected badly. How should bad Norm be behaving? He's one and the same as the Lord himself." He was saying all this in an irritating high-pitched singsong voice.

"Stop it right now. Just stop it for God's sake."

Becky picked up his journal and saw what he had written. Perhaps there would be some clues there to explain his madness.

Can the Void in Anita's model be a Void relative to Prakriti? If so, then Purusha could be considered as pure consciousness that existed everywhere in the universe. It would exist in its pure form in the Void and outside the Void it would co-exist with Prakriti. Prakriti being insentient matter and Purusha being pure consciousness would be two totally different entities.

Since Purusha is everywhere it has no movement. From this viewpoint, Purusha in Sankhya is consistent with what Sankaracharya said,

'The difference between God and man is a matter of degrees. Ultimately they are one and the same being. That which is within man is called Atman and That which embraces the universe is called Brahman. They are one and the same.'

Hence, pursuing Sankhya does not go against Sankaracharya or the Word of Lord Shiva.

Norm was singing to himself, "From the unreal lead me to the real, from darkness lead me to light, from death lead me to immortality."

"Dad, I think you better check into the ward for a few days."

When she said that, Norm looked very scared. His face turned a ghostly pale color as he recalled what they had done to him the last time. Then he thought about Chris and decided that his grandson shouldn't see him in this state of his.

"Okay Becky. You win. This time I'll go quietly, no injections please."

He was admitted to the psychiatric ward of the local hospital. The doctors told Becky that he was too old to survive shock treatment and suggested that they were going to increase his medication.

Twenty-six

Upon his release from the hospital, Norm was behaving more normally at home. His dosage had doubled and this helped in soothing the severe headaches. Nevertheless he appeared restless and fidgety when left alone to himself. Becky knew that this would cause further problems and in desperation she called Ken in Wenatchee, and asked him to spend a couple of weeks with Norm. Ken graciously agreed.

The one thing that Norm hated about Ken was his ponytail hair-do. Norm was regular army and would not put up with that kind of insanity. But who was to say who was insane and who was not? After all, he was the one who had been twice to a mental ward, not Ken. The bond between them was their admiration for the beat-generation writers and poets.

"Norm, it's good to see you after all these years. We still talk about your story of the power of science over the masses."

"Good to see you too Ken. How's Sharon?"

"She's doing fine. How's Anita? Alan rarely writes to us so we have to find out about him through friends."

"They're having a great time in Egypt. She's a very smart girl. Always curious."

"Sharon said that if we had a grandson we would vote to name him George. He would then be curious George. Get it? Curious George the monkey. Like the way of the cat and the way of the monkey. Ha-ha-ha."

249

"Very funny Ken. You always have to come up with a monkey joke."

"Becky tells me that you have been doing lots of reading lately. I want to discuss that with you. I think it's pointless to think intellectually about religious truth. When we think that reality is exhausted by our thought patterns we enter the realm of distortion."

"I can't help it Ken. That's my mission, given to me by Lord Shiva."

"You should give it up Norm. Look where the search has taken you. Whether an absolute God exists or not is not of practical importance. If the God of your own experiences does not exist then you're in big trouble."

"But the God of my experience does exist Ken."

"The problem, Norm, is that he exists only in your mind. None of us has seen Lord Shiva."

"Is that my fault?"

"No, it's not your fault. You should adopt a more pragmatic approach to life. The concept of enlightenment of the Hindus and Buddhists is beyond what the mind can think of. Religion is for doing things, not for reading about doing things."

"That's what my wife believed. If enlightenment is beyond what we can think, how do we know it's there? If the ancient Hindus and Buddhists talked about it, it must have been a product of the human mind. If so, then why can't we try to discover it? We're also gifted with a mind and intellect."

"I don't know the answer to that. There are many mysteries to which we don't have the answers Norm—the mystery of the origin of the universe, the mystery of life and nature, the mystery of time, space and gravity, and the mystery of human consciousness. The answers are not important. It's the path we take in our quest that's important."

"I agree with what you are saying. Solving mysteries is what makes life fun. Neither science nor philosophy has answers to these mysteries. We have empirical philosophies that are not religious enough, or we have religious philosophies that are not empirical enough. Your granddaughter's theory comes close to answering some very important questions."

"Is her theory true?"

"Wrong question, Ken. Even science cannot answer a simple question like this. What is important is whether a theory is useful, not whether it is true."

"Okay. I think I understand what you are saying. I guess everybody follows different paths to enlightenment. Sharon and I find great comfort in Taoism. Have you read it?"

"No. I haven't found my way past Hinduism yet."

BEFORE he left Urbana, Ken stopped by at a bookstore and bought Norm a copy of the centuries-old *Tao Te Ching* by Lao Tzu.

"Here, Norm. This is a present from me and Sharon. Please read it. I think it'll be good for you."

"How do you say the author's name?"

"Lao Tzu means Old Philosopher. People of Chinese origin have no trouble saying his last name whether it is spelled Tse, Tze, or Tzu. They're all the same phoneme.

"Legend has it that he was born into nobility but rejected his family and became a curator of the Imperial archives at Loh. All through his life Lao Tzu followed the path of silence. One day he left the archives, presumably to die in the desert. The keeper of Han Ku Pass persuaded him to write down his teachings for posterity.

"The *Tao Te Ching* has been translated by many scholars, although most of them are more enthusiastic about the mystical aspects and do not know much about Chinese thought or language. The translation I gave you is by D. C. Lau who is an expert in the Chinese language, and this version comes closest to its original intent. I hope you enjoy it."

When Ken left for Wenatchee Norm started his study of Taoism. Literally translated, the *Tao Te Ching* meant The Way and its Virtue. The Tao, or Way, of nature was based on the ancient Chinese principles of yin and yang, two opposite but complementary forces in the universe. Yin was the supreme feminine power, characterized by darkness, coldness and passivity and associated with the moon. Yang was the masculine counterpart of brightness, warmth, and activity, identified with the sun. The Tao itself could not be defined: it was nameless and formless. Lao Tzu had said that the Tao was like an empty vessel, a river flowing home to the sea.

The great Tao flows everywhere, both to the left and
the right.
The ten thousand things depend on it; it holds
nothing back.
It fulfills its purpose silently and makes no claim.

It nourishes the ten thousand things,
And yet is not their lord.

Norm observed the similarity between the Tao of Taoism and
Purusha of Sankhya. Both were similar to the Quality of Robert
Pirsig. Timeless. Boundless. The key to the mystery of existence.

FRIDAY, April 9, 1993 was the eleventh anniversary of Joann's
death. Every year on that day, Norm would read a few pages from
the New Testament. It was something Joann had strongly believed in
and by reading it Norm cherished the memories of her spirit. His
bookmark was at the Gospel of John.

* *In the beginning was the Word, and the Word was with*
God, and the Word was God.
* *He was in the beginning with God.*
* *All things were made through Him, and without Him nothing*
was made that was made.
* *In Him was life and the life was the light of men.*
* *And the light shines in the darkness, and the darkness did*
not comprehend it.
— John 1: 1–5

As he read these first five verses, he was suddenly struck by
their similarity with concepts of the Sankhya philosophy. John was
one of the original twelve apostles of Jesus Christ and his writings,
therefore, were first hand, so different from the Gospels of Mark and
Luke. The life that was the light of men was the same as the twenty-
fifth principle of Sankhya, namely Purusha. What was the first verse
alluding to?

Something called the Word that was present in the beginning.
Could that be the revolving substratum that Anita had described?
Could that be the uniform motion that was eternal?

He recalled a recent passage from Lao Tzu's *Tao Te Ching*.

There is a thing confusedly formed,
Born before Heaven and Earth.
Silent and void
It stands alone and does not change,
Goes round and does not weary.

Tao Te Ching, Verse 25.

There it was, again, a reference to the Void and uniform motion of Anita's theory. Norm's eyes nearly popped out of their sockets. The madcap had stumbled onto something.

The previous year in November he had read *The Rubaiyat* of Omar Khayyam.

The Moving Finger writes; and, having writ,
Moves on: nor all thy Piety nor Wit
Shall lure it back to cancel half a Line,
Nor all thy Tears wash out a Word of it.

These had been Bill Kaplan's last words when he died in Korea. Omar Khayyam was a poet, astronomer, and mathematician who lived in the latter part of the 11th century A.D. Westerners have portrayed Khayyam as a hedonist, drinking his way through life. But in his native Persia, Omar is recognized as a great mystic and spiritual teacher. As is the case with Sufi poetry, it often has two meanings, one on the surface and one cloaked in metaphors.

Norm wondered whether the Moving Finger could refer to a cosmic principle that governed the universe. Something that maintained a universal order and moved on. The revolving substratum?

He remembered something similar from the *Bhagavad Gita*.

Presided over by Me, Prakriti brings forth the world of moving and unmoving things; for this reason, O son of Kunti (Arjuna), the world revolves. — Bhagavad Gita 9:10.

This did not refer to the revolution of the earth around the sun. It referred to the revolving substratum!

253

Religion indeed had answers to the mysteries of the universe. The ancient writings were not myths or poetry handed down to posterity but embodied knowledge that had to be interpreted correctly to decode their hidden message. Lord Shiva was right. His Word had been on earth for centuries. The Tao was 2600 years old. And the *Gita* was older than that. The Word of God was not always present in the organized tradition of religion that was being practiced.

NORM was not a religious expert but he was sure that scholars of theology would find passages in other religions similar to what he had just read. One had to truly seek the Word of God and not be dogmatic about one's own religion being superior to others. The search for Truth transcends religious boundaries and the Word of God has always been there since the early daybreak of civilization. It's the path that people are made to follow to seek it that is questionable.

Norm believed there were several paths to that Truth. Joann's path was one of faith—not a path of religious rites, not a path of prayer for personal gain, but a path of single-minded devotion to God. His own path was one of knowledge. People needed to focus more on the correct interpretation of the sacred writings rather than take them literally. Anita had given him the code to unravel their hidden message.

FROM his study of Hinduism, Norm recalled another symbol—the symbol Om, which produced the sounds of A-U-M. It has deep philosophical significance and its chant has an extraordinary effect on human beings. It produces harmony, peace and bliss by bringing the individual being in perfect attainment with the eternal being. It is the key that unlocks the kingdom of heaven. Contrary to popular belief that its origin lies in Sanskrit, Om is nature's word, nature's *mantra*. It does not belong to any particular language, but occupies a very prominent place in all languages of the world. Omniscient, Omnipotent, and Omnipresent are the highest names for God. Many prayers begin and end with the utterance of Om in some form. Amen in English. Amin in Persian and Arabic.

HE wrote the following lines in his journal.

The sound Om.
In the beginning was the Word.
Symbolized by the cosmic drum of Lord Shiva.
Silent and void.
The force of creation.
The basic frequency of the cosmos.
The revolving substratum of the universe.

Norm knew at this time that he was one step closer to fulfilling his mission, but he had to proceed very cautiously. All he had done was to compare his understanding of various philosophies with his understanding of Anita's theory. There was no guarantee that any of it was true. People could easily say that they were mere ramblings of an insane freak. His record in that department was not altogether exemplar.

No, he told himself, the unraveling of the mystery would have to be carried out on the battlefield of science. Science on one pan of the balance of Truth, religion and philosophy on the other.

Twenty-seven

The winter in Egypt was mild compared to Urbana and for the most part Anita got by with a light jacket. In the summer she visited the Valley of the Kings in Western Thebes, the burial site of many Egyptian kings dating back to 1600 B.C. Several royal tombs had been found and plundered there except for the tomb of Tutankhamen, which was discovered intact by Howard Carter in 1922.

Other than a few bouts of diarrhea, their stay in Egypt was wonderful. Alan had worked with the physics faculty and arranged for one of them to visit Urbana the following year.

Towards the end of summer 1993, they planned to return to Illinois. Norm told Becky and Chris not to tell Anita or Alan about his mental relapse. "She won't be able to handle it," he said. "Don't worry about me. I'll take my medication and behave normally."

He drove to Chicago to pick them up.

"How was your trip?"

"Fantastic. You must visit Egypt, Major Kay."

"Call me Norm from now on."

"Okay. Did you read up on Sankhya?"

"Yes. It's answered many of my questions and opened doors I never knew existed. How did you know about it? It's not something that's in the mainstream of Hindu thought."

"I don't know. I was reading your books on Hinduism and I noticed a similarity with my theory."

"Will you give it a rest?" snapped Alan. "We've had peace and quiet for a whole year, and now it's back to your discussions on philosophical crap. Frankly I'm tired of all this nonsense. I talked to some physicists and they don't think Anita's theory has any merit whatsoever. Anisotropy in em-propagation is simply not tenable with the observed evidence."

"And what about the accelerating and revolving substratums? Are they also not tenable?"

"Yes. There's no solid evidence for either of them. The carousel is merely an analogy. As I told you before, analogies are useless. Just leave these questions to the specialists. The Standard Model gives us a very accurate picture of the universe, although it has a few minor problems. But they will soon be fixed and we will put an end to science."

"When Alan?" asked Norm, somewhat rankled. "Civilization has been around for 12,000 years and we still don't have the answer. When are you specialists going to figure out the answer?"

"Break it up, all of you," interrupted Meg who had received a letter from Becky explaining Norm's mental condition and relapse. "We're approaching home sweet home now. Why don't you rest for a few days? We all have jet lag and may say something now that we'll later regret."

WHEN Chris met Anita a couple of days later, he was taken aback. She was looking so grown-up now and her breasts had matured.

"Hi Chris. I've got some nice things for you." Her voice, too, had cracked just like his.

"Thank you Anita. You look great."

"What did you do last year?"

"I learned computer programming. It's very interesting. You can make computers do whatever you want them to do."

"Can you take them for a walk and show them the soft lines of the hills?"

"You know what I mean."

"Here, I got an ancient papyrus for you from Alexandria. See, it's even got some writing on it."

Chris examined the fragment and noticed it had two numbers. He wrote them on a piece of paper.

5 9 3 5 4 5 4 5 5 4 8 5
4 8 3 2 3 9 7 9 8 5 3 5 6 2 9 5 1 4 1

"What do you suppose these numbers are?"

"How should I know? You're the computer geek. Go figure it out."

"What's the writing on the side? It's not in English."

"Beats me. I got it from a bazaar in Alexandria. When I went to pay for it, the shopkeeper had vanished from sight."

"Did you see King Tut's tomb?"

"Yes. We saw a part of it. It was pretty scary at first when the guide told us about the curse."

"What curse?"

"The one that killed the people who excavated the tomb."

"By the way, what are you doing tomorrow?"

"I don't know. Why?"

"Maybe we can go see a movie in the mall."

"Okay. Sounds like a good idea."

The little kids had suddenly grown up. They were now attending eighth grade in middle school. For no apparent reason and no matter what they did, they and their friends were considered obnoxious by the rest of the world. Anita had been in Egypt during seventh grade and did not know how to dress to be accepted in the circle of friends she used to know from elementary school. It took her a while to learn the rules of behavior, the language to be used, and the clothes to wear. She was forced to downplay her interest in math and science—she didn't want to be called a geek.

Chris was getting romantically attached to Anita, but not confident enough to ask her out. He would pretend to be interested in science and hang out with her and Norm as often as he could.

AFTER a couple of weeks everyone had settled into their fall schedule. Anita and Chris took a bus to school and back. Meg was tired of working in the mall and applied for a job as an executive secretary to the university President. The interview was in October and she was very happy when she learned that she got the job.

Her boss was a biologist by training but Meg soon found out that he was a stark anomaly to Charles Darwin's theory of evolution. If natural selection and random mutations had played a role in the formation of his cells, it was difficult to explain why there were not more of his kind on campus. He was the only complex organism she knew who could articulate through both sides of its mouth with a gusto that was unsurpassable by the finest of Darwin's modern-day greyhounds.

There were days when she became dizzy just thinking about what was common between them: they were both fit and both surviving or were both fit because they were surviving or both surviving because they were fit. On some occasions she thought about asking him whether fish discovered water to ensure their survival, a question she had wondered about since high school. Then she thought better of it and abandoned the idea. She didn't want the President to think that she was stupid—after all, the job paid well and the benefits were excellent.

EVER since Norm had found a religious connection to the revolving substratum, he had been searching for a scientific one. All his life he had never accepted religious writings unless they stood up to scientific scrutiny. He approached Alan to discuss his ideas.

"Alan, do you think we can construct a formal scientific model for Anita's theory? I've noticed a pattern in religious literature that can be interpreted as the revolving substratum."

"We need a lot more than ancient mumbo-jumbo Norm. Besides, her theory has no mathematical basis. There's already a model that answers all the interesting questions. It's the Standard Model of particle physics."

"Is it possible to have alternative cosmologies that conform to the observed evidence?"

"There is a very slim chance, but I wouldn't bet on it."

"Is there anybody in your department who may be interested?"

"The only person I know is Michell. I'll ask him."

"Thanks Alan."

IN November that year, Norm asked Anita an aspect of her theory that was foggy in his mind. Chris made it his business to be present at this meeting.

"One thing that is not clear in your theory, Anita, is the explanation for the microwave background radiation. This

259

background temperature is the only evidence that supports the Standard Model."

"Okay, I'll try to explain it. Big Bang is the night of the universe and Big Crunch is the day of the universe. At the Big Bang, the universe completely dissolves into ether and this transfer of mass and energy produces a very high temperature. The universe starts to expand and at this stage only the substratum ether is present and the manifested universe is non-existent. It continues to expand, resulting in cooling the substratum, until the Void gains enough energy to balance the expanding rate.

"Subsequently, the ether is drawn towards the Void and this is when the Big Crunch starts. It is at this stage that matter and light are formed. It is also the stage when the gravitational field manifests in the universe. As the ether starts contracting and the manifested universe evolves, fluctuating waves are produced in the substratum until a stable state is reached."

Chris interrupted them by saying, "Are these fluctuations the ones that were recently detected by COBE?"

"COBE? What's that Chris? And how do you know about it?" asked Norm.

"I was reading a newsgroup on my computer that described the Cosmic Background Explorer satellite. It said that this probe had detected tiny fluctuations in the microwave background radiation."

Anita smiled at Chris and continued.

"So the microwave background radiation just gives us a time stamp for the evolution of light. There is no light during the Big Bang and during the expansion of the universe. There is just total darkness until the process of Big Crunch begins. It is at this time that both matter and light are formed.

"To link the microwave background radiation with events that may have happened at the Big Bang is speculation. All that you can conclude from this radiation is the time when it started. It need not have started at the Big Bang but could have started at the Big Crunch. That's why I believe the universe is contracting right now, eventually leading to the Big Bang when all the matter and energy will be returned to the substratum ether of the universe."

"My, my, this is a bold theory, Anita. But what about the law of conservation of energy? Surely your model ought to satisfy the law of conservation of energy," said Norm.

"It does," she said, "if you account for all the forces involved. That's something you have to figure out."

NORM decided to look into the forces required to support Anita's model. For the law of conservation of energy to hold good through big bang and big crunch, Anita's theory would have to account for three forces: a single unit of the gravitational or centripetal force, a single unit of the anti-gravitational or centrifugal force, and a single unit of the revolving force. So there would have to be a total of three units to be accounted for.

Professor Michell was a difficult person to get hold of. He was almost never in his office. When Norm finally managed to contact him, Michell told him to come and see him during the winter break.

"What a small office you have," remarked Norm when he entered Michell's room.

"Yes. It's small and dingy. I keep it that way to get a black-hole effect."

"I'm here to ask you for your help with a possible theory on the origin of the universe."

"Sure. I'll listen."

Norm spent a few minutes explaining Anita's theory in quite some detail. When he described the duality of the accelerating and revolving substratums, Michell suddenly perked up.

"Fascinating," he said. "This is going to be difficult to validate, but we may have one hope."

"What's that?"

"Computer simulation. The dependence of theoretical science on mathematical deduction impedes our ability to answer basic questions. One way out of this mess is to use computational science."

"What do you mean by computational science?"

"Theoretical science, as we know it, is an Aristotelian tradition. Experimental science, a Galilean tradition, is useful in determining things that cannot be predicted by theory alone, like the electric charge on the electron. Computational science, which is quite new, is useful in simulating a number of different models on the computer and evolving them in simulated time steps to see if one of them produces a universe like the one we observe today."

Michell's answer and positive attitude was comforting to Norm.

"Would we be limited by the uncertainty principle?" he asked Michell.

"No, we would not because we can make the computer program do whatever we want it to do."

"Is it possible to write this program and carry out the simulation?"

"In principle, yes, but it may not be easy in practice. There is a way to start out with a data set of N particles and subject it to any kind of model. It's called the N-body approach."

"How does that work?" asked Norm.

"Well, you start out with N point-size masses and examine their behavior in accordance with the laws of any scientific theory. There has been some work done using this approach with Newton's law of gravitation."

"What would be the difficulties in writing such a computer program?"

"The main difficulty would be in the time taken by the computer to perform the simulation."

"I thought computers are very fast."

"Yes, they are. In some cases, though, they are not fast enough. You've heard of frequent flyer miles, haven't you?"

"Sure, everybody has."

"Prior to 1982 we had to worry only about death and taxes. Since then we have had to worry about death, taxes, and frequent flyer miles. Let's say that you work for the government, and plan to inspect twenty facilities around the country to see whether they are in compliance with federal regulations.

"Naturally you want to choose an order in which to visit these facilities so that you get the most frequent flyer miles. The only airline you would not travel by is Air Force One."

"Why not?"

"Because that doesn't give frequent flyer miles."

Norm burst out laughing.

"Your main problem," continued Michell, "is with the accountants who check your travel expense report. If by any chance you happen to visit the same city twice, you would raise red flags in their office. There would be all kinds of paper work required to justify your trip, when your main goal is not to attract attention to yourself.

"To choose this order, Norm, appears easy at first but gets harder and harder as you increase the number of destinations. The fastest computers today cannot solve this problem in enough time.

"I will start working on the mathematical formulation of your theory right away, but I need help with the actual programming. I'm mainly a theoretician and don't really know how to use computers."

"I could ask my grandson to help with that. He's only in school but he's very interested in computers. He took a programming class last year at Northwestern. If you mentor him in this project, I'm sure he will enjoy it."

"Great idea. Sounds good. Ask him to call me at home. That's where I get most of my work done. I have to hide there to avoid pesky undergraduates who just want homework points without any true understanding. Our education system has been crumbling for many years but nobody seems to care. Nobody even seems to notice its decline."

Twenty-eight

In the fall of 1994, Anita and Chris entered high school. Both took a class at the university, philosophy for Anita and advanced computer programming for Chris. Their middle school woes were over and this was the start of a new four-year phase. Suddenly it was too "dorky" to ride the school bus so once again Norm became their chauffeur. In Anita's philosophy class, a good portion of the time was spent studying the Great Books of India. When she came back from school she and Norm would discuss the many facets of Hinduism. Norm gave her his notes on Sankhya and told her why it was considered atheistic.

"It's the lack of a Supreme Being principle that makes it untenable to the Vedantist school of thought," he said.

"Let me study it. If I have any questions, I'll ask you."

"Good. Please read it objectively as I'm not sure if I have the correct interpretation of Purusha and Prakriti."

Chris met with Professor Michell twice a week to work on the computer program. With his uncanny abilities to snoop around the Internet, he found a web site that had an N-body simulation program for the Standard Model, and promptly downloaded it for free.

"What we need now, Chris, are two things, the correct equations and the initial configuration," said Michell.

"If I can help in any way let me know. I'm not that much up on my knowledge of physics."

"Nonsense. You can easily understand what we are trying to do. The initial configuration consists of a couple of numbers. We need to figure out the value for the initial energy to determine how big the tornado grows before contracting. And we need to figure out how much time elapses from the moment of the Big Bang before the contraction starts."

"Why can't we use the numbers from the program I downloaded?"

"Because that's based on a different model. In the Standard Model, the universe is in a stage of expansion and the elapsed time is roughly 12 to 15 billion years. We're trying to find a new model."

"How do we test the program to see if we have done the right thing?"

"Excellent question, Chris. That's from a third number. The simulation computes a number for the density of observed matter in the universe. If it's close enough to the observed density, then we conclude we have done the right thing."

"But there can be hundreds of ways to compute that third number," exclaimed Chris.

"Yes. One can formulate hundreds of models to compute the third number."

"What is the result we should get for the density?"

"I don't know, Chris."

"What do you mean you don't know? You're kidding, right?"

"No, I'm not. I truly don't know."

"We've got to have some way to check whether the program computed the correct answer."

"Unfortunately we don't have an exact value for the current density. If the program returns an answer which is fairly close to what we think the actual density is, we accept it."

"You mean the answer lies within a certain range?"

"Yes, within a certain interval and with a certain probability."

"I thought science would be a lot more accurate than that."

"Compared to other things in life it is. We have lies, damn lies, statistics," . . . Michell's voice trails off, "computer programs, campaign promises, cosmology . . ."

DURING the fall semester Chris was busy debugging the computer program. The interface was clumsily done in FORTRAN and Chris decided to modify it using the language *C*. He had taken a course on graphical interfaces and spent a good amount of time making it easy for a user like himself to interact with the program. The UNIX operating system on Michell's workstation was very cryptic compared to the Macintosh he was used to, but it did not present any major obstacles. As Chris was sorting out his junk one day, he found the papyrus Anita had given him and showed it to Michell.

"Are these the kinds of numbers you might be interested in?" he asked the professor.

"Show it to me," said Michell, grabbing the papyrus from Chris's hand. He could barely see the following numbers.

5 9 3 5 4 5 4 5 5 4 8 5
4 8 3 2 3 9 7 9 8 5 3 5 6 2 9 5 1 4 1

"Where did you get it?"
"My friend Anita brought it for me from Egypt."
"Anita? Alan's pesky daughter?"
"Yes."
"She took a class from me and always asked the difficult questions I couldn't answer. These numbers seem to be the right size. I think the smaller one should give us the number of time steps, and the larger one may be the value for the initial energy."

"There's no way the program would accept them. They're much too big."

"Can't you input the digits one by one?"
"No Professor Michell. Eventually they have to be stored in memory. Even the smaller number is too big for your computer."

"Okay. Let me think about how to scale these down. Good work Chris."

AS the academic year progressed, Chris was still nervous about asking Anita out to the movies. One of his classmates sent a letter to Anita without his knowledge.

It said, 'Darling, don't you know I have a crush on you? Your good friend, Chris.'

At first Chris was pissed off when he found out about the prank, but upon later reflection he thought it was all right. At least Anita now knew that he was attracted to her. They started seeing movies together.

During spring break of 1995, while they were eating ice cream after a movie, Chris told Anita, "Let's do something wild together. I mean really wild. I want to do more than just eat ice-cream cones."

"Relax Chris. What we're doing is just fine."

"Come on Anita. We've been going out for quite a while now."

"Okay Chris. If you want something wild, I'll show you something really wild. Let's wait till next month."

On Friday, April 14, 1995, Anita called Chris over to her house after school. Her parents were at work and nobody was home.

"Here, Chris, I want to show you something really wild."

She got out a sanitary napkin soiled with her menses.

"Smell this Chris. Do you still want to come near me when I smell like this?"

"TAKE IT AWAY. Just take it away. You're grossing me out."

"Why Chris? That's part of me," she remonstrated. "You can't have the good parts and reject the bad parts. I suggest you think about what you really want from me."

"Why are you doing this? Is this some kind of joke?"

"No. I'm serious. Sexuality is not about having fun. It's about understanding the sanctity of life."

"I was just trying to do what everyone else does."

"That is not enough. If you want to elevate yourself beyond the body and search for God, you should remain free of worldly attachments. Love beauty for its own sake and let not the fruit of action be your guide."

Poor Chris. At first he was angry. It wasn't fair on her part to treat him to such an abusive show. Anita had changed quite a bit since she returned from Egypt. He had heard his grandfather talk very highly of her abilities. It slowly dawned on him that she was a special girl. He remembered the time he had first met her when he moved to Urbana. He had been mute in his early childhood and she had heard him speak his first words at the library. They had been good friends for many years. Chris was not going to let what just happened come

267

in the way of all the good times. He continued their Platonic friendship with a newfound admiration for her wisdom.

OVER the Memorial Day weekend Anita was helping Norm fertilize the lawn.

"Have you understood Sankhya completely?" she asked him.

"No. I can't say that of anything I know. There's always more for me to understand about any topic."

"Can you tell me why the grass is green?"

"What other color could it be?"

"That's not an answer to my question."

"Okay. I don't know why it is green."

"I'll tell you. When light shines on the grass it absorbs all the colors of the spectrum except green. Green is the only color it reflects back to us. That's why the grass is green."

"Very good Anita. Thanks for letting me know."

"Now, Norm, what is the color of grass?"

"Green, right?"

"Wrong. Green is the color the grass doesn't want and reflects back to us. So its real color is all the others it does want and does not reflect back."

"Very tricky Anita. You got me. Where are we going with all this?"

"I'm coming to that. It's to do with Sankhya philosophy. What is the goal of science, Norm?"

"To find out how the universe has evolved."

"There are two aspects to knowledge about the universe: *how* it has evolved and *why* it has been evolved. Science lays total stress on the how aspect to the exclusion of the why aspect. Sankhya lays stress on the how aspect only to the extent necessary to explain the why aspect."

"I don't quite follow what you are saying."

"Let's go back to the color analogy. Pretend there is a colorless being in association with white matter. If there is no other matter or color, what would the colorless being conclude about her color?"

"White?"

"Exactly. Since there is no color other than white, she would have no chance to begin an inquiry into her real color.

"Now let's introduce a few colors other than white. The colorless being will now grasp the concept of color and by seeing other colors will conclude, 'I am not this color,' 'I am not this color,' and so on. She will then be able to begin an inquiry and ask the question, 'Am I this white color or am I different?'

"Thus she can ultimately realize by way of reasoning that she is colorless."

"What's this got to do with Sankhya?"

"As Prakriti and Purusha were all-pervading and existed everywhere, the Purusha in this combination would never have had the opportunity to begin an inquiry about his existence as pure consciousness, separate and independent of Prakriti. Purusha, which is sentient consciousness, is what Sankhya believes to be God. Prakriti is insentient primal matter. Insentient objects must have a subject in whose consciousness they gain existence, and a subject must have different objects by discarding which he comes to know himself. Just as in the color analogy.

"Therefore, the universe has been evolved by the Great Lord to teach a part of Himself what He really is."

"How do you know all this?"

"I'm writing a term paper for my philosophy class and my topic is Sankhya. However, I've found other sources in Hinduism to back up my views. I found the following passages in the *Bhagavad Gita*:

From the Unmanifest all manifested beings are born at the advent of Brahma's day, and at the approach of His night they get merged in that very thing called the Unmanifest.
— Bhagavad Gita 8:18.

Neither the gods nor the great sages know My birth; for I am the cause of the gods and the great sages in all respects.
— Bhagavad Gita 10: 2.

"I've started studying some Sanskrit and find the word Sankhya used in the *Gita* in quite a few places. It is always translated as knowledge and not as the philosophy. I wonder why."

"I was told by a monk that Sankhya is considered an atheistic philosophy because it does not admit a Supreme Being principle.

269

That's probably why it is not referenced in the Gita. Nobody would want Lord Krishna to mention anything that was atheistic."

"Not true, Norm. It *is* referenced in the original verses of the *Gita*. It's the translations that have missed its interpretation."

The bigger picture of Anita's theory and its connection with Sankhya became clearer to Norm. Brahma's day corresponded to Big Crunch when the universe manifested, and Brahma's night corresponded to Big Bang when the universe dissolved into the Unmanifest substratum ether.

From his study of Genesis in his younger days Norm recalled something similar to Brahma's night. The first chapter of Genesis described a darkness on the face of the abyss. The Hebrew language, however, distinguishes between two kinds of darkness, one named *Khoshekh* and the other *Aphela*. Aphela is what we commonly associate with darkness, namely a state in which light is absent. Khoshekh is a state of darkness having its own physical properties. It denotes a primordial state, one that preceded the appearance of light, or perhaps one from which a secondary phenomenon could emanate.

The link between Khoshekh and Brahma's night was amazing. Beyond coincidence. Genesis and the *Bhagavad Gita* were describing the same thing! A state when the substratum ether expanded and cooled and nothing was manifested. A state when there was no light. From this Unmanifest Khoshekh, matter and light manifest at the advent of Brahma's day or Big Crunch.

The scientific part of Norm, however, was not comfortable with this association. He still could not see how the model satisfied the law of conservation of energy.

As he pondered deep and hard, he started getting a dull headache. It was July 22, 1995.

Twenty-nine

When the leaves started to fall that year, not knowing their true color, there was some excitement in the Supercomputing Center at the university. Alan told them that some colleagues of his were attempting to work on a computer program, similar to the one Chris had been developing for Michell, that would be used to make a film called *Cosmic Voyage*. Viewers would be able to see the effects of the big bang and the evolution of the universe in accordance with the Standard Model.

Michell sat in on Alan's group meetings to learn more about their techniques so that he could use them to formulate his own model with the two numbers from the Alexandrian papyrus. He quickly discovered that it was going to be difficult for Chris. To reduce the time taken for the simulation, Frank Reynolds, the project lead described two main ideas: the first was to use Cray's latest supercomputer which boasted trillions of operations per second, and the second was to develop randomized algorithms to solve some computationally hard parts of the problem. Michell, who had no business attending the group meeting, raised his hand.

"Excuse me," he said, "can some one explain how exactly the Cray computer is going to speed things up?"

"It's very fast, Michell. Here, look at the spec sheets."

Michell pored over the specification sheets but still persisted with his doubt.

271

"I still don't get it. All the spec sheet describes is how fast the processor is. Are we able to get the data to it as quickly?"

"That's not going to be a major problem. The machine's cache will take care of it," replied Greg Summers, who was the hardware person.

"Okay. I hope you fellas know what's going on because I don't even know what a cache is."

There was some laughter in the room as Michell admitted his ignorance. Theoreticians like him had their strict confines and were not expected to venture out in the real world, in the world of practical reality.

IN her philosophy course the previous year, Anita had borrowed Norm's journal to help write the term paper on Sankhya. The journal was still with her and from time to time she flipped through other portions of it to understand where Norm had been and where he was coming from in his inquiry into First Cause.

"Norm," she told him during the Christmas break, "there is an error in your formulation of my model. You've listed only three forces."

"Those are the only forces that support the tornado—the inward centripetal force, the outward centrifugal force, and the revolving force."

"There is one extra force due to the revolving substratum."

"Isn't that what spins the tornado?"

"In a sense it does. But this force is present through Big Bang and Big Crunch and produces uniform motion. Without this momentum the tornado would not be able to form again once it collapsed. So there are four forces and you should consider all of them in applying the law of conservation of energy."

"Well, I'll be a son of a snapper," he cried out loud. "How could I have missed such an obvious thing? Excuse me, Anita, I have to tell Professor Michell right away."

The fourth force was certainly helpful to Michell in his formulation of the Einstein-de Sitter model of positive curvature. The computer simulation, however, had completely stalled. There was no way Michell could scale down the constants unless he cracked their code, unless he knew the origin of the numbers on the papyrus.

JANUARY of 1996 brought some extremely cold temperatures to the Midwest. On the 26th of the month, as the nation was gripped in the middle of an Arctic cold blast, Anita got a severe headache. She developed high fever and was bedridden for a whole week.

It was then that she told her mother that when she died she wanted to be cremated, not buried. Meg, somewhat alarmed at hearing this, admonished her to refrain from such thoughts.

Anita's spirits were uplifted on January 31st when the sighting of a new comet was reported in the newspaper. Chris told her that an amateur Japanese astronomer, Yuji Hyakutake, whose name means a 'hundred samurai,' had unexpectedly discovered the comet southeast of Corvus and in the vicinity of M101.

"When can we see this comet?" she asked Chris.

"It should be easily visible during the last week of March."

Anita's fever soon disappeared but a dull headache, which she didn't tell anyone about, still persisted. She had always been interested in astronomy and the night sky, and eagerly waited for clear nights so that she could track the comet with her binoculars.

In March that year she followed the comet with great interest as it continued to brighten along the northern byway of the sky, from Arcturus to the Big Dipper's handle, through Ursa Minor, and on into Perseus. One weekend she stayed up all night with Chris and Norm watching Hyakutake's long tail from dusk till dawn. On Monday, March 25th, the comet made its closest approach to Earth, a mere 9 million miles away. Its peak brightness would continue into the month of April as it put on a spectacular show for viewers in the Northern Hemisphere.

When the first spring showers hit the ground, it was Sunday, April 7th. Anita had gone over to help Norm in the yard.

"What's your favorite smell, Anita?"

"I like the smell of rain falling on dry sand," she replied.

"Me too."

"Norm, do you know what your legacy in life is?"

"My legacy? That's a funny question Anita. My legacy is for others to determine after I'm dead."

"No, that's not true. We all carry our own cosmic legacy. Our spiritual purpose is to find out what this legacy is before we die, not for others to describe it after we are gone."

"Sounds mighty strange to me."

"Not at all. Hasn't your inquiry into First Cause burned you out all these years?"

"Yes it has."

"You've been desperately looking for an answer in religion and science, haven't you?"

"I'm trying to find the Word of God. That's my mission."

"Norm, the Word of God you have been looking for is everywhere. It is in science as well as in religion. It is also within you. There's been so much rhetoric between science and religion that they continue to operate in different modes, not knowing that there is only one true vision of reality.

"Their words may sound different, but the sense is the same."

There was a pregnant pause as Norm let that sink into his head.

"Do you know what your legacy is?" he asked her.

"Yes I do. Soon it's going to be your turn. I'm confident that you will find it."

"Thank you Anita. I hope I do. Michell's still stuck with the formulation. Even with the fourth force the equations don't come out right."

"There you go again, persisting with your scientific validation. Why don't you worry about God's thoughts? If all else fails you can always tell the truth. The details will take care of themselves."

"I'm afraid that won't work for me."

"Okay, okay. Whose definition of force are you using to satisfy the law of conservation of energy?"

"Newton's definition of course. Force is proportional to rate of change of momentum."

"Wrong. Newton's definition of force is applicable to motion that occurs relative to the substratum. It's a definition of force that is accepted because we can validate it by experiment.

"For the substratum itself, you have to apply Aristotle's definition. Force is proportional to rate of change of acceleration, not momentum.

"Excuse me now, I have to go help my mom. I'll see you later."

NORM had been silenced many times by her in the past, but this was the deadliest blow of all. The definition of force that was in vogue since the days of Galileo and Newton was very fundamental to physics. Anita had trashed it, saying that it was not applicable to the substratum, and suggested using Aristotle's definition of force: that which changed the state of rest or inertia of matter. Would this definition validate her model?

Aristotle, Plato's great pupil, occupied a revered place in the history of philosophy. He took an empirical approach to knowledge and believed that the soul consisted of reason, sensation, and appetite, with reason the controlling power. He was a brilliant formal logician and believed that the earth was at the center of the universe and that the sun, moon and stars revolved around it. His definition of force and his ideas on scientific classification had gone unchallenged for hundreds of years. It was with the invention of the telescope that the Italian astronomer Galileo was able to disprove the notion of an earth-centered universe.

But Aristotle was also guilty of breaking man's connection with Nature. 'Plants,' he had said, 'exist for the sake of animals, and brute beasts for the sake of man . . . . Since Nature makes nothing purposeless or in vain, it is undeniably true that she has made all animals for the sake of man.' It was this domination of man over Nature that became a central part of Western philosophy and separated it from the more holistic view towards Nature taken by Eastern doctrines.

Robert Pirsig had railed at Aristotle in *Zen and the Art of Motorcycle Maintenance*. There was a passage that Norm had read so many times that he remembered it intact.

> *Aristotelian ethics, Aristotelian definitions, Aristotelian logic, Aristotelian forms, Aristotelian substances, Aristotelian rhetoric, Aristotelian laughter . . . ha-ha, ha-ha.*
>
> *And the bones of the Sophists long ago turned to dust and what they said turned to dust with them and the dust was buried under the rubble of declining Athens through its fall and Macedonia through its decline and fall. Through the decline and death of ancient Rome and Byzantium and the Ottoman Empire and the modern states—buried so deep and with such ceremoniousness and such unction and such evil*

*that only a madman centuries later could discover the clues
needed to uncover them, and see with horror what had been
done. . . .*

WHATEVER failings Aristotle may have had as a scientist and a philosopher, he was not around to defend himself. The positive thing for Norm to do would be to try his definition of force instead of Newton's. He called Professor Michell and went over to discuss its ramifications.

On May 1, 1996, Michell was finally able to reconcile the laws of conservation of energy and momentum using Aristotle's definition. Norm was elated. The only thing remaining was for Chris to write the computer program and crack the code of those impregnable constants. Chris was somewhat preoccupied during the last two weeks of April, looking forward to his date with Anita at the junior prom on Saturday, May 4th.

DISASTER struck from the least expected quarter. On Thursday, May 2nd, just two days before her first prom and roughly two weeks before her sixteenth birthday, Anita died in her sleep. She had experienced dull headaches since the end of January and they had persisted all along. It was a heart-wrenching moment for Meg and Alan. Norm cried openly for the first time in his life and there were tears in Alan's eyes.

"Oh, why did she have to die so young?" sobbed Meg. "Alan, can you please get the fire going? I'm so cold."

"I wish I was the one who had gone," choked Norm. "I'm at the right age for death, not a young girl like her."

"I'll miss all the good times we had," said Chris remorsefully. "I'm going to frame the papyrus she brought me from Egypt and hang it in my room."

"What papyrus?" asked Norm.

"This one, Grandpa," said Chris, showing it to him. "Didn't you know that it's the source of the numbers we are trying to use in the computer program?"

"Meg," said Norm, examining the fragment, "tell me where she got this?"

"In Alexandria I believe. We were at a bazaar and a strange thing happened. A peddler gave it to her and when she came to find me to get the money, he had disappeared."

"Hmmm. Did anything else happen while you were there?"

"Her usual phobia of libraries, of course. She fainted when the bus tour passed by the famous Alexandrian library."

"Enough," exclaimed Norm. "I should kick myself in the pants for not knowing who your daughter was."

"What do you mean?" asked Alan.

"Don't you see it?" blurted Norm, in a loud voice, still filled with grief. "She was an ancient martyr sent to us from the past, from a long time ago. Her birth was so special but we all missed its significance."

"What on earth are you talking about, Dad? Please slow down," begged Becky, nervous about him having another breakdown.

"Haven't you heard of Hypatia of Alexandria?" he asked them.

Nobody in the room knew who she was.

"It's a long and tragic story but you have to listen to it. It begins in Egypt and dates back to 332 B.C.

"The city of Alexandria was founded by Alexander the Great. He respected the gods of several countries and was very open-minded in the pursuit of knowledge. His tutor in philosophy was none other than Aristotle. When Alexander died around 323 B.C. the Ptolemys inherited his empire. It was during the reign of Ptolemy II that the library and museum were established. Scholars from other nations were encouraged to visit the library and the emperor funded their stay in the museum. It was expected that these scholars would produce original pieces of research and publish them on scrolls of papyrus.

"For many centuries the tradition of inviting scholars was carried out by the emperors of the Ptolemy dynasty. The library and museum in Alexandria became the research and literary hub of the Hellenistic and Roman eras. The Ptolemys sometimes went to great lengths to acquire original scrolls from other countries. Money was not a limiting factor when it came to getting a prized original of a document they valued.

"When Julius Caesar invaded Alexandria in 48 B.C. his armies supposedly set fire to the library. Historians believe that this story is apocryphal and while Caesar's armies did burn some buildings containing scrolls, the originals of these scrolls were still safe in the library. During the Roman occupation of Alexandria, the city saw many fine scholars. A couple of centuries later, Christianity gained strength and several Christian-Pagan religious clashes broke out in the city.

"Hypatia lived in Alexandria when Christianity began its domination over other religions. She was the daughter of Theon, the last great mathematician and caretaker of the library and museum. Her father taught her all the religions of the world and she shared his passion in the quest for answers to the unknown. She herself became a mathematician, physicist, and astronomer and was one of the leading proponents of the Neoplatonic School of philosophy. Neoplatonism focused on avoiding the material world and concentrated on the perfection of the soul, which it felt could be successively reincarnated, until at last it achieved enlightenment—just like *moksha* in Hinduism.

"She soon excelled her father in mathematics, especially in the theory of cones and conic sections, and edited the work *On the Conics of Apollonius*. Astronomy to her was the queen of all the sciences. This was an extraordinary accomplishment for a woman in male-dominated fields of study.

"Like Pythagoras and Plotinus, the founders of Neoplatonic thought, she abstained from flesh-eating and advocated asceticism and chastity in order to purge the soul of its impurities. There is an incident in her life when she resolved to punish a student for falling in love with her by showing him her sanitary napkin.

"The growing Christian Church was attempting to eradicate all pagan influence and culture and around 412 A.D. there was a new Archbishop in Alexandria, named Cyril. Cyril just could not stand the concept of a woman doing scientific work, work that was identified with paganism by the church. He convinced his followers that Hypatia was a witch who used black magic to influence people. Even though she was in great personal danger, Hypatia's indomitable spirit would not let her give up teaching and publishing. One day in 416 A.D., Hypatia was driving home in her chariot from one of her lectures.

"A fanatical mob of Cyril's followers attacked her and she was killed in the library. It was a gruesome death. Her clothes were torn off her body, she was publicly flayed, her bones dismembered and then burned. All her work was burned along with her and Cyril became a saint for destroying the last remains of idolatry in the city.

"Soon after this occurred, as though it was an omen from the Gods for this dastardly deed, the remnants of the library and museum were consumed by a fire that wiped out whatever civilization had learned over a period of seven centuries. A million handwritten papyrus scrolls turned into dust. It signaled the beginning of the Dark Ages of science until the advent of Copernicus and Kepler in the early 16th century.

"Her death was a sad event in itself but the loss of the library was incalculable. Much of the Old Testament was written from documents stored in the library. Civilization has forever lost the treasures of its ancestors unless the desert sands give up some of their secrets in the form of lost papyri.

"Hypatia had not been put to rest in a proper manner and I think Anita embodied her spirit—risen from the ashes of the volcano and come forth to set things right. To make sure that she finds her rightful place in the world. To make sure that she is properly put to rest.

"I simply have to believe that the volcanic eruption in 1991 awakened some hidden memory within her, and it is in this memory that we are going to find answers to the mysteries of the universe—or at least that portion which was known to her centuries ago."

TEARS flowed freely down Norm's cheeks as he finished and everyone reached for a Kleenex. The embers in the fireplace blew out a wisp of smoke that smiled as it headed towards the rafters.

Thirty

At the funeral Norm was noticeably nervous. For a couple of days he had suffered from the heebie-jeebies, not knowing what he would say at the memorial service. The words finally came as he described Anita's indomitable spirit in repairing the breach between the mystics and the scientists. He concluded with a verse from Palladas, an Alexandrian poet of the fourth century A.D.

Whenever I look upon you and your words, I pay reverence . . .
For your concerns are directed at the heavens, . . .
You who are . . . the beauty of reasoning,
The immaculate star of wise learning.

On her daughter's sixteenth birthday that year, Meg went to church to pray for her soul. For the first time in his adult life Alan accompanied her. It took until Memorial Day for the tears to dry from the outside. It would take a lot longer for them to dry from the inside.

Alan took a break from his duties at school to mourn the loss of his daughter. When her inquisitive voice no longer echoed from the walls of the house, the silence was impossible to bear. At moments like these neither the mystics nor the scientists know why someone's clock stops ticking.

NORM had lost a good friend and was in a pensive mood. He started drinking more than his usual quota of scotch. One evening, as he sipped his drink and observed Venus peeking out of the western sky, he decided to take a closer look at the Alexandrian papyrus. The numbers were strange, one much larger than the other, but the writing on the side was also intriguing. It was not in English and hard for Norm to decipher. As he stared at it some more, it suddenly struck him that it looked awfully similar to the original verses he had seen in the *Bhagavad Gita*. He got out his copy and began scanning each verse to look for a match. It quickly became an impossible task. The next day he went over to a neighbor of his, Professor Pai, an electrical engineering professor of Indian origin, who told him at once that the phrase on the papyrus was indeed in Sanskrit.

"Can you please read it to me?" Norm asked him.

"Sure. It contains two words, Purusha and Prakriti, on beside the other. The funny thing about them is that they're written backwards."

"What do you mean backwards?"

"They're in right to left order instead of left to right order."

"Holy kullolee. Thanks a lot. Excuse me please." So saying Norm rushed home and called Michell.

"I think I can help you crack the code of those numbers," said Norm.

"How? What can you say about them?"

"Try to see if they make sense in right to left order. Read the numbers backwards."

"Why? Why do you think they're backwards?"

"I just found out what the writing on the side is. It's a phrase in Sanskrit and it's written backwards."

"That's weird."

"No, I don't think so. It must have been scribed by someone of Persian origin, and over there they write in right to left order."

"For numbers, too?"

"No, not for numbers. It probably was an apprentice scribe who might have got carried away. At any rate, it can't hurt to check the numbers backwards, can it?"

"No. I'll ask Chris to look into it."

WAS the papyrus was an original fragment of Sankhya philosophy, wondered Norm? Alexander the Great, who had plundered many countries, was not only a soldier but also a student of world religions. His tutor in philosophy was Aristotle and there was a slim chance that the fragment Norm was looking at was a piece of an original that Alexander might have taken back during his conquest of India. The Alexandrian library would have been the logical place to archive it.

Michell told Chris to look at the numbers in reverse order and see if they made sense. After staring at them for an hour, Chris came up with an answer.

"I've got it," he shrieked. "I figured out one of the numbers."

"Which one?" asked Michell.

"The larger one. The digits are the first 19 decimals in the expansion of π."

"Hmmm. By golly, you're right Chris."

"But what does it signify, professor?"

"It is the value for the initial energy just as I suspected. Do you know how π is defined?"

"Yes. It's the ratio of circumference to diameter of a circle."

"That's one definition, Chris. There's another definition that is going to be more useful to us. Π is twice the one and only number between zero and 2 whose cosine is zero."

"Why is that a useful definition?"

"Let me explain it to you." Michell wrote down something on a piece of paper and showed it to Chris.

$3.1\ 4\ 1\ 5\ 9\ 2\ 6\ 5\ 3\ 5\ 8\ 9\ 7\ 9\ 3\ 2\ 3\ 8\ 4 * 10^{19}$

"That's π multiplied by 10 million trillion. A bit more than the current national debt but we'll soon overtake it. The initial energy for the big bang is suspected to be close to the Planck energy which is 10^{19} giga-electron volts."

"What's a giga-electron volt?"

"One giga-electron volt is one billion electron volts, one followed by nine zeros. Nobody knows what the exact value for the initial energy ought to be. This number has something else rooting for it."

"What's that?"

"In our model, there are four units of energy, two for the potential energy and two for the kinetic energy. The electric and magnetic fields are 90 degrees out of phase, the electric field being a cosine function and the magnetic field being a sine function.

282

"At the beginning of creation, the electric field is zero everywhere and the magnetic field is maximum. This occurs when the cosine function is zero. It ties in nicely with our model."

"How many giga-electron volts can you generate in the laboratory?"

"Peanuts, Chris. Peanuts. We can go only as high as 1,000 giga-electron volts. That's why we need a computer simulation."

"Then the other number represents the number of time steps."

"You got it buddy. Get to work on that."

CHRIS reported his discovery to Norm. Their efforts now shifted to deciphering the second number on the papyrus. Written backwards, that number was

5 8 4 5 5 4 5 4 5 3 9 5.

When Alan heard about the value for the initial energy, his interest was sparked by Michell's explanation. He decided to join the group and Norm gave him his usual flak.

"Is the great physicist now into mystical stuff?" he asked Alan.

"Enough, Norm. I've heard enough from you. I'm investigating this to see if there is any merit to my daughter's theory. It's the only thing I can do to cherish her memory."

"But you've always told us that what we were doing was too spooky. That it didn't have any scientific basis."

"Norm, I think you are the one who has a sour attitude towards science. You think that all we do is publish meaningless papers. They appear senseless on the surface but these papers add incrementally to our knowledge of the universe. They provide an objective way of looking at things. The mysteries of nature are as intriguing to science as they are to religion.

"I've heard you quote many mystics in the past but I bet you haven't heard what Henri Poincaré, the great mathematician, had to say,

> *The scientist does not study nature because it is useful; he studies it because he delights in it, and he delights in it because it is beautiful. If nature were not beautiful, it would not be worth knowing, and if nature were not worth knowing, life would not be worth living.*"

"I'm sorry Alan. I wasn't trying to be facetious. I was just trying to get honest answers to basic questions."

"Okay Norm. No offense taken. This second number that represents the time is off by an order of magnitude. In our simulation we are working with 15 billion years as the age of the universe."

"Alan," said Michell, "your model is the hot big bang model of the universe. Our model is an oscillating model with Big Bang and Big Crunch. Naturally the time will be different."

"If it's oscillating," said Norm, "why don't we see whether it's got anything to do with Brahma's day and Brahma's night? Anita had mentioned this when she was writing a term paper on Sankhya."

"Brahma's day and Brahma's night?" interrupted Chris. "I seem to have heard that somewhere but I can't remember right now."

A couple of weeks later Chris was bubbling with excitement. He had cracked the code for the second number. He set up a meeting with Michell and Alan to discuss it at home.

"I think I've got it," he exclaimed. "I've deciphered the second number."

"Go ahead Chris. Tell us," said Norm.

"I learned about the Tower of Brahma in a computer class at Northwestern. The professor was explaining recursion and told us a story. In a temple in India, on a brass plate beneath a dome that marks the center of the universe, there are 64 disks of pure gold and three needles. The disks are all of different diameter and each disk has a small hole in its center. Initially, the disks are all placed on one of the needles, with the largest disk at the bottom and the smallest one at the top, forming a tower of disks.

"This tower is called the Tower of Brahma and signifies the beginning of the universe. The priests in the temple are busy carrying disks, one at a time, between the three needles. Their goal is to transfer the tower from the initial needle to another needle.

"But in the process of transferring disks, they have to obey Brahma's Law: no disk may ever be placed upon a disk smaller than itself. When the last disk is finally in place, once again forming the tower on another needle, it signifies the end of the universe."

"Does the second number represent the time taken to do this?" asked Alan.

"It's not that straightforward. The number of moves necessary to move the tower from one needle to the other is two raised to the power 64 minus one. It is a huge number," said Chris, showing them how big it was.

18, 446, 744, 073, 709, 551, 615

"Chris, that's not the number on the papyrus," said Michell.

"I'm coming to that. If a priest were to take one second to make a move, this number represents the total number of seconds it takes to transfer the disks to another needle. Our number, however, is the number of years it takes."

"Okay," said Alan, "let's divide this by the number of seconds in a year, which is 60 times 60 times 24 times 365."

"What about leap years Alan?" asked Norm.

"Let's use 365.25 days to include the leap years. What I get is

5 8 4 5 4 2 0 4 6 0 9 0.6 2 6."

"That's still not the number on the papyrus," objected Michell.

"It can be," said Chris smiling, " if you do it right."

"Did I make a mistake?" asked Alan.

"Yes. In the Gregorian calendar, years like 1800 and 1900 are not leap years but years like 1600 and 2000 are. The number of days in a year is actually 365.24219 and if you use that you get

5 8 4 5 5 4 5 4 5 3 9 5.2 1 1.

If we drop the fraction, then we have the number on the papyrus."

"Good job Chris," said Michell. "Now we can begin work on the program."

"Let me take over from here," said Alan. "These numbers are way too large for your workstation, Michell. I'll use the supercomputer to crank out the program."

"But I don't have the funds to get time on the machine," cried Michell.

"Don't worry about it. I'll get around the bureaucracy by running it as a test case for the *Cosmic Voyage* project. Nobody will find out."

The headaches that afflicted Norm in July 1995 had continued for a whole year and were slowly beginning to intensify. He was smart enough now not to tell Becky lest she have him confined again to the mental ward.

Thirty-one

The computer simulation began in earnest on November 25th. Several glitches occurred during the development and testing of the large program that Alan had written based on Michell's formulation. The strategy to use the supercomputer was to first make the program work on a scaled-down version of the problem and then, after testing it for correctness, run the full version.

Getting a block of uninterrupted time on the supercomputer was difficult and expensive, but Alan managed that aspect of it. On Thursday, March 27, 1997, Alan called Norm from his office around 6:30 P.M. He asked him to come to his office right away with Chris.

When they got there, Michell showed them an image on Alan's computer screen. "There it is guys," he exclaimed. "A picture of the modern universe. Quite consistent with the observed evidence."

"Where, Michell? I can't find our solar system in it."

"Grandpa, the computer program is not that sophisticated. All it shows is the density of evolved matter. What Michell is telling us is that this density is close to that predicted by the Standard Model."

"Exactly," said Michell.

"Then is Anita's theory correct?" Norm asked Michell.

"I can't give you a right answer to that question. Anita's theory appears to have no inconsistencies at the macroscopic and microscopic levels. Her model predicts a value for the density that is as good as the prediction made by prevalent big bang cosmologies. She permits electromagnetic radiation to be anisotropic in her theory, whereas in conventional cosmology it is assumed to be isotropic."

Michell added, "The reason why it should be isotropic remains a matter of controversy. It is a hypothesis that is very accurately satisfied for the microwave background radiation but it has not been tested for other matter in the universe. Some researchers have suggested that the universe started off being highly anisotropic but evolved to isotropy on the large scale.

"In fact, there is some evidence to indicate anisotropy in electromagnetic propagation, but we haven't even gone to our own sun to measure its parameters at the epoch of emission."

"What is Stephen Hawking's position on isotropy?" asked Norm.

"Stephen Hawking argues that if the universe were not isotropic then galaxies would not form and we would not be here. Thus, his argument is that the universe is isotropic because we are here."

"How can both Anita and Stephen Hawking be right?"

"It's not a question of who is right and who is wrong. It's a question of which theory best approximates the observed evidence. Certainly Anita's theory merits scrutiny from a broad scientific community."

"Are you telling me that her theory can be a valid theory of the origin and fate of the universe?"

"Yes, Norm. I believe it can be. All the theories reduce finally to a number. Either it is the Baryon number or the net electric charge, or the density of observed matter. Our program has computed another number that is within the expected range for the density.

"The physicist, although he would not admit it, shows a lot more faith than the priest. He readily accepts many postulates and principles, all the time claiming to rely on observed evidence. Yet, when it really matters, there is very little observed evidence with which to accept a theory. More often than not there is a wide leap of faith and mass consensus by other scientists. It is best to remember what Abdus Salam used to tell his graduate students, 'When all else fails, *you* can always tell the truth.' "

NORM slowly sat down on a chair. The excitement added to the throbbing pain in his head. He asked Alan for a glass of water.

"Well Norm, you and Chris and Michell did it. Are you going to write a scientific paper describing this work?" asked Alan.

Norm thought for a few moments before replying.

"No, Alan. I don't think I am going to write a paper. I am not a professional in physics. I'm a retired officer of the United States Army. I have mowed people's yards to make a living. Who on earth is going to believe that I have anything useful to say about the universe?

"I suggest you and Michell write the paper. You have more credibility in the field of physics than I. Write it up and submit it for publication. The review process would bring out any mistakes that might have been made. Nobody is perfect. Make sure you acknowledge your daughter's contribution. After all, the entire theory was her idea.

"Be careful, though. The ideas in this work are bold and imaginative. If Anita's model is more accurate than the Standard Model, it will no doubt herald an era of sweeping changes in conventional physics. These changes will take time to settle down. In all my years of gardening, I have noticed that planting a young sapling was much easier than uprooting a mature tree. Science, with its deep roots, will have to undergo significant changes to accommodate this theory.

"If the computer program proves to be correct Alan, then you and I would have been the first ones to have taken a ride on the carousel of scientific progress. I consider myself very fortunate, blessed with a wonderful family and good friends. This picture on your computer screen brings me an inner peace of mind that I cannot describe."

The discussion soon drifted towards computer-ese and Norm excused himself.

"Alan, will you please drop Chris on your way home? I know that he would love to discuss the computer program with you. I'm leaving now."

"Sure Norm. No problem. I'll bring Chris back."

WHEN he left Alan's office, Norm had a deep inner conviction from his philosophical readings that the model just had to be correct. Perhaps a few details needed to be worked out. That was all.

He thought about the clues that Nature had left about her own existence. The tornado was Nature's signature. He thought about the many people who had dedicated themselves to discovering the mysteries of the universe right from the dawn of civilization. He reached home and prepared his first drink. So many scientists and philosophers had pondered the origin and fate of the universe. Norm recalled a verse from one of his favorite poems, *Elegy Written in a Country Churchyard* by Thomas Gray:

> *But Knowledge to their eyes her ample page*
> *Rich with the spoils of time did ne'er unroll;*
> *Chill Penury repress'd their noble rage,*
> *And froze the genial current of the soul.*

Science and philosophy had long been considered the playground where men excelled—men like Aristotle, Galileo, Newton, Poincaré, Einstein, Heisenberg, Sagan, Hawking, and many others. These men had dedicated their lives to the study of Nature. In their pursuit of her secrets, scientists had kept their blinders on. They had ignored clues present in religion and philosophy, dismissing them as mere myths. The history of science has shown, time and time again, that real advances come only from ideas that move it laterally. Imaginative and bold ideas whose source is intuition. A domain that has been and continues to be one where women excel. Women like Anita who show the world that the reality most acceptable to science is understandable by even a small child, provided it is explained properly.

NORM started writing in his journal.

> *The truth that I have been seeking all along is at the interface between science and religion. Dualism is a fundamental principle of Nature. It is present in several places in religious philosophy and science:*

Purusha and Prakriti of Sankhya philosophy;
Tonal and Nagual of the Yaqui Indian;
Yin and Yang of Chinese philosophy;
Khoshekh and Aphela of Genesis;
Lila and Nitya of Hinduism;
Wave and Particle of quantum mechanics; and
Accelerating and Revolving substratums of the universe.

All along, the answers to First Cause were in religion but they were hidden so deep that I had to seek them out for myself.

Norm got out his notes on the Gospel of Thomas. Thomas was one of the original twelve apostles of Jesus Christ, but his Gospel is not part of the New Testament because it was discovered only in 1945. Unlike the synoptic gospels of Matthew, Mark, and Luke, the Gospel of Thomas is in a raw, un-canonized form. It consists of questions and answers, as if the living Jesus was speaking directly to the apostle Thomas. In his journal, Norm wrote his interpretation of some of the passages.

Jesus said: ". . . But the kingdom is within you, and it is outside of you."
This is so similar to the principle of Purusha in Sankhya philosophy.

Jesus said: "I am the light that is above them all. I am the all; the all came forth from me, and the all returned to me."
A clear-cut reference to the Void and the collapse of the universe.

His disciples said to Him: " . . . on what day will the new world come?" He said to them: "What you await has come, but you do not know it."
An implication that the universe was contracting, as predicted by Anita.

Then Norm read his notes on Sankhya and saw how the philosophy related to aspects of Anita's theory. He continued writing in his journal.

Sankhya philosophy has been buried because of a misunderstanding regarding its principles. It is a philosophy that preaches dualism. The two principles are Purusha or sentient Consciousness, and Prakriti or insentient Primal Matter.

These two subtle principles being eternal and all pervading existed everywhere in association with each other as there was no Void. As they were everywhere, there was no room for these principles to move. In such a total state of rest, time and space were absolute.

According to Sankhya, sentient Consciousness is God.

The Creator has expended two units of energy in creating the Void in Primal Matter by lifting Primal Matter and displaying Its Omnipotence. The Void is a void relative to Primal Matter since Primal Matter does not exist in the Void. With the creation of the Relative Void, the Primal Matter gains motion and the universe evolves from insentient Primal Matter. Anita's theory has shown how the universe would be self-contained once it evolved, oscillating between Big Bang and Big Crunch.

The sentient Consciousness exists in the Relative Void in Its pure form unalloyed with Primal Matter. So does It exist in the relative voids of all evolutes, including humans, in Its pure form.

This Consciousness is present in the tappets of a motorcycle engine, in the petals of a flower, in the many statues of God worshipped everyday, and inside each and every one of us. It is that which is the movie screen as well as the audience in the Cartesian theater of the brain. It is that which enables a Mother Teresa or a Swami Vivekananda to see the Godhead in each human being.

The unmanifest Purusha, being different from Prakriti, can never present Itself to beings like us unless It manifests in

291

human form. That is why God has to descend on earth, time and time again, as a human. Our ancestors have been enlightened by avatars like Adi Sankaracharya, Buddha, Jesus Christ, the Prophet Mohammed, and many others.

Sankhya's doctrine of causality explains cause as that in which the effect subsists in a latent form. The evolution of the universe (which is the effect) subsists in the cause (which is the dissolution), and the dissolution of the universe (which is the effect) subsists in the cause (which is the evolution).

Effect subsists IN the cause.

What is the first cause whose effect is the birth of the universe?

First Cause is the lifting of Primal Matter and the creation of a Relative Void. Thereafter, all effects follow from this cause without intervention.

The search for Truth is not complete with the unification of subjects and objects through Quality and Goodness. That constitutes one aspect of reality—Lila or the relative reality. There is another aspect to reality—Nitya or the absolute reality, as explained in Sankhya.

Karika 10: The Manifested has a cause; it is neither eternal nor pervading (universal); it is active (mobile or modifiable), multiform, dependent, predicative (or characteristic), conjunct, and subordinate. The Unmanifested is the reverse.

Karika 11: The Manifested has three constituent Attributes *(gunas),* it is indiscriminating, objective, generic (or common), non-intelligent (or insentient) and productive. So also is Nature. The Spirit is the reverse, and yet also (in some respects) similar.

Karika 13: Goodness is considered to be buoyant and illuminating; Foulness is exciting and versatile (mobile); Darkness sluggish and enveloping. Their action, like a lamp, is for a single purpose.

Karika 54: Among the beings of the higher plane Goodness predominates; among those of the lower plane predominates Dullness; in the middle reside those predominating in Foulness—these constituting the whole universe, from Brahma to the tuft of grass.

Purusha coexists with Prakriti everywhere, except in the Relative Void wherein It exists all by Itself as Pure Consciousness. The sentient Purusha, being Consciousness, is the subject in whose Consciousness Prakriti and the evolved universe gains existence as the object. Insentient objects must have a subject in whose consciousness they gain existence, and a subject must have different objects by discarding which it comes to know itself.

How can they understand Goodness who do not know Foulness or Darkness? A colorless being in association with white matter will conclude his color is white because he has no concept of different colors. If other colors are introduced, the colorless being can understand the concept of color and begin an inquiry into what his real color is. He will see different colors and conclude 'I am not this color,' 'I am not this color,' etc. Then he may ask himself, 'Am I this white color or am I different?' Thus he will proceed with his inquiry to find out his true color till he ultimately realizes that he is colorless.

The universe has been evolved so that the subject gets to know Itself by discarding insentient objects, by isolating the object from the union of subject and object—by transferring the 'I-ness' of subject, which manifests as egoism leading to bondage between subject and object, back to the subject to whom It really belongs.

Our spiritual purpose is to help the Purusha inside us emancipate Itself by realizing Its independent existence, separate from Prakriti. When we do this, Purusha is liberated, and Prakriti has no further reason to indulge in action. Hence, the universe exists so that the Supreme Consciousness can teach Itself what It really is. This has been summed up in the Hindu doctrine Tat tvam Asi, which literally means 'Thou Art That.'

It has also been summed up in Karika 21 of Sankhya:

Karika 21: For the Spirit's contemplation of Prakriti, and its final emancipation, the union of both take place, like that of the halt and the blind; and from this union proceeds creation.

Halt is the inert Consciousness meaning lame and blind refers to the insentient Prakriti. When a lame person sits on the shoulders of a blind person, they both move forward, the blind person using his feet and the lame person using his eyes. Science, which is lame, can move forward by sitting on the shoulders of religion, which is blind.

Thus, our essential nature is Pure Consciousness, and we have been endowed with the gift of human life, along with intellect and mind, to find our permanent legacy. There are many paths to emancipate our spirit. Scientists follow the path of knowledge, carefully observing things and applying reason to figure out absolute reality. Mystics follow the path of meditation, believing that absolute reality is beyond description of natural language.

FOR many years Norm had wrestled with empirical philosophies that were not religious enough, or religious philosophies that were not empirical enough. Anita's theory had given him the closure he had been yearning for all his life.

As he put down his pen and fixed his second drink, the bigger picture of existence and its ultimate meaning loomed in front of him. He could now hear some music in his head—a divine music he had never heard before.

It was the sound of the plants blooming.

The sound of the cosmic background radiation.

The sound of silence.

A sound that his wife Joann had been able to hear so easily, but had taken him so many years. By her pragmatic approach to religion and God, she had led an enlightened life Norm could hardly fathom. She had never allowed organized religion to interfere with her spirituality.

Her daily ritual of kindness towards others was not merely the source of her strength but also her beauty. Like the wind in her native Midwest, it had carried her through the river of life. There had been no conflict in her mind between ritual and freedom.

Ritual, to her, was the one and only indivisible order operating in the universe. A moral as well as spiritual order, known to ancient Hindus as *Rita* or cosmic order. The Hebrew-Christian ritual of *confirmation* that initiates one into the faith, the Hindu ritual of *upanayanam* that invokes the sun from within oneself, the Moslem ritual of *Ramadan* that enforces a month of daytime fasting and abstinence from drinking, smoking, and sex, the daily ritual of work to provide for one's family, the endless ritual of household chores, the monk's ritual of meditation, the scientist's ritual of research, and the primordial ritual of reproduction are mechanisms that have evolved over centuries to preserve and improve society. Life, as we have come to know and understand it, is nothing but one ritual after another.

Three other rituals foster spiritual growth. The ritual of sacrifice produces creative energy when we give up our most precious offering—egoism and its brood of greed, fear, anger, hatred, and pride. The ritual of truth produces results when there is complete accord between thought, word, and deed. The ritual of prayer releases love energy and uplifts the entire human race.

Through the Sankhya philosophy, through the *Bhagavad Gita,* through the Gospels of John and Thomas, through the *Tao Te Ching* of Lao Tzu, through Anita's scientific theory, and through the writings of philosophers like Robert Pirsig and William James and scientists like Stephen Hawking and Carl Sagan, Norm had achieved the essential ideal of philosophy and science—a religious experience.

295

HE concluded his journal with the following words.

Aristotle was right when he said that we were at the center of the universe. Each one of us is at the center, each one of us a privileged observer of the cosmos. Our dharma is to seek the discriminative knowledge that explains the nature of God. Mystics who contend that this knowledge is beyond us are blind—why else are we endowed with an intellect and mind? Scientists who contend that religion is a myth are lame—why else would the Word of God have appeared in so many places? Wisdom and enlightenment come to us when we gain the insights to put this knowledge into action.

The Great Spirit that breathes through our bodies is our permanent cosmic legacy. Our purpose in life is to emancipate this Spirit and help It understand Its true nature—that of pure Consciousness. Not by committing suicide that kills only biological cells, but by leading a life based on the rituals of sacrifice, truth, and penance. This spiritual uplifting of humanity should be our utmost priority—a force for change in a changing world—one by which our human experiences can be enriched in quality. A world where we should idealize the real, not realize the ideal.

Epilogue

Four kinds of people who have done virtuous deeds worship Me. . . . the distressed person, the aspirant after knowledge, the seeker of wealth and the man of knowledge. . . .To the man of knowledge I am very dear indeed, and he is dear to Me.

— Bhagavad Gita 7: 16, 17

On Sunday, March 30, 1997, Norm was sitting at home in an easy chair and thinking about the dramatic events of the previous week, his head stinging from the persistent headaches. On Thursday Michell had shown him some interesting results in Alan's office. Anita's theory had been verified by the computer simulation—the program that Alan ran on the supercomputer admitted the possibility of an accelerating substratum and a revolving substratum. Norm's Easter egg hunt was finally over. The dark matter he had been searching for was Prakriti, and he had finally understood his own legacy.

CHRIS is in the family room watching a rerun of *Welcome Back, Kotter* on TV. As the show starts, Norm can hear a fragment of the theme song:

. . . Welcome Back, to that same old place that you laughed about,
Well the names have all changed since you hung around
But those dreams have remained and they've turned around
Who'd have thought they'd lead ya
Who'd have thought they'd lead ya
Back here, where we need ya
Back here, where we need ya . . .

His eyes shut and a panorama of his entire life flashes before him as the song plays. Right from the time he was born, his childhood, his teenage years, his college days, his army career, his retirement in Florida, and his years in Urbana. He dreams that his birth mother is beckoning him—she's the one that he can hear singing the line, "Back here, where we need ya."

Norm follows her to the mountaintop where he meets Lord Shiva once again. It has been a long and arduous journey for him to get there. Lord Shiva tells Norm, *"You have fulfilled My mission and are now ready to enter My abode."* Norm stands still, refusing to move. He tells Lord Shiva that he has a few more questions. What a persistent bastard. But that was his nature and he couldn't help it.

"I know now *how* the universe came into being, O Lord. But I still don't know *why.* Why did You create the universe and why did You create us? And if evolution and dissolution of the universe is a cyclic process, is it deterministic? Will it be the same the next time around?"

"That's for Me to know and you to find out."

It is Anita's childhood voice that answers his question and Norm can now see Her face within Lord Shiva's face. That is his last living memory on earth. The headaches vanish from his consciousness. The clock reads 1:37 P.M.

JOANN had died on a Good Friday; Norm passed away on an Easter Sunday. Like Anita, he too was cremated. The funeral was simple and sparsely attended, no military honors after his ignominious departure from the army, no ceremonial flag to drape his now listless body, no gun salute to herald his eternal silence. In society's eyes he would never be regarded as a hero or celebrity to warrant any kind of extravagant send-off. Except for an innate persistence in his inquiry into First Cause, he did not contribute anything of value to civilization's coffers. He had lived the life of an ordinary soldier, pounded on the door of knowledge that was opened for him by a young girl, only to realize that enlightenment was a process of disappearing into the world and becoming indistinguishable from it.

His ashes were dropped by the side of a small stretch of Highway 127 near Murphysboro, Illinois. In the heart of tornado alley. They had been returned to the holiest of holy places—the place whence he commenced the ritual of breathing.

AMIDST a peaceful and quiet gathering of family and friends, Chris said a few words about Norm: "I stand before you today, deeply humbled by my grandfather's ordinariness. I can't find words to describe his life. Like his best friend Bill Kaplan, he was a poet at heart, and I am going to recite a few verses from poems I found in his journal. The first two are from *Elegy Written in a Country Churchyard* by Thomas Gray.

> *Here rests his head upon the lap of Earth*
> *A Youth to Fortune and to Fame unknown.*
> *Fair Science frown'd not on his humble birth,*
> *And Melancholy mark'd him for her own.*
>
> *Large was his bounty, and his soul sincere,*
> *Heav'n did a recompense as largely send:*
> *He gave to Mis'ry all he had, a tear,*
> *He gain'd from Heav'n ('twas all he wish'd) a friend.*

"The next one is from *The Rubaiyat* of the Sufi poet, Omar Khayyam.

> *The Moving Finger writes; and, having writ,*
> *Moves on: nor all thy Piety nor Wit*
> *Shall lure it back to cancel half a Line,*
> *Nor all thy Tears wash out a Word of it.*

"Now a piece from the *Bhagavad Gita*.

> *To work alone you have the right, but never claim its results.*
> *Let not the results of actions be your motive, nor be attached*
> *to inaction.*

"I conclude with a verse from the *Tao Te Ching* of Lao Tzu.

> *When Tao is lost, there is goodness.*
> *When goodness is lost, there is kindness.*
> *When kindness is lost, there is justice.*
> *When justice is lost, there is ritual."*

FROM the fading glow of sunset, a yellow-white light slowly crept out to witness Norm's death. It was a celestial object, a marker in the night sky, comet Hale-Bopp, which on that day approached a very bright perihelion. First sighted at the end of July 1995, it was intrinsically brighter than Hyakutake but much farther away at closest approach to Earth.

For many centuries, philosophers and scientists have engaged in a calumnious ritual of vilification that has propagated the dichotomy between them. In their relentless pursuit of truth, oftentimes by blatantly flouting conventional wisdom, their patterns of thought are in danger of being wiped out from our memories. But the ghosts of civilization's ancestors would not permit that. They would rise from the ashes to repair the breach between the mystics and the scientists. The ghosts of countless ordinary souls who nurture the cosmic consciousness into producing great souls.

By selflessly following the rituals of their lives.

By accepting the harmony in an unseen order of things.

By succumbing to the world, not conquering it.

Acknowledgments

I thank you, the reader, for enduring the unusual pattern of thought presented in this book. Although I have cogitated the issues discussed here for 30 years, the short time it took to craft the narrative bespeaks a heavenly Finger that took over the writing process. The words seemed to appear from a mysterious source and many times I got the feeling that I was listening to dictation.

There are many I need to thank but I must single out a few who greatly facilitated its creation.

—My father, Major K, who has persisted with this inquiry for more than 50 years and whose life since birth has been marked by melancholy.

—My mother who, like Joann, died tragically of breast cancer.

—My guru and granduncle, Swami Vireswarananda, who taught me all I know about Hinduism, spirituality and the practice of religion. Sitting at his feet in the Ramakrishna Ashram in Madras during summer vacations, I recall myself as an obnoxious maverick questioning his every word until one day he told me, 'You talk too much. If you would only stop and listen, then maybe one day you too will hear the sound of silence.'

—My wife, Gitanjali, and two angels, my children Krishna and Mythili from whom I learn constantly.

—Professor Charles Thomas Wright, my colleague, jogging partner, bridge coach, and best friend for 17 years, who died in a tragic car accident as this book went into production. He was a physics major, and all my scientific explanations had to first pass "Charlie's test." Rest in peace, my dear friend.

—Vikram Rao, Sona Pai, Somenath Biswas, Rivka Israel, and Mary Jo Brearley for giving me a reality check on early drafts of the manuscript.

—My senior editor, Prem Kumar, for being ruthless and brutally honest in his efforts to polish the material. Any weaknesses that remain should be credited entirely to me.

—Dawn Adams for shaping many of my spiritual ideas.

301

—Professor Albert Baker for simplifying my role in a course we taught together when the first draft was created.

—Francesca B., a devout Catholic woman, for sharing her early school experiences and encouraging me throughout the writing of this book.

—Professor Ramesh Rao for being a strong advocate and posting his pre-publication review on www.sulekha.com.

—My advance readers for their kind words and suggestions.

—The authors who penned the following masterpieces that I used for my research:

The Gospel of Sri Ramakrishna by Mahendranath Gupta (M)
The Complete Works of Swami Vivekananda
The Bhagavad Gita translated by Swami Vireswarananda
Spiritual Ideals for the Present Age by Swami Vireswarananda
A treatise on Sankhya by Major G. K. Prabhu
The Tao Te Ching by Lao Tzu
The Rubaiyat by Omar Khayyam
Zen and the Art of Motorcycle Maintenance by Robert Pirsig
Pragmatism by William James
Mister God, This is Anna by Fynn
Cosmos by Carl Sagan
Quasars, Redshifts, and Controversies by Halton Arp
A Brief History of Time by Stephen Hawking
Hypatia of Alexandria by Maria Dzielska

www.anitaslegacy.com

Order Form (in India)

From www.amazon.com

From www.bn.com

Purchase orders may be faxed to: 080-5512335 or sent via e-mail to marianne@bgl.vsnl.net.in. Phone number: 080-5300605.

Please send me _____ copies of *Anita's Legacy.*

Name: _____

Ship To Address: _____

_____

City: _____ State:_____ Zip:_____

Indian Price: Rs. 225 per book (*postage & packing extra*)

Payment:

Please make check out in favour of **Arc Publications** and mail to:

 Arc Publications
38 Castle Street
Richmond Town
Bangalore 560025

www.anitaslegacy.com

Order Form

From www.amazon.com

From www.bn.com

Purchase orders may be faxed to: 515–292–0600 or sent via e-mail to vireshpubns@hotmail.com. Phone number: 515–292–6009.

Please send me _____ copies of *Anita's Legacy.*

Name: _____

Ship To Address: _____

City: _____ State:_____ Zip:_____

Country: _____Phone_____

Price: U.S. \$13.95 per book. Please add sales tax 6% for buoks shipped to Iowa addresses. Domestic shipping in U.S. is \$3.00 per book. Call or e-mail us for volume discounts.

Payment:

Please make check out to **Viresh Publications.**

Address:

> **Viresh Publications**
> P.O. Box 2439
> Ames, IA 50010-2439